Getting Started with Salesforce CRM Analytics

A Beginner's Guide to Building Interactive and Complex Dashboards

Second Edition

Johan Yu

Apress®

Getting Started with Salesforce CRM Analytics: A Beginner's Guide to Building Interactive and Complex Dashboards, Second Edition

Johan Yu
Singapore, Singapore

ISBN-13 (pbk): 979-8-8688-0478-6 ISBN-13 (electronic): 979-8-8688-0479-3
https://doi.org/10.1007/979-8-8688-0479-3

Copyright © 2024 by Johan Yu

This work is subject to copyright. All rights are reserved by the Publisher, whether the whole or part of the material is concerned, specifically the rights of translation, reprinting, reuse of illustrations, recitation, broadcasting, reproduction on microfilms or in any other physical way, and transmission or information storage and retrieval, electronic adaptation, computer software, or by similar or dissimilar methodology now known or hereafter developed.

Trademarked names, logos, and images may appear in this book. Rather than use a trademark symbol with every occurrence of a trademarked name, logo, or image we use the names, logos, and images only in an editorial fashion and to the benefit of the trademark owner, with no intention of infringement of the trademark.

The use in this publication of trade names, trademarks, service marks, and similar terms, even if they are not identified as such, is not to be taken as an expression of opinion as to whether or not they are subject to proprietary rights.

While the advice and information in this book are believed to be true and accurate at the date of publication, neither the authors nor the editors nor the publisher can accept any legal responsibility for any errors or omissions that may be made. The publisher makes no warranty, express or implied, with respect to the material contained herein.

Managing Director, Apress Media LLC: Welmoed Spahr
Acquisitions Editor: Aditee Mirashi
Development Editor: James Markham
Coordinating Editor: Kripa Joseph

Cover designed by eStudioCalamar

Cover image by Freepik (www.freepik.com)

Distributed to the book trade worldwide by Apress Media, LLC, 1 New York Plaza, New York, NY 10004, U.S.A. Phone 1-800-SPRINGER, fax (201) 348-4505, e-mail orders-ny@springer-sbm.com, or visit www.springeronline.com. Apress Media, LLC is a California LLC and the sole member (owner) is Springer Science + Business Media Finance Inc (SSBM Finance Inc). SSBM Finance Inc is a **Delaware** corporation.

For information on translations, please e-mail booktranslations@springernature.com; for reprint, paperback, or audio rights, please e-mail bookpermissions@springernature.com.

Apress titles may be purchased in bulk for academic, corporate, or promotional use. eBook versions and licenses are also available for most titles. For more information, reference our Print and eBook Bulk Sales web page at http://www.apress.com/bulk-sales.

Any source code or other supplementary material referenced by the author in this book is available to readers on GitHub (https://github.com/Apress). For more detailed information, please visit https://www.apress.com/gp/services/source-code.

If disposing of this product, please recycle the paper

To my wife, Novida, and my son, Jeremy, thank you for your love!

Table of Contents

About the Author xi

About the Technical Reviewer xiii

Acknowledgments xv

Introduction xvii

Chapter 1: CRM Analytics: Introduction 1

Getting the Right Term 2

Integration with Salesforce 2

Why CRM Analytics? 3

Environment and License 4

CRM Analytics Permissions 5

Navigating CRM Analytics 6

    Lightning Page 6

    Analytics Tab 6

    Analytics Studio 7

    Mobile App 8

CRM Analytics Components 8

    Apps 8

    Dashboards 8

    Lenses 9

    Datasets 9

Understanding Data Manager 10

    Jobs Monitor 11

    Data Assets 13

    Recipes and Dataflows 13

TABLE OF CONTENTS

    Usage 14

    Connections 15

Summary 16

Chapter 2: Data Sources 19

Getting Data into CRM Analytics 20

CSV File 21

    Hands-On: CSV Data Load 22

Local Salesforce Data 26

External Data 27

Existing Dataset 29

Salesforce Trend Report 29

    Hands-On: Trend a Salesforce Report 30

External Data API 35

Summary 35

Chapter 3: Recipe 37

Dataflow 37

    1. Open Dataflow 38

    2. Convert to Recipe 38

    3. Save and Run 39

Recipe User Interface 40

Creating a Recipe from Scratch 42

    Use Case 42

    Building Concept 43

    Hands-On: Create a Recipe 44

Backup and Restore Recipe 48

Data Transformation in Recipe 49

Input Data 49

Transform 51

Filter 54

Aggregate 55

Join	56
Append	61
Update	62
Output	62
Summary	63

Chapter 4: Dataset 65

Dataset Properties	65
Dataset Fields	68
Extended Metadata File	69
Rename the Field Label	70
Hide Fields	70
Edit Values	71
Format Numbers	72
Default Fields	73
Specify the Dataset Grain Label	74
Replace and Restore Dataset	75
Configure Actions for Dataset	76
Summary	79

Chapter 5: Lens 81

CRM Analytics App	81
Creating App	82
Run App	83
Share App	84
Exploring Dataset	84
Using Chart in Lens	85
Using Table in Lens	87
Saving Lens	89
Present Lens	90
Clip Lens to Designer	90

vii

TABLE OF CONTENTS

    Share and Download Lens 91

        Get URL 91

        Post to Feed 92

        Download 92

    Add Lens to Subscriptions 93

    Add Lens to Collection 94

    Add Lens As Favorite 95

    Explore with Conversational 97

    Summary 98

Chapter 6: Building Dashboard 101

    Permission 102

    Layout 102

    Template 105

    Widgets 108

        Chart 108

        Table 110

        Filter 111

        Container 112

        Date 113

        Link 115

        Image 116

        List 117

        Number 118

        Range 119

        Text 120

        Toggle 121

        Navigation 122

    Page 124

        Sharing Widget 125

        Dataset Filter 125

Dashboard Tab	125
Performance	126
Adoption and Maintenance	126
Faceting	126
Global Filter	127
Using Multiple Datasets	129
Summary	131

Chapter 7: Exploring Dashboard 133

Dashboard Inspector	134
Set Notifications	137
Annotations	140
Following Annotations	140
Hands-On Annotations	141
Share Widget	142
Show Details	144
Explore	145
Hands-On Explore Widget	146
Widget Built with SAQL	147
Embedding CRM Analytics Dashboard to Salesforce Lightning Page	148
Hands-On Adding Dashboard to Lightning Home Page	150
Hands-On Adding Dashboard to the Record Page	152
Summary	155

Chapter 8: Applying Security 157

Permission Set Assignment	157
Apps Level Sharing	159
Security Predicate	160
Syntax	160
Hands-On Security Predicate	161
Role Hierarchy Access	163

TABLE OF CONTENTS

Sharing Inheritance 166
    Enable Sharing Inheritance 167
    Configure Recipe 167
    Sharing Inheritance Coverage Assessment 168
Summary 170

Chapter 9: Advanced Topics 171

Recipe Nodes 171
    Edit Attributes 172
    Drop Columns 174
    Custom Formula 175
    Filter Node 177
    Append Node 179
    Join with Multiple Value Lookup 180
Salesforce Direct Data Queries 181
    Hands-On 181
JSON 182
    Dashboard and Lens 183
    Recipe 184
    Dataset 185
SAQL 186
Binding and Custom Query 188
    Hands-On Binding and Custom Query 188
Widgets 193
    Input 193
    Repeater 195
    Component 197
Summary 199

Index 201

About the Author

Johan Yu has more than 25 years of experience working in the IT sector across multinational corporations (MNCs) and a leading Salesforce consulting company in the Asia-Pacific region. He has spent more than 19 years working with Salesforce technology, starting his career as a developer, team leader, architect, and technical manager, among many other challenging roles.

Based in Singapore, Johan holds 19x active Salesforce certifications, ranging from Administrator to Architect/Designer certifications, including CRM Analytics and Einstein Discovery Consultant. In his spare time, he enjoys writing blogs and volunteering in the Salesforce Trailblazer Community.

In May 2014, Johan became the first Salesforce MVP from Southeast Asia. He is also the leader of the Salesforce Singapore User Group for more than a decade.

About the Technical Reviewer

Venkata Karthik Penikalapati is a seasoned software developer with over a decade of expertise in designing and managing intricate distributed systems, data pipelines, and MLOps. Armed with a master's degree in Computer Science from the University at Buffalo, his knowledge spans the realms of machine learning, data engineering, and workflow orchestration. Venkata thrives in the world of distributed systems, continually pushing the boundaries of innovation.

Currently, Karthik is a valuable member of the Salesforce team within the Search Cloud division. Here, he's at the forefront of cutting-edge developments, spearheading the integration of the latest advancements in artificial intelligence (AI).

Acknowledgments

I would like to take this opportunity to recognize and say thank you to everyone who directly and indirectly contributed to this book. Writing the second edition of this book was not as simple as I thought, but I enjoyed sharing my knowledge, and it has been a great journey authoring this book. I am grateful for every opportunity, support, and input from

- My family
- My manager and teammates: Adrian, Eileen, Masako, Swapna, Jesus, and Joel
- Venkata Karthik Penikalapati for the review and feedback to make this book better
- Sayantani Mitra, the technical reviewer in the initial edition; Alexander Waleczek; and all team members of CRM Analytics #WorkoutWednesday
- Shonmirin, Aditee, and Kripa from the Apress team
- All Salesforce CRM Analytics Product Managers
- My church and cell group
- All Salesforce Singapore Trailblazers

Introduction

Salesforce is known to be the most friendly user interface for enterprise applications; it is the pioneer of cloud applications; over 25 years, Salesforce has evolved from a simple cloud CRM application to a comprehensive enterprise application for Sales, Service, Marketing, and so on, including Analytics.

One of the most liked features by Salesforce platform users is the report and dashboard. Users are able to create and edit reports and dashboards on their own easily using drag and drop. Furthermore, the result generated is based on real-time data from the Salesforce platform, and the user will get the result in seconds, including sorting, grouping, adding chart, subtotal, bucket field, row-level formula, summary fields, etc. The dashboard is built using a report created as the data source for each dashboard component.

Salesforce reports and dashboards serve well in generating simple real-time operational reporting, but Salesforce is not designed to work with large amounts of data, nor as a data analytics and exploration tool; it does not support the creation of reports and dashboards with complex logic, and it cannot connect and retrieve data directly from external or other Salesforce organizations. Therefore, Salesforce introduced CRM Analytics to fill the gap for complex analytics needs.

CRM Analytics is hosted in the Salesforce core cloud, so it is tightly connected to the Salesforce core platform; it is also able to get and sync data from external systems, including from multiple Salesforce organizations.

The CRM Analytics dashboard is built using datasets stored in the CRM Analytics platform; in this book, we will learn how to build the dataset using recipes, where you can combine and transform data from multiple sources. We will also learn how to store, share, and secure the assets, including each user's permissions and licenses.

The best method to learn CRM Analytics is to be hands-on with all the features introduced, so you need to have access to the platform from the beginning. If your organization has not purchased CRM Analytics licenses, you can register for a free Salesforce Trailhead Developer Edition organization with CRM Analytics enabled; you will learn that in this book.

INTRODUCTION

Thank you for purchasing this book; if you read till the end of the book and follow all the hands-on provided, you will know and absorb all the features offered by CRM Analytics and know how to build interactive dashboards for your organization or clients. Happy learning!

CHAPTER 1

CRM Analytics: Introduction

CRM Analytics is a visualization platform from Salesforce that allows you to build complex and interactive dashboards. The dashboard will let you and your users get insights and make smarter decisions from Salesforce and external data. Furthermore, it can also give you predictions and recommendations by analyzing the data.

The data visualization built will work in the web browser and mobile app. As the Salesforce admin, you can add the CRM Analytics dashboard to other Salesforce products, such as Sales Cloud, Service Cloud, Experience Cloud, Slack, etc. This empowers your Salesforce users to access the dashboard seamlessly from the Salesforce platform, which allows the user to analyze data without the need to switch platforms. You can also embed the dashboard into a record page, such as the Account or Opportunity page, so the dashboard will only show insight that is relevant to a particular record open. Additionally, if your organization is using Slack, you can also integrate CRM Analytics into Slack with a simple setup.

If you are familiar with building reports and dashboards in Salesforce, you need to reset your mind when learning to build dashboards with CRM Analytics. The concept of building a CRM Analytics dashboard is different from building a dashboard in the Salesforce platform. In CRM Analytics, you do not need to have reports to use as source data for the dashboard widgets because it will pull data directly from the CRM Analytics data source.

This book is written for Salesforce admins, analytics specialists, business intelligence professionals, data analysts, business analysts, and reporting analysts who want to learn to build CRM Analytics dashboards without any prior experience with CRM Analytics. This book is also intended for the managers and decision-makers who use and explore CRM Analytics dashboards in their daily jobs, so that they can make the most out of the platform.

CHAPTER 1   CRM ANALYTICS: INTRODUCTION

Throughout this book, you will learn step-by-step instructions to guide you in exploring dashboards and building interactive and complex dashboards, from preparing datasets, creating recipes, building dashboards, and implementing security.

By the end of this chapter, you will learn the following:

- Introduction to CRM Analytics and relation with the Salesforce platform
- Setting up the environment, licensing, and permission
- Navigating CRM Analytics and components of CRM Analytics
- Understanding Data Manager

Getting the Right Term

In the past, CRM Analytics was also known as **Tableau CRM**, **Einstein Analytics**, and **Wave**. Since the Salesforce Summer '22 release (around June 2022), this product has been called **CRM Analytics**. Thus, if you see those terms mentioned in older blogs, YouTube videos, or discussion forums, they refer to the same product, so the content may still be applied, but you will need to be cautious as some content may no longer be valid as of now.

Integration with Salesforce

If you have experience working in the Salesforce platform, the knowledge of Salesforce permission, objects, and fields will benefit you in learning CRM Analytics. However, CRM Analytics is a platform by itself; the data is stored on the CRM Analytics platform, not in the Salesforce platform. Therefore, only the data needed by dashboards has to be "brought" into CRM Analytics. Ideally, not all fields and objects in Salesforce will be available in CRM Analytics. However, for specific needs, you can query data in real time from Salesforce objects.

Because CRM Analytics is tightly integrated with the Salesforce platform, it offers the Salesforce admin the ability to embed the CRM Analytics dashboard easily into the Lightning App Builder. Users with CRM Analytics permissions will be able to explore embedded CRM Analytics dashboards from a Lightning page. For dashboards that are not embedded in a Lightning page, users can access the dashboard from the **Analytics** tab in Salesforce.

As a dashboard builder, you need to open the **Analytics Studio** app to create or edit a dashboard or work with recipes. Select the Analytics Studio app from the Lightning App Launcher (nine-dot icon) at the upper-left corner of the Lightning platform; see Figure 1-1. The Analytics tab and Analytics Studio app will only be visible for Salesforce users with CRM Analytics permission.

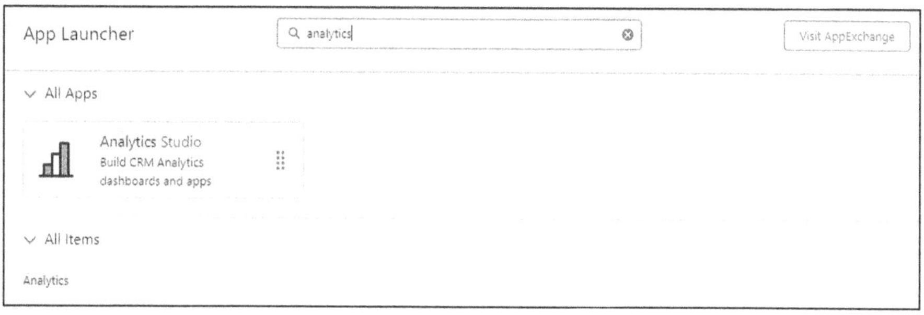

Figure 1-1. Analytics Studio app and Analytics tab in the Salesforce Lightning App Launcher

If you are unable to locate Analytics Studio from the App Launcher, you probably have not been assigned the permission set to access CRM Analytics; we will cover permissions related to CRM Analytics later in this chapter. Another reason is that your Salesforce profile has not been enabled with the Analytics Studio app; reach out to your Salesforce admin to enable it.

For the CRM Analytics admin, CRM Analytics configuration and user-related permissions are configured from the Salesforce setup menu. Type `Analytics` in the setup search box to configure it, while user permissions are granted with the Salesforce permission set.

Why CRM Analytics?

With CRM Analytics, users are empowered to ingest, explore, and analyze data on their own. The CRM Analytics dashboard does not depend on the Salesforce object's structure; therefore, as a dashboard designer, you are free to create datasets, recipes, dataflows, and dashboards with your own creativity. The CRM Analytics platform is designed to handle millions of records, and it supports users in interacting and analyzing data by faceting/broadcasting selected data across components.

CHAPTER 1 CRM ANALYTICS: INTRODUCTION

Salesforce comes with great standard reports and dashboard features, so why do we still need CRM Analytics? It depends on the dashboard's purpose.

Table 1-1 is the comparison between CRM Analytics and standard Salesforce Report and Dashboard.

Table 1-1. Comparison of CRM Analytics with Salesforce Report and Dashboard

	CRM Analytics	**Report and Dashboard**
Data Source	Salesforce and external	Salesforce
Object Relationships	Many levels	Three levels
Count of Rows	Millions	2,000 (display)
Data Availability	Schedule	Real time
Usage	Insight	Operation
Mobile App	Analytics	Salesforce
Data Load	External Data API	SOAP/REST/Bulk

Environment and License

CRM Analytics is hosted in the core Salesforce platform; if you are an existing Sales Cloud or Service Cloud customer, you need to purchase additional CRM Analytics licenses for each user to build or access CRM Analytics; reach out to your Salesforce Account Executive (AE) for the pricing and information on the different editions of CRM Analytics. After acquiring the CRM Analytics license, you should learn or test it in a sandbox environment.

However, if your company has not purchased CRM Analytics and you would like to learn CRM Analytics, there is nothing to worry about; you can learn CRM Analytics by signing up for Trailhead with free CRM Analytics–enabled Developer Edition from the following URL: `https://developer.salesforce.com/promotions/orgs/analytics-de`. This environment allows you to learn almost all the items that will be discussed in this book.

Note To check if your Salesforce environment has CRM Analytics enabled, navigate to **Setup** and type `Analytics` in the **Quick Find** search box; if you see the **Settings** under the **Analytics** menu, your environment (Salesforce organization) has CRM Analytics enabled. Another option is to navigate to **Company Information** in the setup menu and look for **Analytics Platform** in the **Permission Set Licenses** box; see Figure 1-2 to see the numbers of Analytics Platform licenses purchased and remained.

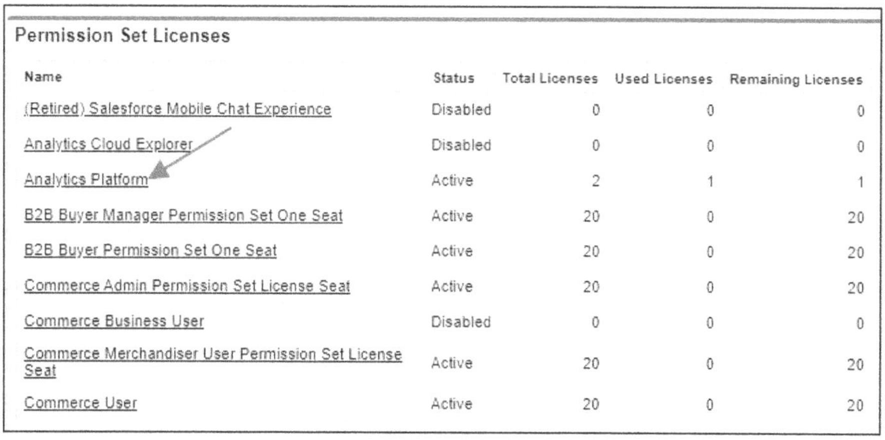

Permission Set Licenses

Name	Status	Total Licenses	Used Licenses	Remaining Licenses
(Retired) Salesforce Mobile Chat Experience	Disabled	0	0	0
Analytics Cloud Explorer	Disabled	0	0	0
Analytics Platform	Active	2	1	1
B2B Buyer Manager Permission Set One Seat	Active	20	0	20
B2B Buyer Permission Set One Seat	Active	20	0	20
Commerce Admin Permission Set License Seat	Active	20	0	20
Commerce Business User	Disabled	0	0	0
Commerce Merchandiser User Permission Set License Seat	Active	20	0	20
Commerce User	Active	20	0	20

***Figure 1-2.** CRM Analytics license information in Salesforce Company Information*

CRM Analytics Permissions

As the CRM Analytics license is in addition to the Salesforce license, each Salesforce user needs to have a CRM Analytics license to access CRM Analytics dashboards; otherwise, the users will not be able to build or explore CRM Analytics dashboards. And vice versa, each CRM Analytics user needs to have a Salesforce license as well; the Salesforce license type can be a "cheaper" one, such as a platform license.

In CRM Analytics, the license for a dashboard builder and a dashboard explorer is the same. To check if a user has been given a CRM Analytics license, go to user detail in Salesforce, scroll down to the **Permission Set License Assignments** related list, and look for **Analytics Platform** or **CRM Analytics Plus**, as shown in Figure 1-3. This license

CHAPTER 1   CRM ANALYTICS: INTRODUCTION

name depends on the editions of CRM Analytics you purchased. We will discuss CRM Analytics user permission further in Chapter 9, which will include hands-on instructions to assign the user the correct CRM Analytics permissions.

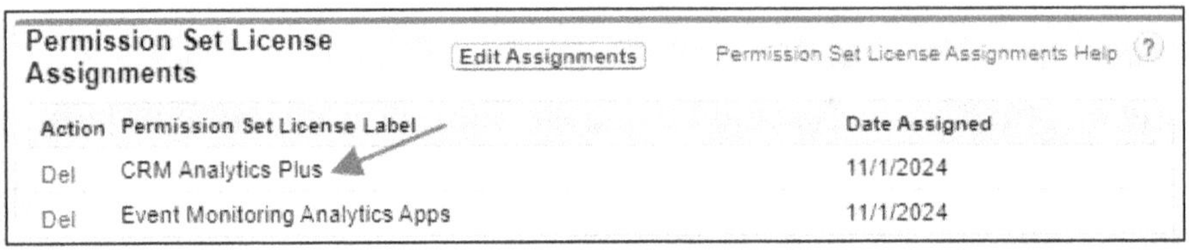

Figure 1-3. CRM Analytics licenses on a user

Navigating CRM Analytics

Since CRM Analytics is a Salesforce product, it integrates well into the Salesforce platform. A Salesforce user can access CRM Analytics dashboards from multiple places in Salesforce.

Lightning Page

A Salesforce admin can add CRM Analytics dashboards to any Lightning page, such as the Home page or a record page (Account, Opportunity, etc.). To add the dashboard to a record page, Salesforce can pass the record ID as a filter to the dashboard, so the dashboard only shows the relevant data. The Salesforce admin needs to edit the Lightning page, then add the **CRM Analytics Dashboard** component, select the dashboard, and configure the component property.

Analytics Tab

Once CRM Analytics is provisioned, the **Analytics** tab will be added to your Salesforce organization. Your Salesforce admin needs to configure the tab visibility, either by profile or permission set; this is similar to the standard Salesforce tab; your Salesforce admin can set it as Default On, Default Off, or Tab Hidden.

From the Analytics tab, users can explore all apps, dashboards, and lenses that users have access to. Also, users can track Notifications, Subscriptions, Watchlists, Collections, and Favorites of items added.

CHAPTER 1   CRM ANALYTICS: INTRODUCTION

Analytics Studio

The Analytics Studio app is primarily for dashboard builders to build or edit CRM Analytics dashboards, starting from building the dataset to defining security and so on. Dashboard builders can open **Data Manager** from Analytics Studio or the App Launcher; we will discuss Data Manager later in this chapter. Figure 1-4 shown a sample of Analytics Studio user interface with the Home tab.

Business users will be able to access Analytics Studio if their profile or permission set allows; from here, the users can explore apps, dashboards, lenses, and datasets. There are two ways to open the Analytics Studio app:

1. **Analytics Tab**: Open a dashboard or lens, then click the "Open Analytics Studio" icon at the upper-right corner.

2. **Analytics Studio App**: Click the App Launcher (nine-dot icon at the upper left in Salesforce Lightning), then click Analytics Studio.

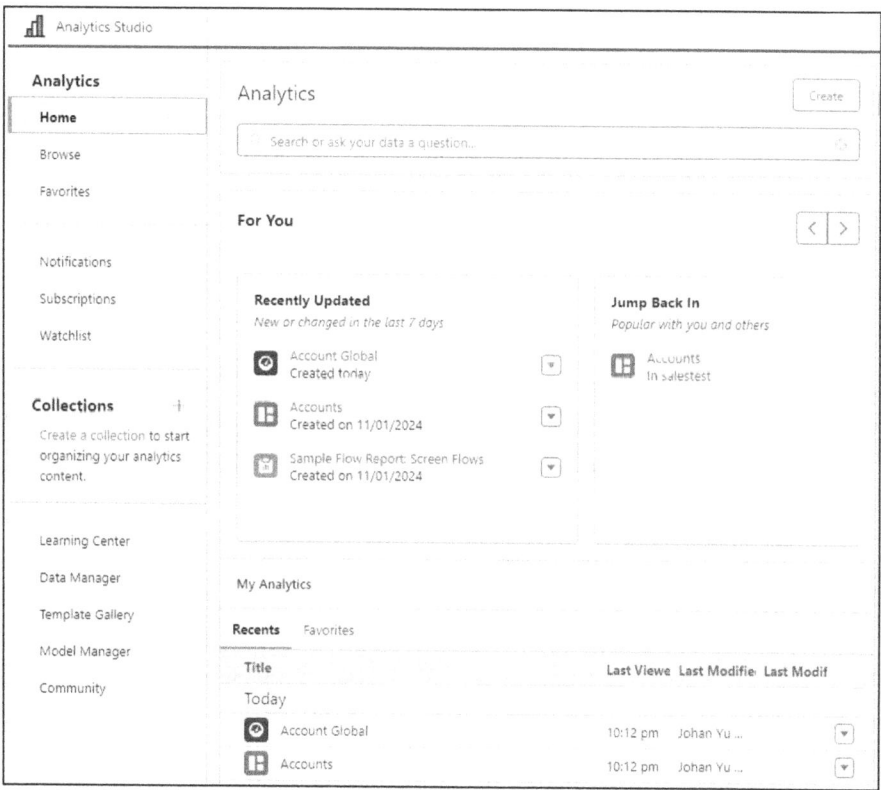

Figure 1-4.   Analytics Studio user interface

Mobile App

Users can download the **CRM Analytics** mobile app from the App Store or Google Play Store. In the mobile app, users will be able to open all dashboards and lenses to which the users have access.

As the dashboard builder/designer, you should design dashboard layouts that are optimized for mobile or tablet devices. If you do not create the mobile or tablet layouts, the mobile app will be using the default app for web browsers, where some widgets will not visualize well on mobile/tablet devices.

CRM Analytics Components

We discussed that the dashboard is the visualization for users to explore and analyze data, but behind that, many components build a CRM Analytics dashboard. We briefly mentioned Apps, Lenses, Widgets, Datasets, and Data Manager. Now, let us go through each component of CRM Analytics.

Apps

Suppose you are familiar with the Salesforce report and dashboard; each report and dashboard are stored in a folder, and the folder controls user accessibility of the reports and dashboards that are stored in that folder. An app in CRM Analytics is like a folder in Salesforce, where it controls who can view, edit, or manage items within the app.

The app is similar to containers that can hold multiple types of items, from dashboards, components, lenses, and datasets. Ideally, you should put all related items within an app; then, you can configure the app sharing to users who need to access the dataset, dashboard, or lens.

Dashboards

A dashboard is a collection of widgets that may contain charts, tables, repeaters, text, numbers, links, components, containers, images, filters, lists, inputs, toggles, dates, ranges, and navigation. Ideally, a dashboard is the result of what we want to achieve, and then it is published to a group of users, where users will explore and analyze the data. You can build a dashboard that contains multiple pages.

However, not all business needs are required to build a dashboard; for example, if the users simply need to get the data into a table or a chart, we can use Lens, which explores data from one or multiple datasets.

Lenses

A lens is a visualization of dataset; it can be presented as raw data, grouping, pivot table, and multiple types of charts. The lens can be saved to an App and shared with other users.

The lens is similar to that of Salesforce's report. However, the CRM Analytics dashboard does not need a lens to build the widgets as a data source; the widget gets the data directly from the data source.

A lens can be created by exploring a dataset or by exploring a widget from the dashboard. When the user explores a widget from a dashboard, it will not impact the dashboard itself, but it will create a new lens, and the user is able to save the lens if needed for future usage or analysis.

A lens can be visualized in the form of a chart or table. Many types of charts can be used in a dashboard; the same type of charts is available to use in a lens.

Datasets

A dataset is a collection of data stored in a tabular format. The data can come from multiple sources, such as Salesforce objects, other Salesforce organizations, external systems, and CSV files.

Everything you need to build a dashboard or lens starts from the dataset. The dataset contains the data itself and **extended metadata** (XMD).

You can configure dataset extended metadata by exploring the dataset, such as setting field formatting, relabeling field names, hiding fields, setting default fields, and editing data values (but this is not bucketing).

By opening the dataset, you can get dataset information such as the API Name, created date time, data last refreshed, data last queried, the number of rows, source, app, usage, and security predicate. Additionally, you can perform actions such as backing up and restoring the extended metadata, configuring actions, restoring the dataset, and replacing data (for CSV data load).

CHAPTER 1 CRM ANALYTICS: INTRODUCTION

If a dataset is created as a result of a recipe or dataflow, whenever possible, design the recipe or dataflow that produces data that can be easily used in the dashboard, where all the heavy lifting works are performed in the recipe or dataflow, not in the dashboard, such as by performing SAQL (Salesforce Analytics Query Language). Figure 1-5 show CRM Analytics architecture, from data sources, recipe to dashboard.

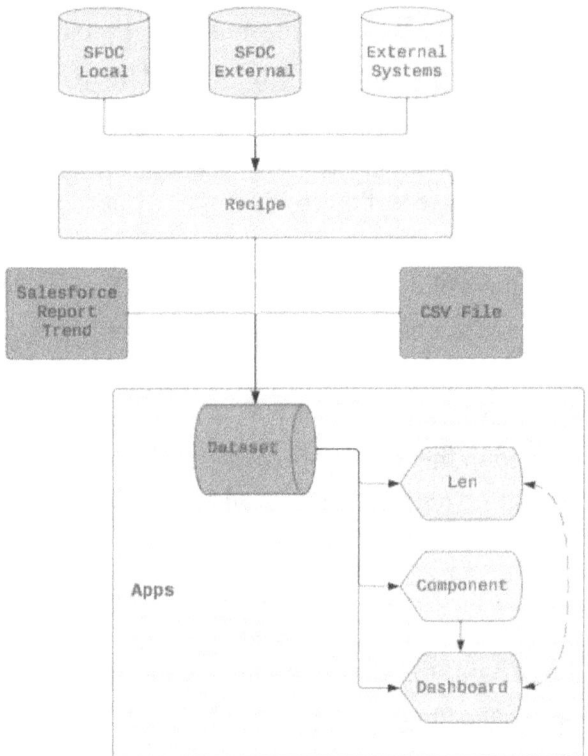

Figure 1-5. *CRM Analytics architecture*

Understanding Data Manager

You can access the Data Manager from **Analytics Studio** or the **App Launcher** (nine-dot icon in the upper-left corner). Data Manager is meant to be used by dashboard builders, CRM Analytics super users, or CRM Analytics administrators to manage data connection and scheduler.

CHAPTER 1 CRM ANALYTICS: INTRODUCTION

From Data Manager, you can create and schedule recipes, create and schedule dataflows, monitor job runs, monitor data assets, monitor usages, manage connections, and schedule data sync. If you have permission to access Data Manager, click the gear icon at the upper-right corner of Analytics Studio, then select Data Manager; see Figure 1-6.

Figure 1-6. *Accessing Data Manager from Analytics Studio*

Jobs Monitor

Jobs Monitor is the default page when opening Data Manager. Jobs Monitor will show all the history and current jobs that are running, including Recipe, Dataflow, Data Sync, Trend, and File Upload. At the top bar, you can click one of the six tabs to filter the jobs quickly based on job status: All, Succeeded, Failed, Warning, Running, and Queued. For a sample of Jobs Monitor and Data Manager user interface, see Figure 1-7.

11

CHAPTER 1   CRM ANALYTICS: INTRODUCTION

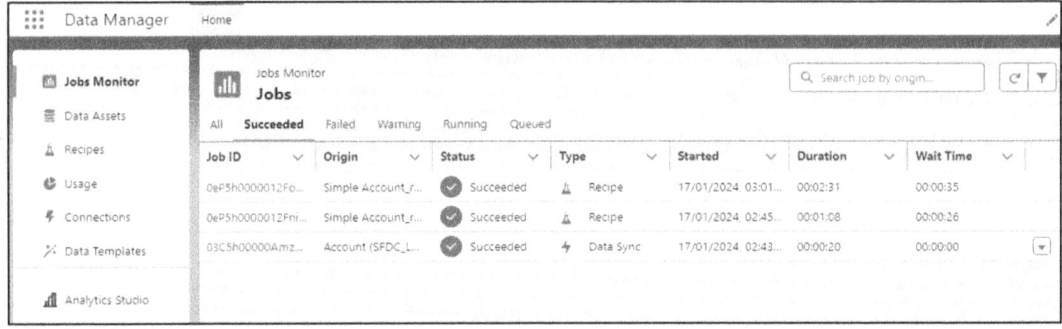

Figure 1-7. *Data Manager user interface*

Click the **filter** icon at the upper-right corner to filter the job history and run. Click the **refresh** icon (next to the filter icon) to refresh the latest status of jobs run. Information from Jobs Monitor will include

- Job ID
- Origin
- Status
- Type
- Started
- Duration
- Wait Time

Click the Job ID to get details from each job, so you can monitor which nodes take lots of time, and you can try to optimize them:

- Name
- Status
- Type
- Started
- Duration
- Rows In
- Rows Out
- Rows Failed

CHAPTER 1   CRM ANALYTICS: INTRODUCTION

Data Assets

From Data Assets, see Figure 1-8, you can view all datasets that exist in the CRM Analytics platform, as well as Salesforce (and external) objects that are connected to CRM Analytics.

For datasets, you can see where the datasets are stored, who created the dataset, the number of rows, creation date time, last refreshed, and last queried; click the header to sort it. For Connected data, you can see the title, the connection source, and the last data sync.

You can also create a new dataset from a CSV file by clicking the New Dataset button at the upper-right corner; this is similar to creating a dataset from Analytics Studio.

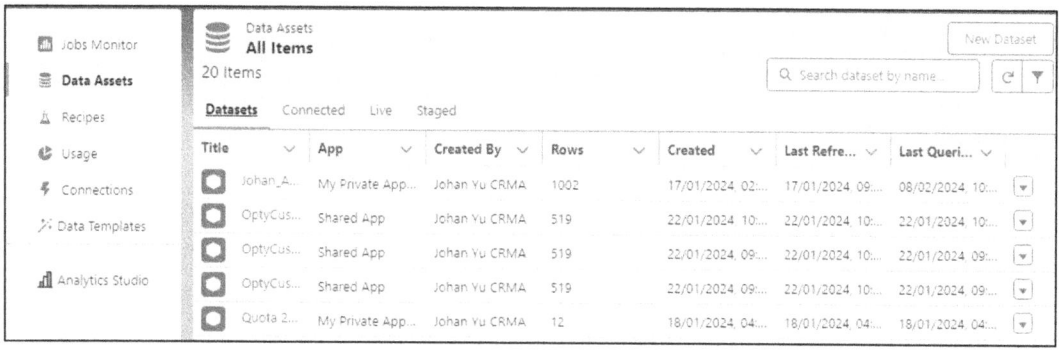

Figure 1-8. Data Assets user interface

Recipes and Dataflows

Recipe is the primary data transformation tool in CRM Analytics. Use the recipe to transform and enrich data before loading it as datasets or other targets. When building a recipe, you can preview the results as you build it. When you are done building the recipe, run the recipe to write the result as datasets or other targets, such as CSV or Salesforce objects.

The dataflow used to be the primary data transformation tool before the recipe was enhanced with many features. There are many benefits of the recipe compared to the dataflow, which we will discuss in depth in Chapter 3.

By default, the Recipes tab will list all recipes built; click the arrow at the far right of the recipe name:

- **Edit**: This is the same as clicking the recipe name.
- **Delete**: Please note that you cannot restore a deleted recipe.
- **Run Now**: Run the recipe, and you can monitor the progress in Jobs Monitor.
- **Schedule**: Select time based (hour, day, week, month) or event based.
- **Notifications**: Send notifications when the recipe runs and ends with warnings, failure, or all events.

Similar to Jobs Monitor, you can click the header to sort, type in the search box, refresh, and filter the list of recipes. To create a new recipe, click the **New Recipe** button in the upper-right corner of the Recipes tab; we will discuss more on new recipe creation in Chapter 3.

To create a dataflow, make sure "Allow users to access Data Manager (Legacy)" is enabled in the Analytics setting under the Salesforce setup; click "Manage Dataflows" at the bottom left of the Data Manager. However, as Salesforce has transitioned to using recipes as the primary data transformation tool, we will not discuss the dataflow in depth in this book edition.

Usage

In this tab, you can review the data usage at a glance:

- Number of rows used (total of all datasets) and maximum rows allowed for your organization. The maximum rows are based on the CRM Analytics edition and the number of licenses purchased.
- Usage in GB of output to Salesforce and the maximum size allowed in a day.
- Usage in GB of output to CSV and the maximum size allowed in a day.

Synced data does not count toward CRM Analytics usage; only the rows are in All Datasets.

Connections

The Connections tab shows local Salesforce objects that are synced between Salesforce and CRM Analytics; this connection is called SFDC_LOCAL. For each item:

- **Object Name:** This is the Salesforce object API Name.
- **Filter:** Adding a filter here will cause not all data to sync from Salesforce objects.
- **Columns:** Number of columns that synced from each object.
- **Connection Mode:** What is the sync mode for the object?
- **Last Run:** When is the last sync for the object?
- **Status:** What is the status of the last sync?

Similar to the recipe, click the arrow at the far right of the object name to

- **Run Data Sync:** Only run data sync for the select object.
- **Disconnect Object:** This will disconnect the object from the data sync. Data sync will stop pulling data from the data sources.
- **Edit Connection Mode:** This can be set up differently for each object.

You can connect CRM Analytics to external data sources, such as Google Big Query, Microsoft Azure SQL, Amazon RDS, Snowflake, etc., and, of course, you can also connect to other Salesforce organizations.

To create a new connection, click the **New Connection** button on this page, then select the connectors. To schedule the sync, click the arrow next to the connection name and click **Schedule**; this is similar to scheduling recipes. See Figure 1-9; you can select **Run Now** to sync all connected objects for this connection, set Notifications, or Edit Objects.

CHAPTER 1   CRM ANALYTICS: INTRODUCTION

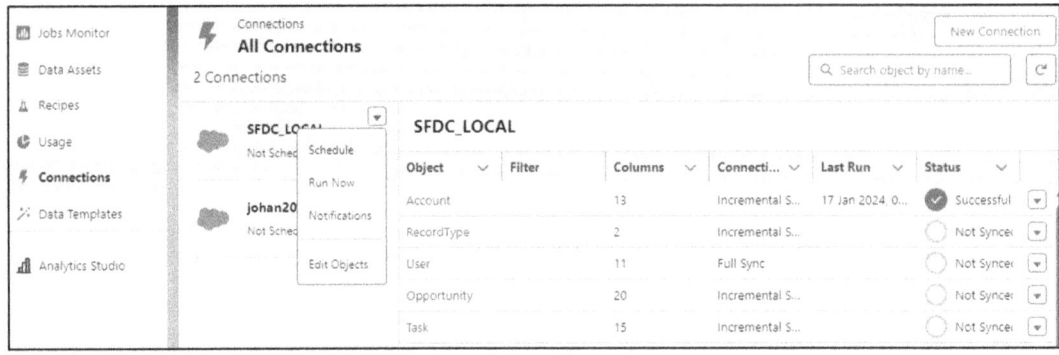

Figure 1-9. *Connections user interface*

When you click an object from SFDC_LOCAL, you will see three tabs:

1. **Columns**: Select fields that you want to sync from Salesforce.

2. **Data Preview**: Preview data for selected columns.

3. **Data Sync Filter**: Add filters to filter out data sync from Salesforce; unless you are working on a specific custom object, do not set filters for main objects, such as Account, Opportunity, etc., as other dashboards (maybe in the future) may need those data. You can filter out unneeded data from the recipe with a filter.

Summary

In this chapter, we learned that CRM Analytics is a platform by itself. The data is stored in the CRM Analytics platform, not in the Salesforce platform, but you can configure the system to sync the necessary fields and objects. We also discussed why we need CRM Analytics and the differences with standard Salesforce reports and dashboards.

CRM Analytics user provisioned from Salesforce user details with a permission set. To access the CRM Analytics dashboard, users need to log in to Salesforce and then access the embedded dashboard on the Lightning page or from the Analytics tab. But to edit or build a dashboard, you must start from Analytics Studio.

You can create a free Trailhead Developer Edition with CRM Analytics to learn CRM Analytics from a basic level; this environment will give you all the items that you need to learn CRM Analytics.

We ended this chapter by walking through permissions, the components within CRM Analytics, and Data Manager. In Chapter 2, we will discuss Data Sources and how we can get data into the CRM Analytics platform, so stay tuned!

CHAPTER 2

Data Sources

In Chapter 1, we learned what CRM Analytics is, the differences with the Salesforce dashboard, and the components in CRM Analytics, including Analytics Studio and Data Manager. In this chapter, we will dive deep into data sources and how to get data into CRM Analytics. As explained in Chapter 1, CRM Analytics stores data on its platform, utilizing recipes to get and transform data from multiple sources, including the local Salesforce platform, external Salesforce organization, and other external data sources.

By the end of this chapter, you will learn multiple methods to get data into CRM Analytics.

CRM Analytics syncs data from Salesforce local and all connected environments within schedules set by the CRM Analytics admin. Each connection can have a different data sync scheduled, and each object from Salesforce local can be configured with a different **Connection Mode** (Full Sync, Periodic Full Sync, and Incremental Sync). As a CRM Analytics admin, you need to decide and set the correct connection mode by analyzing the volume of transactions and the total number of records for each object. I recommend setting Periodic Full Sync whenever possible; this will prevent data drift over time with Incremental Sync.

However, some Salesforce objects, such as User and Group, can only be set with Full Sync; this makes sense as those objects will not have many transactions – the same applies to external connections, with only Full Sync available for all objects. All of this can be configured in the **Connections** tab under Data Manager.

Data that is uploaded manually into CRM Analytics, such as from a CSV file, will be stored as a dataset. You can update the data by opening the dataset and clicking Replace Data, and you can also restore the previous version of data by clicking Restore Dataset.

CHAPTER 2   DATA SOURCES

Getting Data into CRM Analytics

The Dataset in CRM Analytics is the result of data "import" into the CRM Analytics platform; this includes data from the local Salesforce platform, external Salesforce organization, other external data sources, and CSV files. You can create new datasets from Analytics Studio by clicking the Create button at the upper-right corner and selecting **Dataset**.

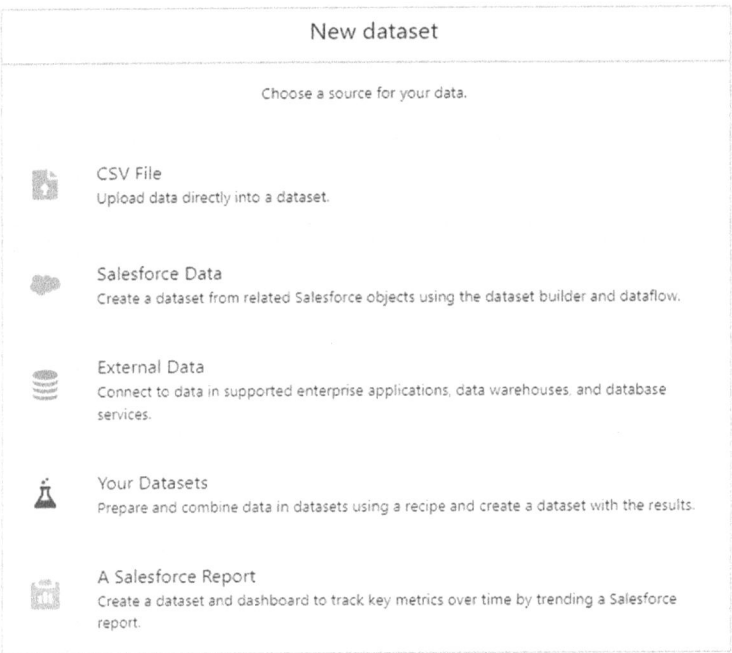

Figure 2-1. *A few options to create a new dataset*

We will walk through each of them. However, if you are using the free Trailhead Developer Edition, you may not see the last option, "A Salesforce Report"; this is only available in the paid CRM Analytics. You can check if the Salesforce organization has the "Trend Report Data in CRM Analytics" permission. See Figure 2-2 for data integration concept in CRM Analytics.

CHAPTER 2 DATA SOURCES

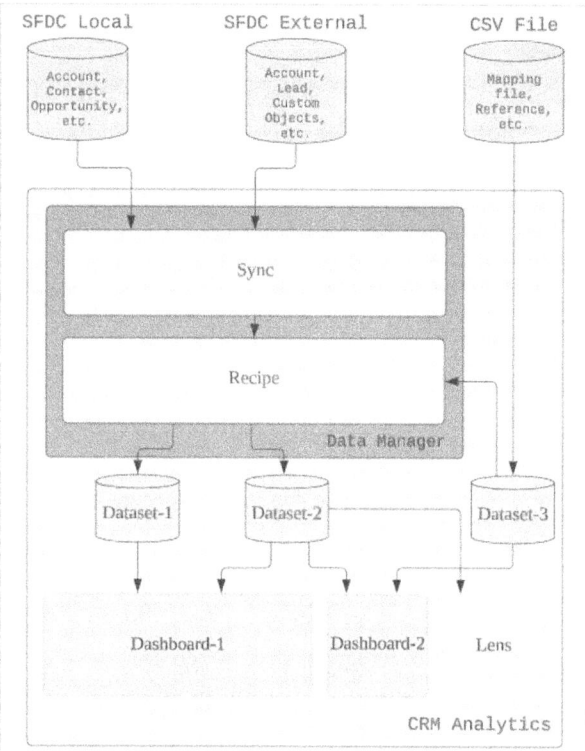

Figure 2-2. *Concept and sample of data integration in CRM Analytics*

CSV File

CSV files are the most basic type of data source. However, it is still widely used as it is standard, simple, human-readable/editable, can be opened with a simple text editor, and is interoperable by many systems. You can directly load data from a CSV file into CRM Analytics from Analytics Studio; this will create a new dataset. If the data is stored in an Excel file, save it in CSV format before the upload process.

CSV files are also suitable for storing simple data without many rows, such as mapping or reference between data stored in Salesforce with output needed in CRM Analytics; this data is supposedly not frequently changed.

CHAPTER 2   DATA SOURCES

Hands-On: CSV Data Load

Let us start with getting our hands dirty by loading a CSV file into CRM Analytics. In this exercise, we are going to load the quota for each sales rep for each quarter. You need to prepare the CSV file as shown in Table 2-1; to create the file quickly, you can use Microsoft Excel and save it as a CSV file.

Table 2-1. Sample Table for Sales Rep Quota

Employee Id	Quota Quarter	Quota Amount
A001	2024-03-31	500,000
A001	2024-06-30	600,000
A001	2024-09-30	650,000
A001	2024-12-31	500,000
A002	2024-03-31	700,000
A002	2024-06-30	750,000
A002	2024-09-30	800,000
A002	2024-12-31	650,000
A003	2024-03-31	400,000
A003	2024-06-30	450,000
A003	2024-09-30	500,000
A003	2024-12-31	350,000

Let us save the data from Table 2-1 as "Quota 2024.csv," then load the CSV file as a dataset in CRM Analytics; follow these steps:

1. Open **Analytics Studio**.
2. Click the **Create** button, then select **Dataset**, see Figure 2-3

CHAPTER 2   DATA SOURCES

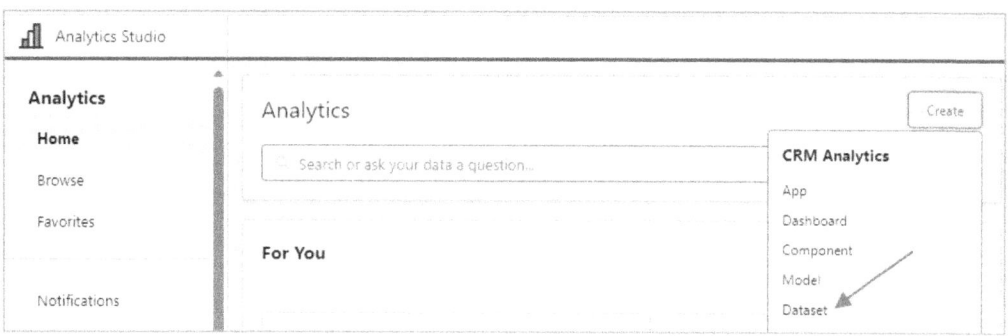

Figure 2-3. *Create a new Dataset*

3. Select **CSV File**.

4. Upload the CSV file by selecting the file or dragging it to the box.

5. Click **Next** to continue.

6. Click **Next** again; for now, let us use the default dataset name and default app, **My Private App**.

7. Click the **Upload File** button; there is no need to change anything on this screen; the system automatically matches each column with field type. Notice there are three types of Field Types:

   - Employee Id: Dimension
   - Quota Quarter: Date
   - Quota Amount: Measure

8. Done; wait for a few seconds, and the system will open the created dataset, see Figure 2-4. Optionally, you can monitor the data load progress from the **Data Manager**.

23

CHAPTER 2   DATA SOURCES

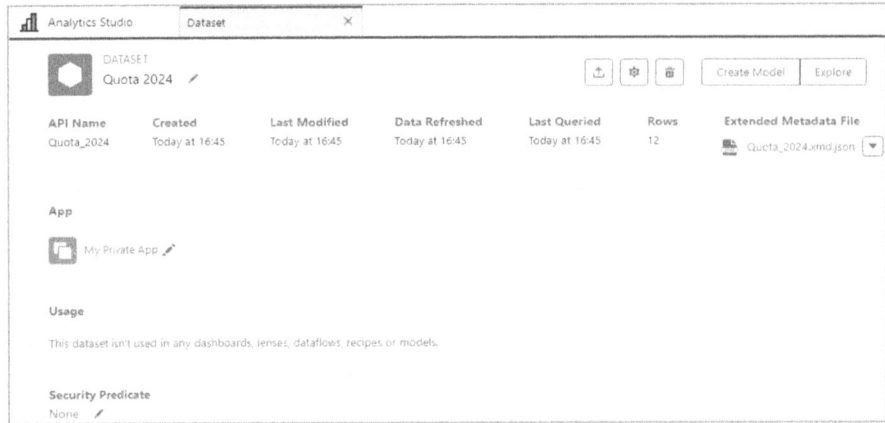

Figure 2-4. *The dataset is created; the pencil icon means that you can change the data*

9. Let's confirm the dataset created by going back to Analytics Studio, clicking the **Browse** tab, and then clicking the Datasets button; you should see the Quota 2024, as in Figure 2-5

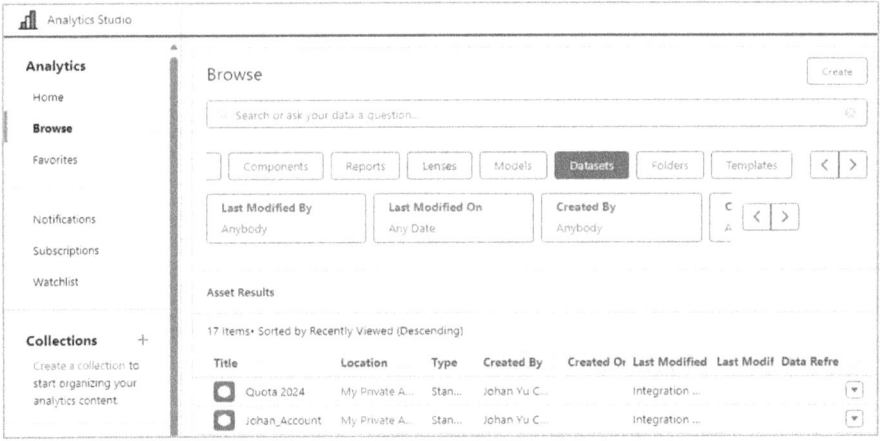

Figure 2-5. *The new dataset is available under the Datasets*

10. Clicking the Quota 2024 dataset will open the dataset as a new lens; by default, it will be a horizontal bar chart with the count of rows as bar length and without any grouping.

11. Click the arrow next to the dataset name and select **Show Fields Panel** to see all available fields for the dataset. See Figure 2-6

24

CHAPTER 2 DATA SOURCES

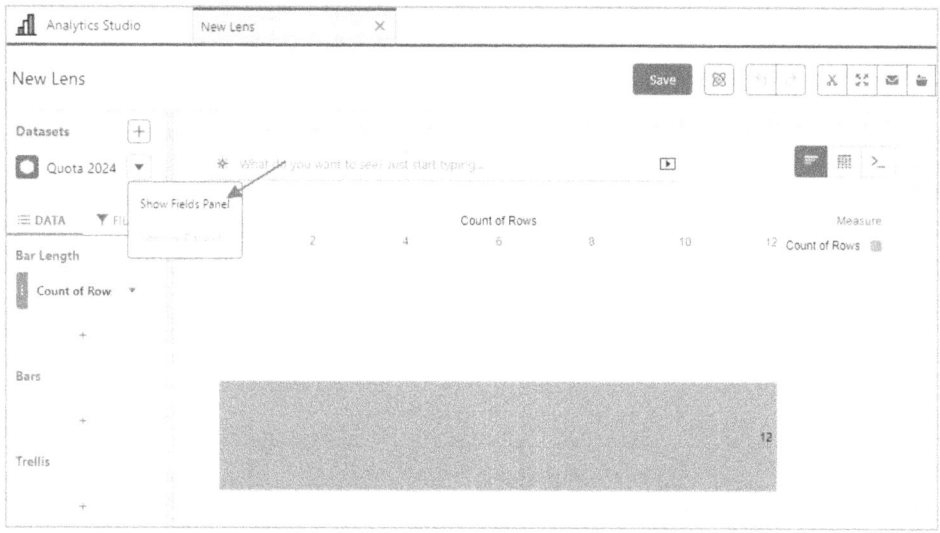

Figure 2-6. *Explore the dataset and show the fields panel*

Here are a few items that we learned from this hands-on:

- The file must be in CSV format, not in Excel format or other formats.

- By default, the dataset name would be the file name and stored in My Private App, but if you click the Create button from an app, the dataset created would be stored in that app.

- There are three types of Field Type:

  - **Dimension**: Data is stored as text; you can perform the string functions in this field.

  - **Date**: Data is stored in a date format; CRM Analytics will auto-split it into year, quarter, month, week, day, hour, minute, and second.

  - **Measure**: Data is stored as numbers; you can set the number format and perform the numerical functions in this field.

- You can monitor the data loading progress via Jobs Monitor in Data Manager.

25

CHAPTER 2　DATA SOURCES

Local Salesforce Data

You probably noticed that I mentioned earlier in this and the previous chapters Salesforce "local" and external Salesforce. Salesforce local means the Salesforce organization where your CRM Analytics is hosted; remember that the user must log in to Salesforce to access CRM Analytics. For external Salesforce, this is another Salesforce organization that is not related to your CRM Analytics; still, you can retrieve the data by adding it to the Connection. Table 2-2 show the difference between Local Salesforce and External Salesforce in CRM Analytics.

Table 2-2. Local Salesforce vs. External Salesforce

	Local Salesforce	**External Salesforce**
Relation with the CRM Analytics platform	CRM Analytics host, although the data is separate	Not related to your CRM Analytics organization
Connection mode	Full Sync, Periodic Full Sync, Incremental Sync	Full Sync
Number of organization	Only one organization, which is local	Connect to multiple Salesforce organization

Whether local or external Salesforce, you need to run/schedule data sync to retrieve data from Salesforce local or Salesforce external organization's objects to CRM Analytics as "sync objects." You cannot see/explore synced data, only the number of columns; however, you can create a simple recipe to pull data from the synced objects and write the output to datasets.

Tip　You can see the number of rows synced in Jobs Monitor, open the succeeded sync job, and look for Rows In and Rows Out.

When a recipe runs, it will not retrieve the data from the Salesforce objects, but from the synced data in the CRM Analytics platform. With this architecture, the data load performance in the recipe runs much faster than that of retrieved data directly from Salesforce, see Figure 2-7.

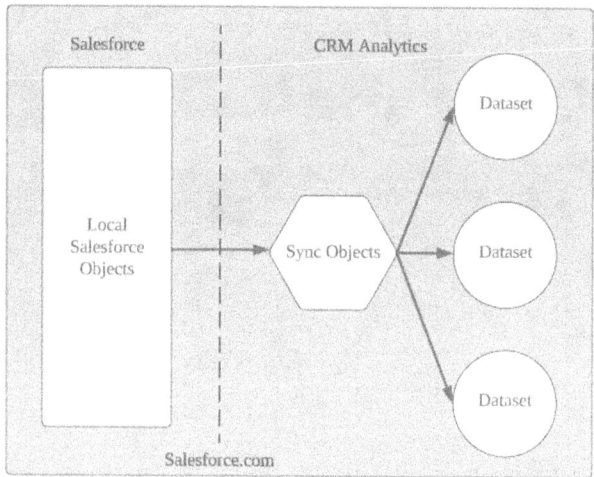

Figure 2-7. *Retrieve Salesforce data to CRM Analytics*

Tip You can create multiple "SFDC_LOCAL" connections, but an object can only be connected to one "SFDC_LOCAL" connection. The purpose of having multiple "SFDC_LOCAL" connections is to have a different sync schedule, for example, SFDC_LOCAL will sync the Account object every two hours, while Opportunity in SFDC_LOCAL_2 will sync every hour. You can move the object across the SFDC_LOCAL connection by selecting **Switch Connection** from the object arrow at the far right.

External Data

CRM Analytics provides multiple connectors to retrieve data from other systems, including the connector to retrieve data from different Salesforce organizations.

From Data Manager, click the **Connections** tab, and you will see all connections and the objects synced for each connection. To add a new connection, click the **New Connection** button in the upper-left corner.

CHAPTER 2 DATA SOURCES

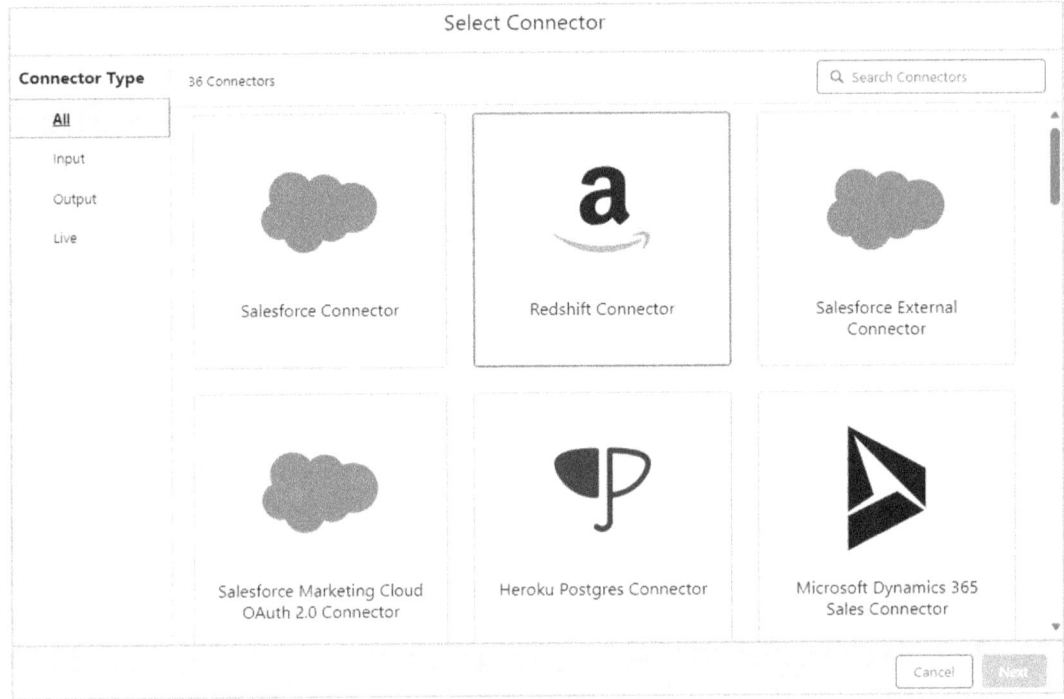

Figure 2-8. *Connector available in CRM Analytics*

For each connection, you can schedule when to sync from the external data source, including from external Salesforce. Figure 2-8 shows that I have three connections; two of them are SFDC_LOCAL, and one is another Salesforce organization, where I named the connection "johan2024." With this, we can set different sync schedules for each connection, see Figure 2-9.

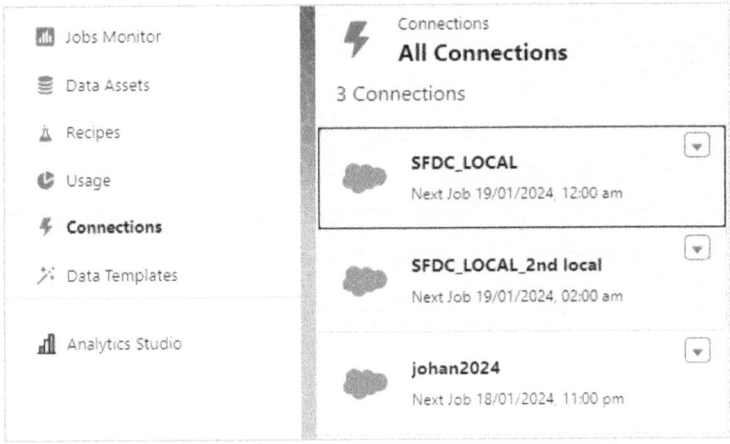

Figure 2-9. *Multiple connections connected to CRM Analytics*

Existing Dataset

In some scenarios, you need to use existing datasets for other purposes, such as to build a new similar dashboard. Another scenario is that it is too risky to change the existing dataset that is used in existing dashboards and lenses. As a solution, you can create a **recipe** to use existing datasets; select the "CRM Analytics Datasets" checkbox when adding input data to create a new enriched dataset; this will not impact the existing dataset and dashboards and is the safest option when the dataset has been used in dashboards or lens.

We will discuss the recipe in detail in Chapter 3.

Salesforce Trend Report

The Salesforce trend report is a compelling feature yet a simple way to trend Salesforce data into CRM Analytics. With the Trend, you can push data directly (in schedule) from a Salesforce report to CRM Analytics as a dataset. You also do not need to know the Salesforce objects and fields; you can use any Salesforce report and click the **Trend** button.

This option also has another benefit, such as if the fields that you would like to push to CRM Analytics are fields that are only available in the report, such as Last Activity, Age, and Fiscal Period in Opportunity report. A recipe or dataflow will not be able to retrieve those fields, but the Trend will serve that efficiently.

Basically, the idea of creating trending is to track key metrics over time so you can see your data growing in a dataset.

After clicking the Trend button, you need to schedule the frequency and time. As for trending, data pushed into CRM Analytics will be kept added, not overwritten like the dataflow or recipe. In addition to creating a new dataset, it will also automatically create a new Dashboard in CRM Analytics.

> **Tip** You can schedule a recipe to run after the Salesforce local connection or external connection sync is completed.

If you are using the Trailhead Developer Edition, you need to check if you have the "Trend Report Data in Analytics" permission in your organization; otherwise, you will not see the Trend button in the report; you may log a ticket to Salesforce to ask for enabling this permission.

Hands-On: Trend a Salesforce Report

Let's get our hands dirty and have an exercise to trend a Salesforce report:

1. **Create a report**

   You can use any Salesforce report for trends. For this exercise, I'll create an Opportunity report and add the Opportunity Name, Stage, Age, and Last Activity, then group rows by Fiscal Period. Fiscal Period, Age, and Last Activity are report-only fields. Hide the Detail Rows, save and run the report, and click the **Trend** button, see Figure 2-10

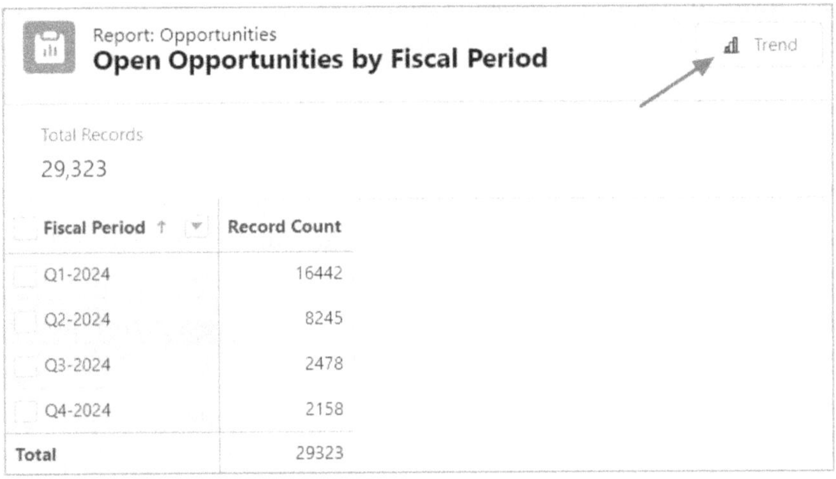

Fiscal Period ↑	Record Count
Q1-2024	16442
Q2-2024	8245
Q3-2024	2478
Q4-2024	2158
Total	29323

   Report: Opportunities — Open Opportunities by Fiscal Period
   Total Records: 29,323

   Figure 2-10. *Trend a Salesforce report*

2. **Configure a Trend**

   In the Trend window, the Dataset name and Dashboard title have been pre-populated; you can change them if needed. Then, you need to schedule for frequency and select the days and times when the Trend will run. You can keep the default dataset and dashboard name; let's change the frequency to Daily 5:00 AM or any time you prefer, then click the **Trend** button at the bottom right of the window, see Figure 2-11.

CHAPTER 2 DATA SOURCES

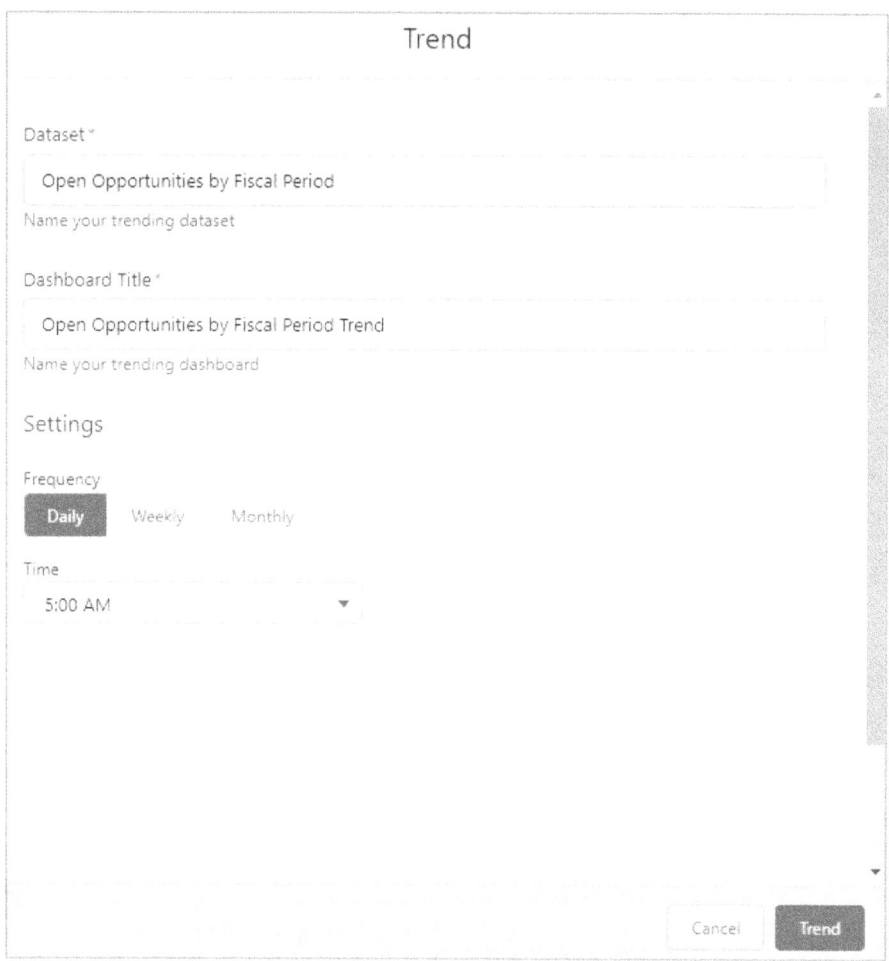

Figure 2-11. *Schedule the Trend from a Salesforce report*

Alternatively, you can also trend a report from Analytics Studio; click Create and then Dataset, and select **A Salesforce Report**; see Figure 2-1.

Note At a minimum, you can only run the Trend scheduled once daily; if you need to run more trends in a day, you can duplicate the report, schedule trends for each report, and then use a recipe to combine the datasets into a new dataset.

31

CHAPTER 2 DATA SOURCES

3. **Verify the Dataset and Dashboard**

   Once you click the Trend button, the dataflow will run immediately (before the scheduled date and time); this will create a new dataset (with the data as in the report) in CRM Analytics. You can monitor the progress for the initial run from Jobs Monitor; see Figure 2-12.

Figure 2-12. Monitor trend progress for the initial trend run

   Once completed, you should see a new Trend dashboard and dataset in My Private App.

Tip If you only need one snapshot of data per day, set the schedule daily before the current time. For example, now is 10:30 PM; if you set the schedule at 11:00 PM, the schedule will run at 11:00 PM on the same day, and you will have two data snapshots for the same day, but if you schedule before the current time, the schedule will only run the following day.

---

4. **On Schedule Date/Time**

   When the schedule runs, the dataset will add data from the report to the existing dataset from the initial run. You can check in Jobs Monitor that the process is a bit different; there is an additional process called **append**, see Figure 2-13. If you recheck the dataset, the count is more than that of the initial trend run.

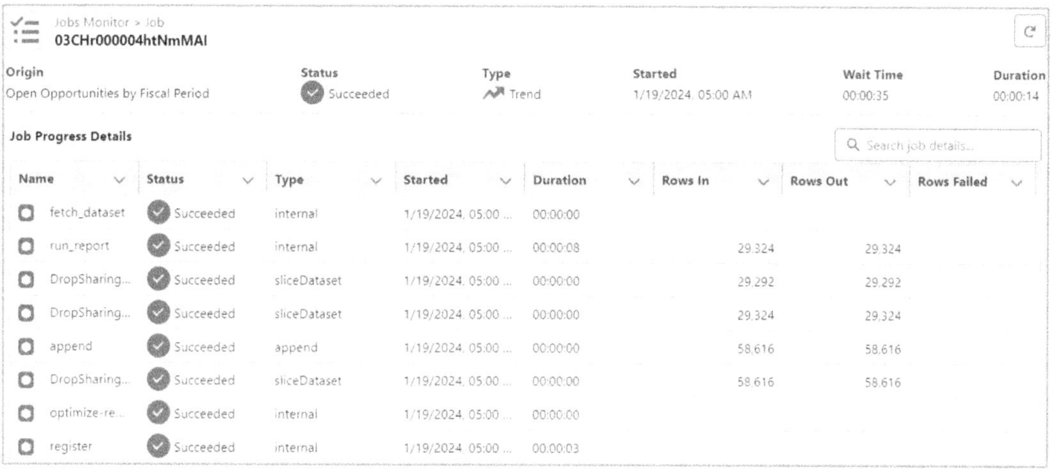

CHAPTER 2 DATA SOURCES

Figure 2-13. Trend job progress detail on schedule trend

5. **Dataset Fields**

    Let us see what fields are created in the dataset from the Trend. Open the dataset as a new lens and change to the table format; you should see all fields from the Salesforce report, including fields used for grouping. Additionally, there is a DateTime field called **Snapshot Date**; this field is useful to mark when the Trend runs when adding new rows in the dataset. See Figure 2-14.

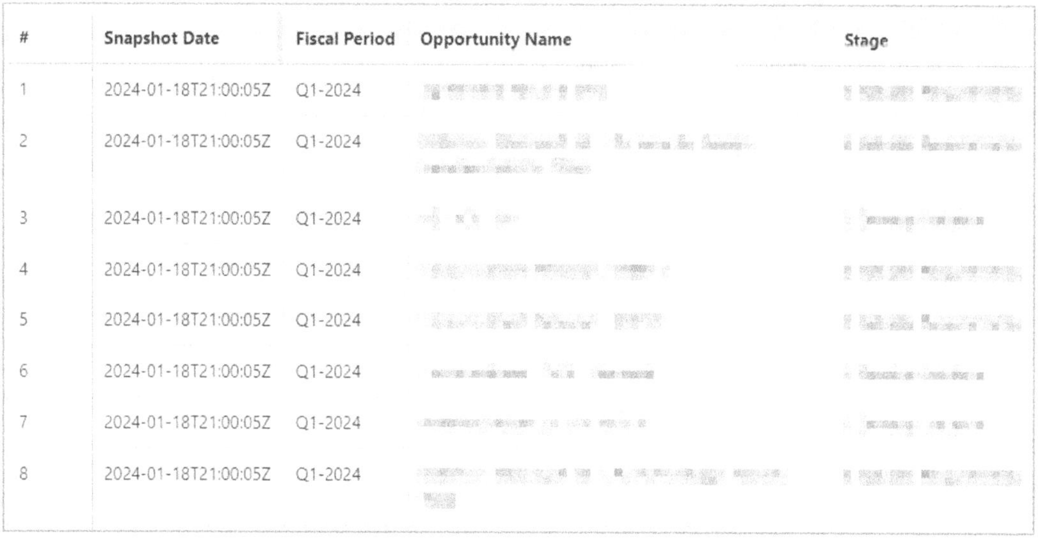

Figure 2-14. The table shows data in the dataset created by Trend

33

CHAPTER 2   DATA SOURCES

6. **Trend Dashboard**

    As part of the Trend process from Salesforce, a simple dashboard is created in CRM Analytics with the data source from the trend dataset. See Figure 2-15.

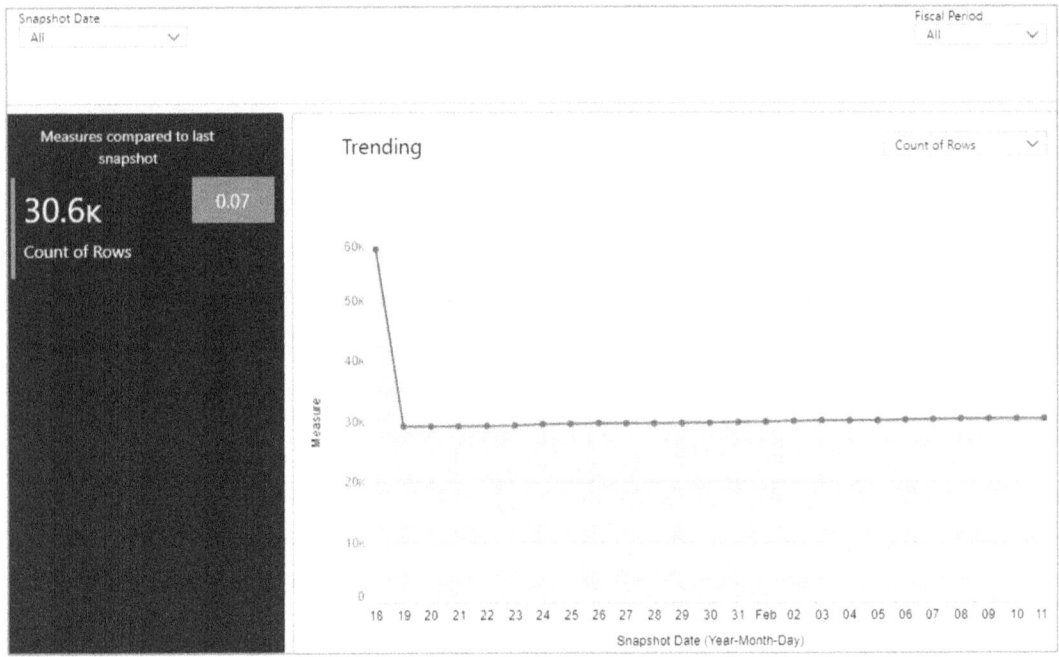

Figure 2-15. *Trend Dashboard*

Tip   If you need to have only the latest data from Salesforce and do not keep adding data to existing rows, you can create a recipe to clean all existing rows and make sure the recipe runs before the Trend schedule runs. Ideally, this should be performed at midnight, when no one is accessing the dashboard because the dataset will blank out between the recipe end and trend end.

External Data API

This option is not available when you click Create Dataset from Analytics Studio, and this is more targeted for developers. The API enables you to upload external data into the CRM Analytics platform, and it can be triggered based on actions in other systems. You need a developer to write a script and use the CRM Analytics API. However, we will not discuss this option in this book; check out this article: https://developer.salesforce.com/docs/atlas.en-us.bi_dev_guide_ext_data.meta/bi_dev_guide_ext_data/bi_ext_data_overview.htm.

Summary

In this chapter, we looked at all possibilities for bringing data into the CRM Analytics platform, from a simple CSV file data load, from local Salesforce data sync, from other Salesforce organizations, from other systems with external connectors, and trends from a Salesforce report. Additionally, we were also able to create a new dataset by using values from the existing datasets with the recipe.

However, there is also a feature that we have not discussed, where we can directly pull local Salesforce data to the dashboard in real time without using a dataset; we will discuss this in Chapter 6.

The next chapter will be more exciting as we will be hands-on with building Recipes from scratch. The Recipe is the most crucial tool for CRM Analytics professionals because it offers you unlimited possibilities to design the datasets. We will also share how to back up and restore recipes and will close with a session to create a recipe.

CHAPTER 3

Recipe

We discussed how to get data into CRM Analytics in Chapter 2. We had a hands-on CSV file data load exercise and also another hands-on with trending data from a Salesforce report; in both exercises, we created a new dataset. But we have not discussed the Recipe, one of the most critical tools for data transformation from multiple sources into CRM Analytics, so let us start now.

Trust me, this chapter will be fun; we will build a Recipe from scratch. You can architect the data transformation, data manipulation, and data enrichment to produce the datasets that are required for your dashboard.

By the end of this chapter, you will be able to build a new recipe from scratch and convert an existing Dataflow into a new Recipe.

Dataflow

The Dataflow used to be the primary data transformation tool; it was when the product was still known as Wave and Einstein Analytics.

As per the product evolution, the Dataflow is no longer available by default; unless your Salesforce/CRM Analytics admin enables it, look for **Allow users to access Data Manager (Legacy)** under the Analytics menu in the Salesforce setup. If you have existing dataflows built and scheduled, they will continue to run as usual. You can still edit or even create new dataflows.

One of the limitations of Dataflow is that you will not see the preview of data transformed along the nodes; after you run the Dataflow and open the Dataset created, then you will see the data, which sometimes takes minutes. While using the new Recipe for data preparation, you will see the data preview for each node, so if the result is incorrect, you can fix it immediately without the need to run the Recipe.

If you have existing Dataflows, you can convert them as Recipes; see the following sample.

CHAPTER 3   RECIPE

1. Open Dataflow

From **Analytics Studio**, click **Data Manager**, then click **Manage Dataflows** at the bottom left of the screen, and you will get into an older version of Data Manager. Click the **Dataflows & Recipes** tab on the left menu, and look for the Dataflow that you want to convert.

2. Convert to Recipe

At the end of the Dataflow, click the arrow button (see Figure 3-1) and select **Convert to Recipe**.

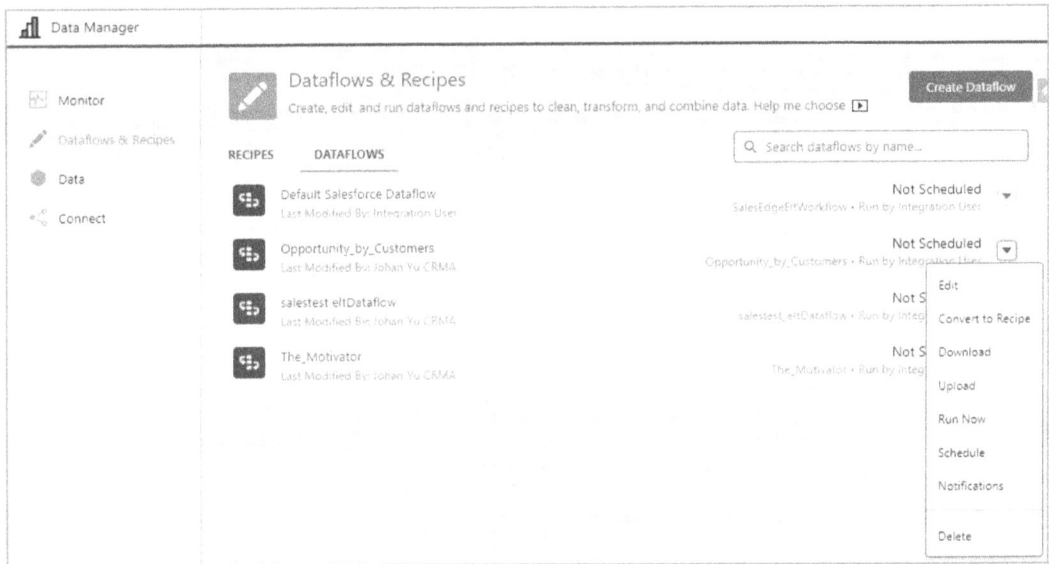

Figure 3-1. *The older version of the Dataflow*

In some instances, the conversion may not be smooth, so you need to edit and fix the Recipe manually.

CHAPTER 3 RECIPE

Here are a few items to note on Dataflow conversion to Recipe:

1. The conversion will run immediately and will take only a few seconds.

2. The conversion will create a new Recipe; by default, the Recipe name is the same as the Dataflow name with the suffix "_R3". You can rename the Recipe before saving it. If you see a warning icon on top of the node, something is wrong with that node after conversion (see filterOpty node in Figure 3-2); you need to fix it.

3. By default, the Dataset created in the converted Recipe will have the same label but a different API Name; you can adjust it manually in the Output nodes.

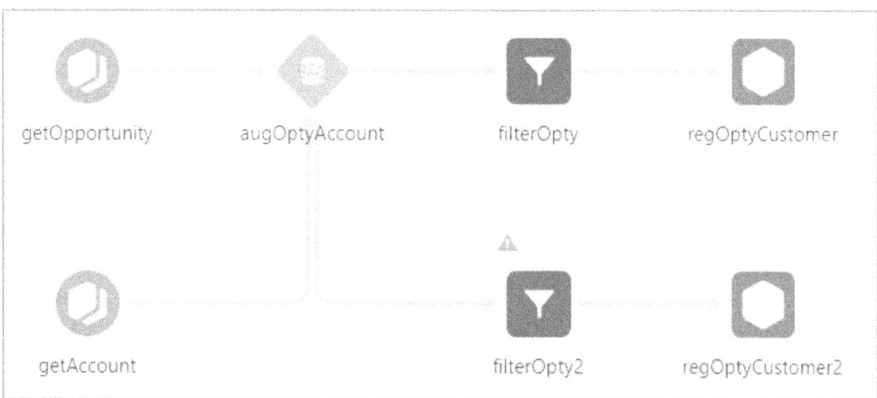

Figure 3-2. Recipe created from a Dataflow conversion

3. Save and Run

Once all the warnings are fixed (if any), click the **Save and Run** button at the upper-right corner to test. You can monitor the Recipe runs in Jobs Monitor under Data Manager.

As mentioned, the dataset output from the Recipe will have a different API Name (and different ID) than the Dataset produced by the original Dataflow, so it will not overwrite the existing Dataset and will not impact the existing dashboards. Once the new Dataset is verified, you can update the Recipe's Output node to have the same API Name as the original dataset name. Once the Recipe run is completed, it will overwrite the existing Dataset, and the dashboard will automatically consume datasets produced by the Recipe. You can verify the dataset source data by editing the Dataset and looking for the **Source** information; see Figure 3-3.

39

CHAPTER 3 RECIPE

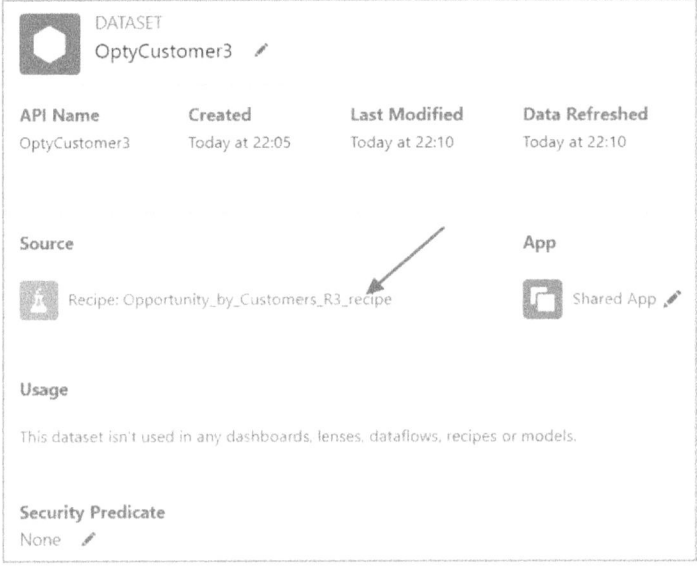

Figure 3-3. Dataset's source

Recipe User Interface

The Recipe user interface is pretty clean and straightforward, see Figure 3-4 for a sample of Recipe. At the very top, there are

- Recipe name at the left, where you can change the name by clicking the pencil icon.
- The search box is at the center, where you can search by node and column name, but unfortunately, it does not search for the description entered in the node.
- Back to the Data Manager link.

At the second row from the top, we can group them into three:

Group of Icons at the Left

- Add Input Data: Click this icon to add additional data input from an existing dataset, Salesforce Local, or external.
- Undo and Redo
- Cleanup Nodes

- Upload and Download Recipe JSON: Click the Download icon to download the Recipe in JSON format and store it on your local computer as a backup. If you want to restore it from the "backup" version, upload the backup JSON file to restore the Recipe.

Group of Icons at the Center: There are five icons in total; they will only appear when you select a node in the Recipe: Copy nodes, Cut nodes, Duplicate nodes, Paste nodes (only when already copied or cut node), and Delete nodes.

Group of Icons/Buttons at the Right

- Information the Recipe last saved
- Gear icon: Refresh preview and disable data previews
- Version History icon: Revert the Recipe to a version previously saved
- Save and Save as New Recipe button
- Save and Run button

In the third row from the top, only on the right, these icons are related to the zoom controls for the Recipe.

At the center of the Recipe is the white canvas for you to architect the Recipe, which is represented by nodes.

The lower part of the canvas will be visible when you select a node; each node will have different properties. However, the right panel will be the same, which is about data preview:

- **Hide or Show Column Icon**: If you are in the **Preview** tab, click the *eye* icon to hide the column. To show the column, go to the **Columns** tab, find the columns, and click the *eye* icon to show the columns (you can select multiple columns at once).

- **Column Profile Icon**: To quickly analyze data based on the selected column.

- **Expand or Collapse Icon**: Click this icon to expand the data preview pane to maximum (override the Recipe canvas).

Tip You can adjust the panel height and width by dragging the horizontal and vertical bars.

41

CHAPTER 3   RECIPE

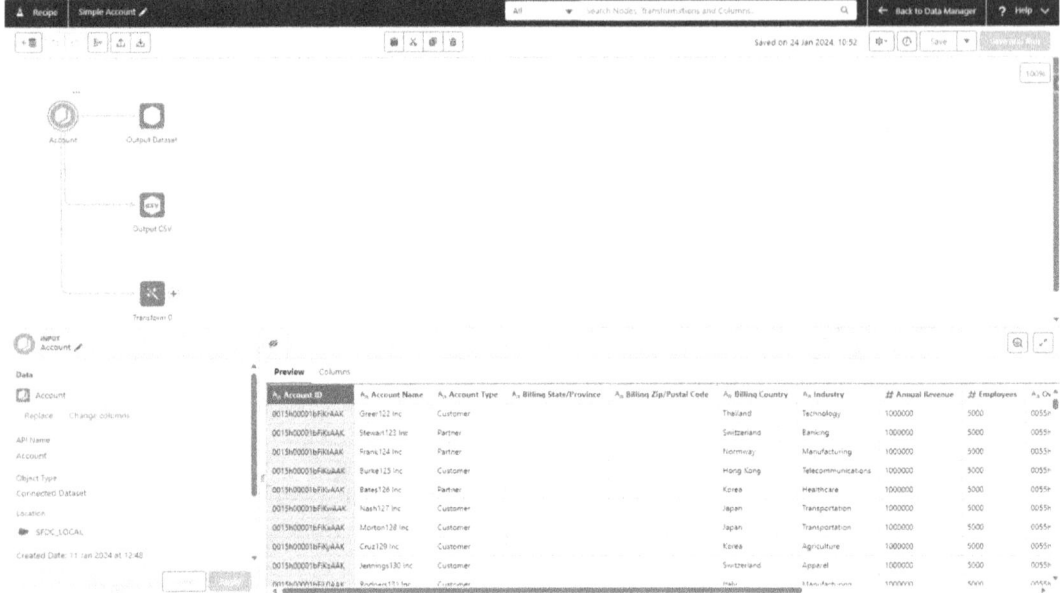

Figure 3-4. *A sample of a Recipe*

Creating a Recipe from Scratch

Instead of reading lots of text, let us build a simple recipe, so this will be fun. We are going to create a new Recipe from scratch to produce a dataset for a dashboard.

Use Case

Build a recipe to create a new dataset that contains the following information from Opportunities:

- Opportunity Id
- Opportunity Name
- Opportunity Owner
- Opportunity Stage
- Account Name
- Amount

Additionally, we need a field called "Is New Business?" and this is not a field in Salesforce; the logic is if the Type contains "New Business," then "Yes"; otherwise, "No."

Also, the Dataset should only have Opportunities of

- Only Open and Closed Won opportunity
- Amount must be > $0

Building Concept

Understand and analyze the data relationship in all related objects and fields:

1. Determine how many objects are involved. For this use case, there are three objects:

   - Opportunity
   - User
   - Account

2. Determine the main object; this will determine the granular level of rows in the Dataset. For this use case, the main object is **Opportunity**.

3. Determine filters for each object:

   - Opportunity Stage <> "Closed Lost"
   - Opportunity Amount > 0

4. Determine fields to extract from each object:

   Opportunity

   - Id
   - Name
   - OwnerId
   - AccountId
   - Type
   - Amount
   - StageName

CHAPTER 3 RECIPE

User

- Id

- Name

Account

- Id

- Name

5. Determine the relationship of each object:

    - Opportunity.AccountId with Account.Id

    - Opportunity.OwnerId with User.Id

6. Determine if we need any formula fields; for this use case, we will create a field called "Is New Business?" in the Recipe.

7. Once you have all the preceding answers, you are ready to rock!

Hands-On: Create a Recipe

Let's get started:

1. Open **Data Manager** from Analytics Studio or the App Launcher.

2. Click the **Recipes** tab, then click the **Create Recipe** button.

3. Name the Recipe by clicking the **Save** button; name it *Open Opportunity more than $0*, Version Description *Initial recipe*, then click the **Save** button.

4. Click the **Add Input Data** button at the center of the canvas.

5. Select only "Salesforce Objects" at the upper-left drop-down box, then select **Account**; at the right panel, only select Id and Name; you can click "Show Only Selected" to deselect the default fields quickly. Perform the same for the **User** object; select only the Id and Name columns. For **Opportunity**, select Id, AccountId, Name, StageName, Amount, Type, and OwnerId.

6. Click the **Next** button to continue.
   Tip: If you want to add fields after clicking Next, you can add them from the Input node.

7. We are free to move the nodes around; to make them look neat, I move the Opportunity node between the Account and User nodes.

8. Look up the Account to Opportunity to get the Account Name, click + next to the Account input node, drag it to the Opportunity node, and then select **Join**. The system will try to match the join keys, but you can change them if they are wrong. I will change the Join node from Join 0 to *joinOptyAcct*, and click the **Apply** button. Since we do not need the Account ID from the Account object, we can remove it from the **Columns** tab. In the Preview tab, you should see the **Account Name** column (with an orange icon) with the data.

9. Perform the same for Lookup from User to *joinOptyAcct* to get Opportunity Owner. Remember to use the latest data stream *joinOptyAcct*, which now contains the Account Name lookup. Rename the node to *joinOptyUser* and click the **Apply** button. As previously, we can remove the User.Id from the **Columns** tab; this is also to ensure the Dataset is clean; also, make sure the join keys are correct. In the Preview tab, you should see the **Full Name** column (with an orange icon) with the data. By now, your Recipe should be similar to Figure 3-5.

CHAPTER 3 RECIPE

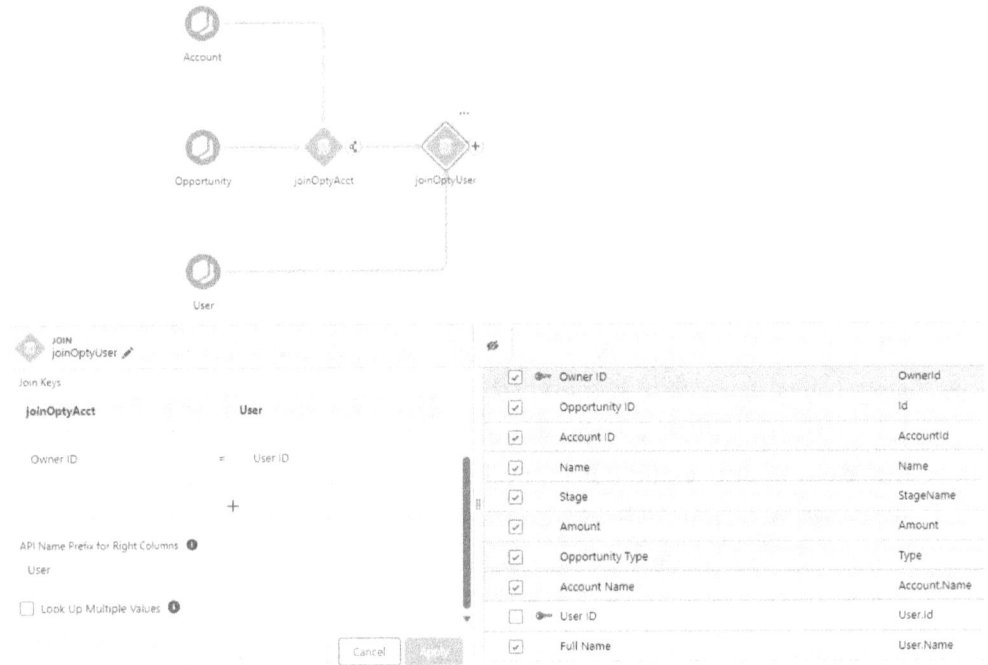

Figure 3-5. *Recipe in progress*

10. Click + at the joinOptyUser node and select **output** from the bottom-left panel:

    - Rename the node to *OutputOpportunity* (click the pencil icon)

    - Write To = *Dataset*

    - Dataset Display label = Open Opportunities more than 0

    - Dataset API Name = Open_Opportunities_more_than_0

    Click the **Apply** button. By now, your recipe should be similar to Figure 3-6.

CHAPTER 3 RECIPE

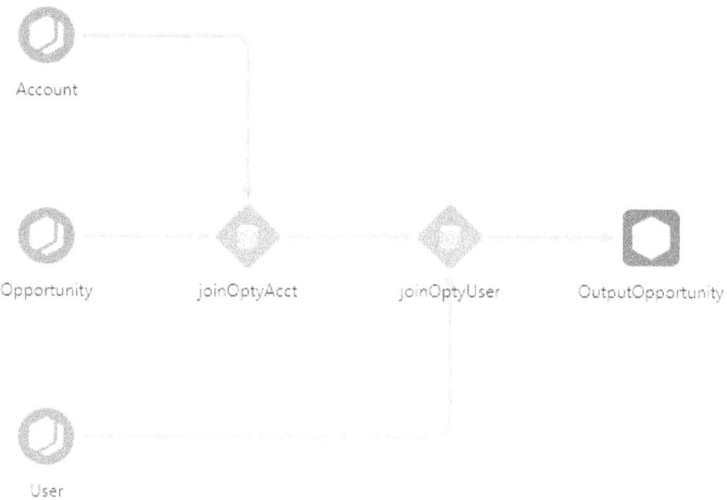

Figure 3-6. *Final Recipe*

11. Click the **Save and Run** button, then click **Back to Data Manager** at the upper-right corner to monitor the Recipe progress. Depending on the volume of data, this may take a few minutes.

12. Once completed, you should see the Status = Succeeded; open Analytics Studio and search for the Dataset with the name "Open Opportunities more than 0"; remember the dataset name set in point 10 iii earlier. See Figure 3-7 for dataset search in Analytics Studio.

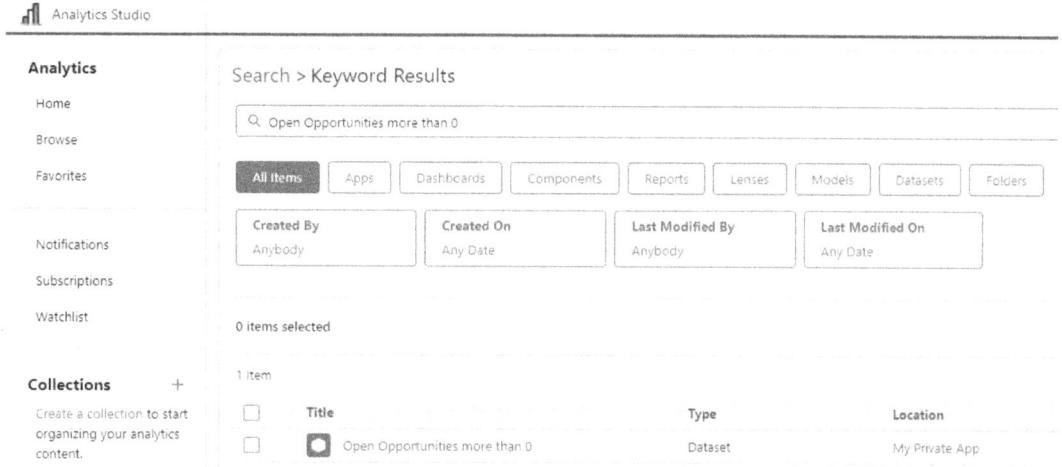

Figure 3-7. *Search Dataset in Analytics Studio*

47

CHAPTER 3   RECIPE

13. Click the Dataset; it will open as a new lens with a bar chart count of rows.

14. Done.

To summarize the preceding hands-on exercise, we create a new recipe that pulls data from Opportunity, Account, and User objects; then, we join the Account to Opportunity to get the Account Name by matching AccountId in Opportunity to ID in Account. Then, we continue to join the User object to the latest data stream (with Account Name) to get the Opportunity Owner.

Backup and Restore Recipe

You can back up a recipe by opening the Recipe and clicking the "Download recipe JSON" icon; this will store the JSON file on your computer drive.

The Recipe also offers the **Version History** feature; by clicking the Version History icon next to the gear icon, the system will show when the Recipe is saved and by whom, see Figure 3-8. You can simply click the stored version to see the Recipe at that time. Clicking the arrow allows you to delete or add a description for that particular version.

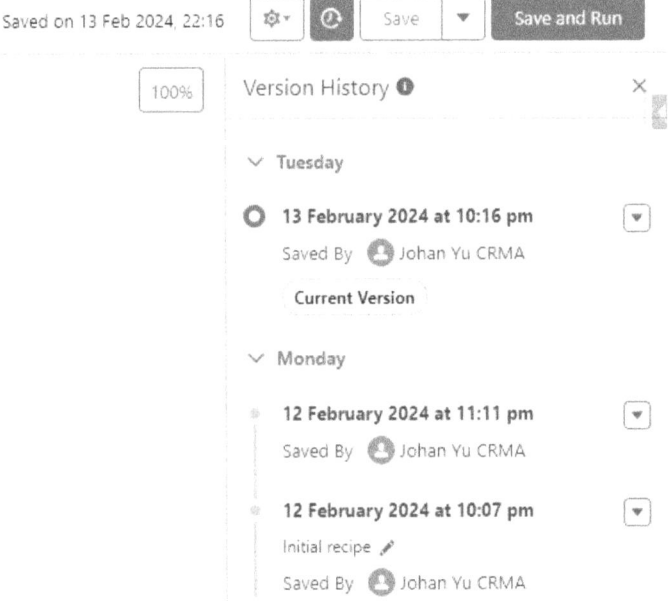

Figure 3-8. *Version History*

Since there is version history, do we still need to have the backup/restore JSON file?

- Because the Recipe is editable by any user with permission, it can be a challenge to find the correct version in the version history, even worse when the correct version has been deleted.

- You can "migrate" the Recipe across an organization, such as between sandbox and production.

- You can edit the JSON file manually using a text editor; for example, when you are using the wrong field in the Recipe or the field API Name is changed in the source, you can mass update the field name in the JSON file using a text editor and restore it (make sure to back up the original JSON file).

Data Transformation in Recipe

In short, the purpose of a recipe is to get data, transform it, and write to output. So, what can we do with a recipe? Any data transformation based on your creativity for a specific purpose.

Input Data

The first and must-have component in a recipe is input data, which is to load data from the data source to the Recipe; a recipe can have one or multiple input data. You must have input data to start building a recipe. The source of data can be from

1. **CRM Analytics Dataset**: These are data already stored as datasets in CRM Analytics.

2. **External Connected Objects**: These are objects from external data, including other Salesforce organizations.

3. **Salesforce Objects**: These are objects of the Salesforce organization that host CRM Analytics.

CHAPTER 3   RECIPE

When you start creating a recipe, you will see a blue button at the center, **Add Input Data**, or click the "Add Input Data" icon in the upper-left corner. Next, you will be presented with the "Add Input Data" window, where you can add and search for the objects that you need. Additionally, you can filter the list by selecting from the drop-down menu for just datasets, external objects, or Salesforce objects - see Figure 3-9. You can differentiate a dataset and object with the different icons in the list.

You can select multiple datasets or objects and then select (and search) all the fields for each object that you want to use in the Recipe; it is good to know the API Name of the fields to make sure you have selected the correct fields. Then, click the Next button.

Figure 3-9. *Add Input Data window*

You can always add new input data when needed, not just upon recipe creation. To add/remove fields from the input node, click the node and click **Change columns** or click **Replace** to change the data source, see Figure 3-10.

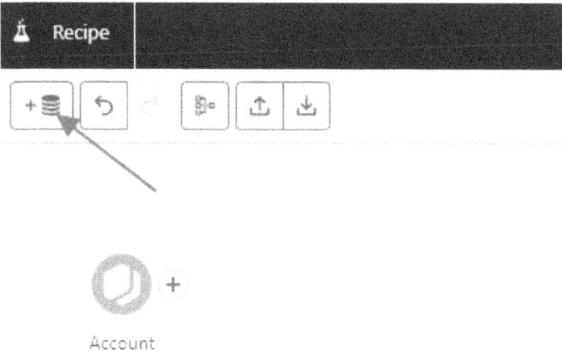

Figure 3-10. *Add Input Data icon*

Tip Scroll down in the input node property; in the **Data Preview Sampling**, select Sampling Mode = **Filtered rows**; this is useful if you need to monitor specific values data only, and all data preview in the following nodes will be based on these filtered rows.

Transform

The Transform node is one of the most used and important nodes in the Recipe. In this node, you can create "columns" based on the logic defined. There are a lot of functions offered by the Transform node; here are a few items you can do in the Transform node:

- **Now**: Return the date and time value in a specific format.
- **Custom Formula**: Calculate and return a value based on the existing value in columns; this is the most useful function to create a new column; many items below can be used with a custom formula.
- **Trim**: Select a dimension field, then select New Column (and Keep Original), New Column (and Drop Original), or Original Column. Use this function to remove leading and trailing whitespaces and set the maximum character length from the left.
- **Substring**: Select a dimension field; use this function to retrieve characters from the specified position and of the specified length.

- **Split**: Select a dimension field; use this function to split a column value into two new values at the specified delimiter.

- **Uppercase and Lowercase**: Select a dimension field, then select New Column (and Keep Original), New Column (and Drop Original), or Original Column. Use this function to get a value in upper- or lowercase for the whole string.

- **Replace**: Select a dimension field, then select New Column (and Keep Original), New Column (and Drop Original), or Original Column. Use this function to replace a specific value with an existing value.

- **Text to Number and Date**: Select a dimension field, then select New Column (and Keep Original), New Column (and Drop Original), or Original Column. Use this function to change the text into a number or date.

- **Format Date**: Select a dimension field, then select New Column (and Keep Original), New Column (and Drop Original), or Original Column. Use this function to convert dates in the selected Text column to the specified format.

- **Bucket**: This function can be used in the dimension and measure field; for the measure (number) field, you can organize values into buckets based on ranges; for the dimension, organize values based on the defined value for each bucket.

- **Edit Attributes**: The purpose of this function is to change field attributes for both columns Label and API Name.

- **Drop Columns**: To remove columns that are no longer needed from the Recipe.

- **Fill**: This function is only available in the number column; use this function to fill in null values in the data with the given replacement value. You can select New Column (and Keep Original), New Column (and Drop Original), or Original Column.

Is Transform node a must-have in a recipe? The Transform node is not a must-have in a recipe; however, a recipe without any Transform node will only add or remove rows or aggregate from the data source, which can be achieved with the **Join**, **Aggregate**, and **Filter** nodes.

It would be best if you renamed the default Transform node name by clicking the three-dot icon above the node, and at the same time, you can add the description for that node. Another way is by clicking the node and then clicking the pencil icon at the node properties to change the node name to something meaningful.

> **Tip** Make sure each node has a unique name that represents what the node does.

In a Transform node, you can add multiple transformations, and they will be run in order, for example, in step 1 you can create a new field called A, then in step 2, you can use field A as the logic for new field B. To make it clear, you can edit the transformation name to reflect what the transformation will do, see Figure 3-11 to edit the node Name and Description.

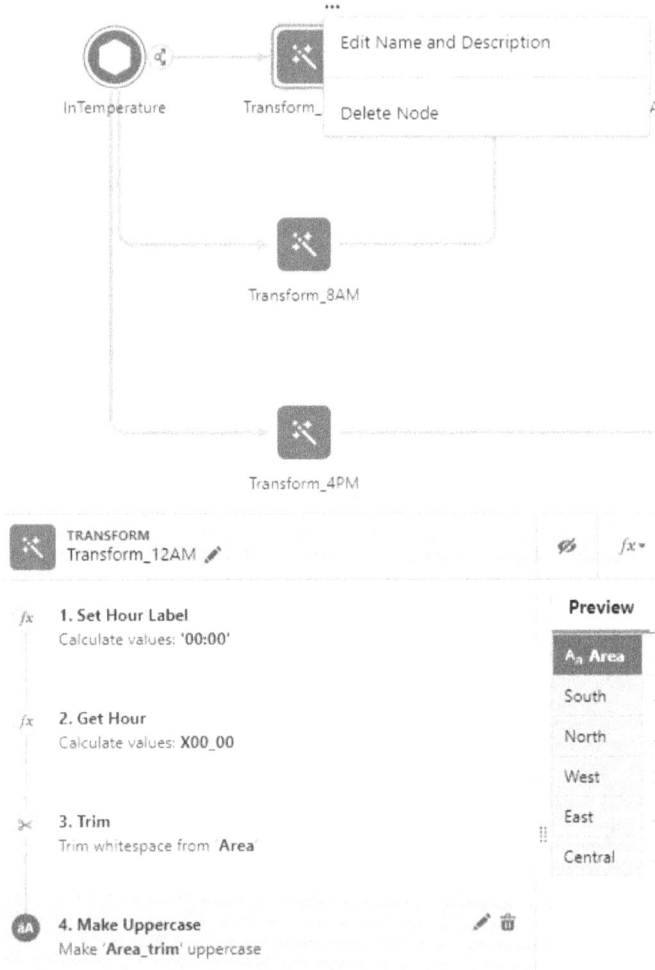

Figure 3-11. *A sample of a Transform node with multiple transformations*

For Custom Formula, you can also work with data across rows; you need to enable **Multiple Row Formula**, and you will be offered a set of "Windows Functions."

Filter

A Filter node is required to filter out rows that are not needed for our dashboard or output. Remember that we usually sync all data from the original data source; unless the data has been filtered out in the Connection setting, this is usually only for objects that are used for a specific dashboard.

You can add Filter nodes anywhere in the Recipe, and you can have it as many as needed. As a best practice, you should put the filter at the start or after the Join node (depending on the scenario), so the Recipe doesn't process unused data.

Adding a filter to the node is very easy; select the field, operator, and value, for example, *Amount Greater Than or Equal To 0*. You can have multiple filters in a Filter node, and by default, all the relation is **AND**. To change the logic to **OR**, click the **Add Standard Filter Logic** from the arrow drop-down in the Filter properties, so if you have multiple filters, you can have filter logic, for example, (1 OR 2) AND (3 OR 4).

Another option is to use **Custom Expression**; this is useful for complicated filters. Click **Add Custom Expression** from the same drop-down menu in the Filter properties, for example, `StageName = 'Closed Won' AND Amount > 0`.

Aggregate

Use this node to summarize large amounts of data with aggregates and groups. You can aggregate the data with

- Unique
- Sum
- Average
- Count
- Maximum
- Minimum

Then, group it by rows and columns (optional). As per the standard in the Recipe, you can rename the node and add a description. In the preview window, see the result after aggregate.

You can add multiple aggregates into a node; each aggregate will create a new column in the output. As you see in the preview, after the Aggregate node, the original raw data will no longer be available, see Figure 3-12. But of course, you can have a branch from the previous node to keep the raw data.

Depending on the needs, the Aggregate node is not very commonly used in the Recipe, compared to the Filter, Join, and Transform nodes, which are very common.

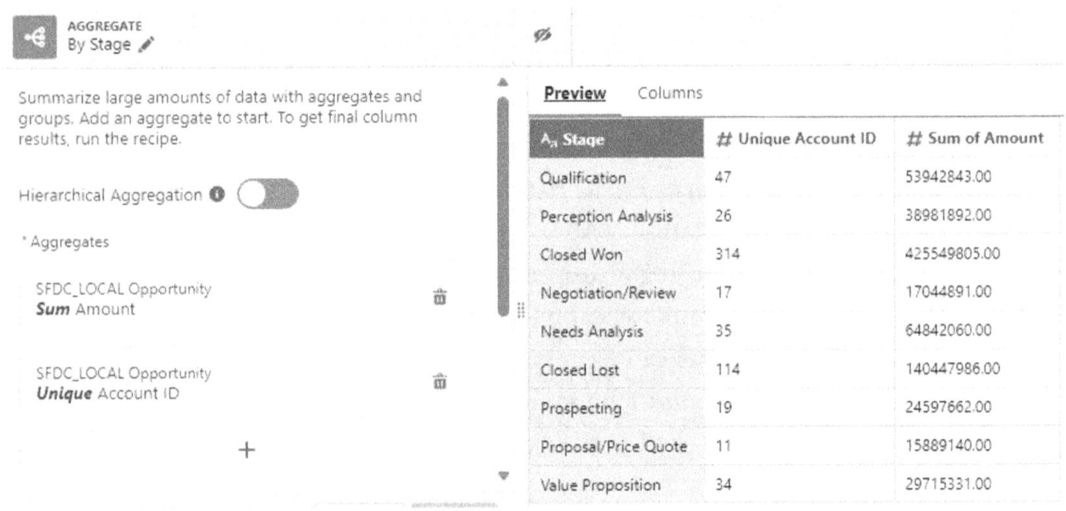

CHAPTER 3 RECIPE

Figure 3-12. A sample of an Aggregate node with multiple aggregates

Join

As per the node name, use this node to join data from two nodes, for example, to get the Opportunity Owner Name; by default, Salesforce only has the "Opportunity Owner Id" field in the Opportunity object, so we need to join Opportunity with the User object to get the Opportunity Owner Name.

To perform join, drag + at the right of the lookup (right) node to the main (left) node, then select Join, see Figure 3-13. Alternatively, click + at the right of the lookup (right) node, select the Connect tab, select the main (left) table, then select Join.

CHAPTER 3   RECIPE

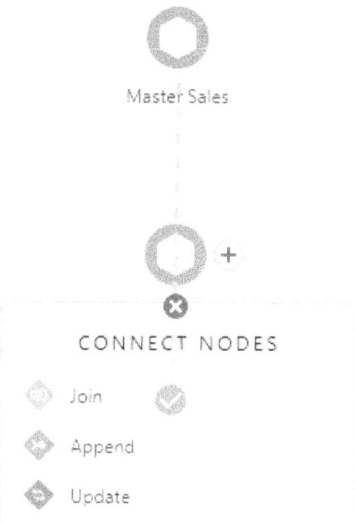

Figure 3-13. Connecting node with Join

For easy visualization and understanding, I will use the two datasets in Figure 3-14 to explain each type of Join and the results.

Master Staff			Master Sales	
ID	Name		ID	Amount
A1	Andy		A1	250
A2	Bryan		A1	300
A3	Charlie		A2	150
A4	Diana		A3	175
A6	Florence		A5	155
			A6	205
			A6	80

Figure 3-14. Sample datasets

The Recipe offers five types of Join; let us look at how it works for each of them:

- **LookUp:** This is the standard Join to get the data from the lookup object, such as to get the Opportunity Owner, as mentioned earlier. LookUp can look up multiple values; you need to select **Look Up Multiple Values** in the join properties. For Look Up Multiple Values, if the lookup field is a number field, the number will be the sum in the result.

57

The lookup type will not change the number of rows of the main (left) node, no matter if there are matched lookups based on the keys. If there is no result, the data will be blank. In Figure 3-15, the Master Staff is the main data. Note that we can see the keys from the preview table.

ID	Name	ID	Amount
A1	Andy	A1	250
A2	Bryan	A2	150
A3	Charlie	A3	175
A4	Diana		0
A6	Florence	A6	80

Figure 3-15. A sample result of LookUp

- **Left Join**: This join type will expand the number of rows of the left table if the lookup from the right table has multiple rows with the same key. In Figure 3-16, the Master Staff is the main data.

ID	Name	ID	Amount
A1	Andy	A1	300
A1	Andy	A1	250
A2	Bryan	A2	150
A3	Charlie	A3	175
A4	Diana		0
A6	Florence	A6	80
A6	Florence	A6	205

Figure 3-16. A sample result of Left Join

- **Right Join**: Similar to left join, but the other way round, see Figure 3-17

CHAPTER 3 RECIPE

Preview	Columns		
ID	Name	ID	Amount
A1	Andy	A1	250
A1	Andy	A1	300
A2	Bryan	A2	150
A3	Charlie	A3	175
		A5	155
A6	Florence	A6	205
A6	Florence	A6	80

Figure 3-17. A sample result of Right Join

- **Inner Join**: Both tables must have the key; otherwise, the rows will be eliminated, see Figure 3-18.

Preview	Columns		
ID	Name	ID	Amount
A1	Andy	A1	250
A1	Andy	A1	300
A2	Bryan	A2	150
A3	Charlie	A3	175
A6	Florence	A6	205
A6	Florence	A6	80

Figure 3-18. A sample result of Inner Join

- **Outer Join**: This Join node will show all results; the one with the missing key will be blank, see Figure 3-19.

59

Preview | Columns

ID	Name	ID	Amount
A1	Andy	A1	250
A1	Andy	A1	300
A2	Bryan	A2	150
A3	Charlie	A3	175
A4	Diana		0
		A5	155
A6	Florence	A6	205
A6	Florence	A6	80

***Figure 3-19.** A sample result of Outer Join*

- **Cross Join**: Each row from the left table will be combined with each row on the right table, so there is no key to match, see Figure 3-20.

Preview | Columns

ID	Name	ID	Amount
A1	Andy	A1	250
A2	Bryan	A1	250
A3	Charlie	A1	250
A4	Diana	A1	250
A6	Florence	A1	250
A1	Andy	A1	300
A2	Bryan	A1	300
A3	Charlie	A1	300
A4	Diana	A1	300
A6	Florence	A1	300

***Figure 3-20.** A sample result of Cross Join*

CHAPTER 3   RECIPE

For all types of Join, except Cross Join, we need to match the keys between the left and right tables. The system will try to auto-set the keys, but we can manually change them if they are incorrect.

For all types of Join, there is a property called **API Name Prefix for Right Columns**; the value here will be added as the prefix in the API Name for the right object fields; for example, if the value entered is Owner, the result field is "Owner.Id". You can see the field API Name from the **Columns** tab, including the field type and source. You can use **Edit Attributes** to change the Label and API Name.

Append

As the name suggests, the purpose of this node is to combine data from two nodes, so the total number of rows will be the total of rows from both nodes. If you have more than two nodes to join, then you need to have additional Append nodes; for example, we need to Append node A, node B, and node C; for this scenario, append A and B, say node D as a result, then Append node D with node C with the final result in node E.

The system will try to map the columns from both nodes, but you can manually fix it if incorrect. You can also select **Map all columns** and then select **Allow schema merge**; this will add columns that do not match as new columns.

ID	Name	Amount
A1	Andy	0
A2	Bryan	0
A3	Charlie	0
A4	Diana	0
A6	Florence	0
A1		250
A1		300
A2		150

Figure 3-21. *A sample result of the Append node with Allow schema merge*

61

CHAPTER 3 RECIPE

Update

Use this node to replace column values with data from another data source when key pairs match. See the example in **Figure 3-22**; instead of using the original Name value, for each key matched, the New Name value will replace the original Name value. However, the column name will stay the original, which is the "Name" in the example.

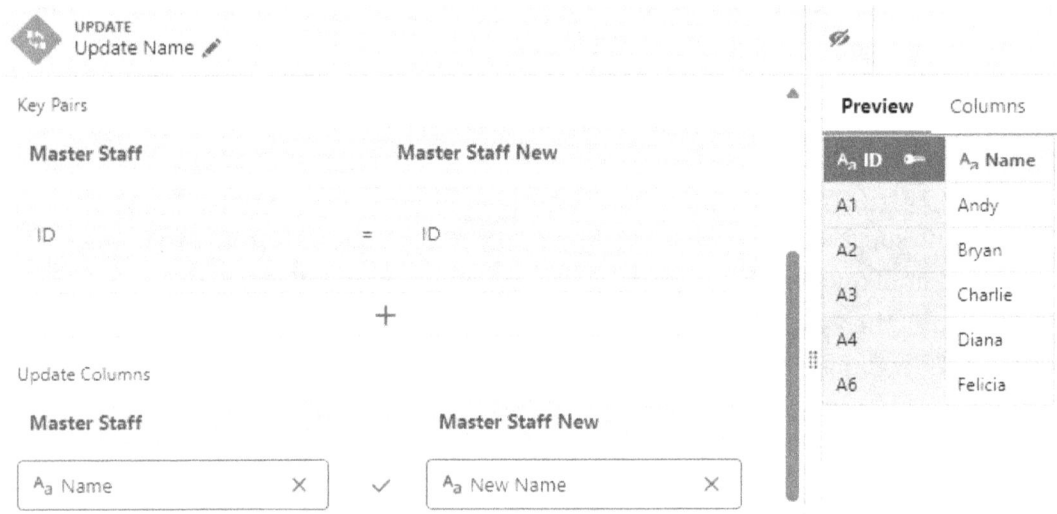

Figure 3-22. A sample result of the Update node

Output

The Output node is the result of the Recipe, and you can have multiple Output nodes in a recipe. There are three output options:

1. **Dataset**: This is the most common output from a recipe, where the output is a dataset and can be used for a lens or dashboard.

2. **Output Connection**: You can write the result to a system, including Salesforce; make sure the admin has selected **Enabled Salesforce output connection** in the setup menu.

3. **CSV**: The result will be written as a File in Salesforce; you will need a developer to write a script with the REST API to retrieve the file.

In this book, we will cover **Dataset** only as the output result. There are a few properties that we need to set in the Output node:

- **Dataset Display Label**: This is the Dataset label.

- **Dataset API Name**: This is the Dataset API Name.

- **App Location**: This is where we want to store the Dataset; ideally, all related assets (Dataset, dashboard, lens) are stored in the same app, so it is easier for us to set the sharing access.

- **Sharing Source and Security Predicate**: These will be discussed in Chapter 8.

Summary

Finally, we learned one of the most powerful items in CRM Analytics. In this chapter, we learned about Recipe. We did hands-on exercises by converting a Dataflow to a Recipe. Lastly, we created a recipe from scratch based on the given scenario.

We learned each node available in CRM Analytics's Recipe by getting data into the Recipe using the Input Data node. Use the Transform node to do data transformation, including work with data across rows. Use the Filter node to remove data that is not needed. Use the Aggregate node to aggregate raw data into groupings and values in summary. Use the Join node to look up or join data from two nodes. Use the Append node to combine data from two nodes, even if they don't have similar columns. Use the Update node to replace data and the Output node to write the data into a Dataset, CSV, or Salesforce.

We also learned how to back up and restore the Recipe using a JSON file and version history.

In the next chapter, we will look into Datasets created in CRM Analytics, which can be created from the CSV file, Dataflow, Recipe, or Salesforce trend report. We will also learn, including hands-on exercises, how to configure dataset metadata so that the Dataset will be displayed as per our business needs.

CHAPTER 4

Dataset

In Chapter 2, we discussed how to get data into CRM Analytics. From Analytics Studio, you can quickly bring the data into CRM Analytics by creating a new dataset, clicking the Create button, and then selecting Dataset; a wizard will assist you in selecting a source of data, with the option to upload a CSV file, using the Dataset Builder to extract Salesforce data from the external data source, create a recipe to use an existing Dataset or connected data, and trend from a Salesforce report.

In Chapter 3, we learned how to use the Recipe as a tool to create Datasets in CRM Analytics; it could be data from Salesforce, from other data sources that synced to CRM Analytics, or from the existing Dataset in CRM Analytics. A Recipe gives you the freedom and creativity to build the dataset model needed for the dashboard. Remember that *Output* is the node that will create/overwrite the Dataset in the Recipe. The Recipe will allow you to have new enriched Datasets, usually from multiple datasets, local/remote Salesforce objects, or connected data synced from other systems.

In this chapter, we will learn everything about the Dataset from

- Dataset Properties
- Dataset Fields
- Extended Metadata
- Replace and Restore Dataset
- Configure Actions for Dataset

Dataset Properties

To see the properties of a dataset, from Analytics Studio, find the Dataset and click **Edit** from the arrow drop-down at the far right of the Dataset, see Figure 4-1.

CHAPTER 4 DATASET

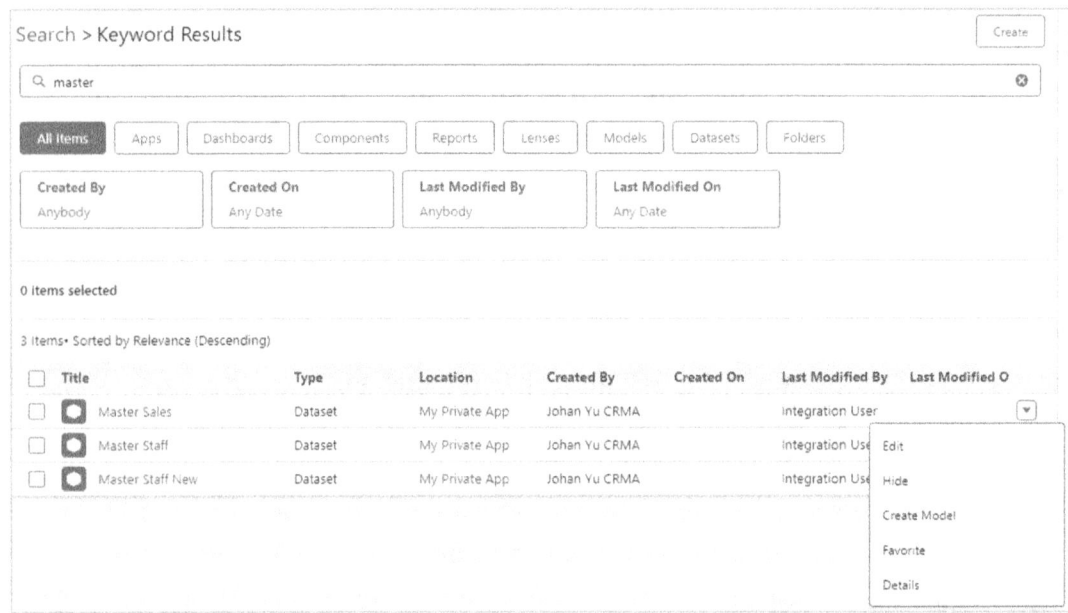

Figure 4-1. Edit Dataset

From the Dataset properties, you can check and perform actions for the Dataset, see Figure 4-2.

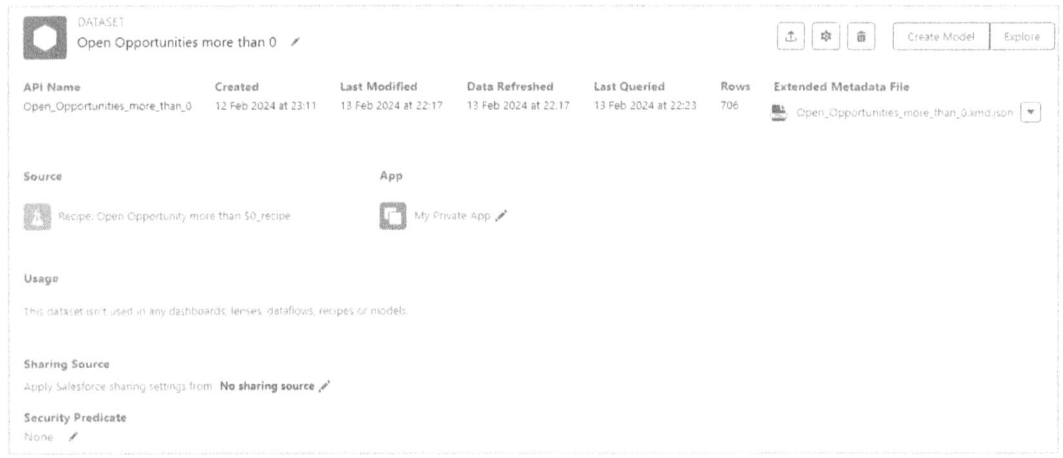

Figure 4-2. Dataset Properties

The following are the information and actions that can be performed on the Dataset:

- **Dataset Label**: Click the pencil icon next to the dataset name to change the Dataset label, but not the API Name. When you explore or work in a dashboard, you will see the dataset label, not the API Name.

- **Dataset Information**
    - Dataset API Name: You cannot change it from here, but from Recipe, or recreate the Dataset for the CSV file.
    - Dataset Created Date Time
    - Dataset Last Modified Date Time
    - Dataset Last Refreshed
    - Dataset Last Queried
    - Number of Rows

- **Source**: Which Recipe or Dataflow creates the Dataset.

- **App**: Where the Dataset is stored; you can move the Dataset to another App by clicking the pencil icon.

- **Usage**: All dashboards and lens use that Dataset.

- **Sharing Sources and Security Predicate**: We will discuss these items in Chapter 6.

- **Download and Replace Extended Metadata File**: We will discuss this item later in this chapter.

- **Replace Data**: This is to replace the Dataset with a CSV file.

- **Configure Actions**: Configure fields in the Dataset when they are open in the dashboard or Lens.

- **Restore Dataset**: Restore the Dataset from the previous two most recent versions.

- **Delete Dataset**: You cannot undelete the Dataset once it is deleted; you also cannot delete the Dataset if it is still in use in a dashboard or Lens.

- **Explore**: This is to explore datasets as a lens, including taking some actions for the Dataset.

CHAPTER 4   DATASET

Dataset Fields

When you load a CSV file as a new dataset or replace an existing Dataset, each column from the CSV file will become a field in the Dataset; you will be prompted for the following:

- Select a CSV file.

- **Dataset Name**: The CSV file name would be the default for the Dataset Name; however, you can change the Dataset Name.

- **App**: This is to define where the Dataset will be stored; by default, the Dataset will be stored in the "My Private App."

- **Field Label**: By default, it will be the same as with the column name, but you can change it if needed.

- **Field Type**: CRM Analytics will try to assign a field type (Dimension, Measure, or Date) for each field based on the value of data; however, you can change the field type as needed, for example, if all value in the column is number, the system will set the field type as Measure (number), but you can change it to Dimension (text).

As mentioned in previous chapters, you can monitor the data load progress from the Data Manager. Once the data is loaded, search for the Dataset name from Analytics Studio.

For the Dataset Created from a Recipe, if no data transformation happens, the field name and field type will follow the Salesforce field name and type. The Dataset API Name and Dataset Label are defined in the Output node. By default, the Dataset will be stored in the "My Private App" app, and you can change it.

Note   The Dataset API Name must begin with a letter, can contain only alphanumeric or underscores, can't exceed 80 characters or end with an underscore, can't contain two consecutive underscores, and is case sensitive.

Extended Metadata File

By configuring the extended metadata file of a Dataset, we can present data stored in the Dataset differently:

- Rename the field label.
- Hide fields.
- Edit field values for the Dimensions field.
- Format numbers for the Measures field.
- Set default fields.
- Specify the Dataset Grain Label.

Now, let us see each of them, but before that, I'll share how to edit the extended metadata easily.

CRM Analytics provides an easy way to update Dataset extended metadata from Analytics Studio. Explore the Dataset (or click Explore from Dataset properties) by clicking the Dataset name; this will open the Dataset as a New Lens. From the left panel, click the arrow next to the Dataset label, then click "Show Fields Panel."

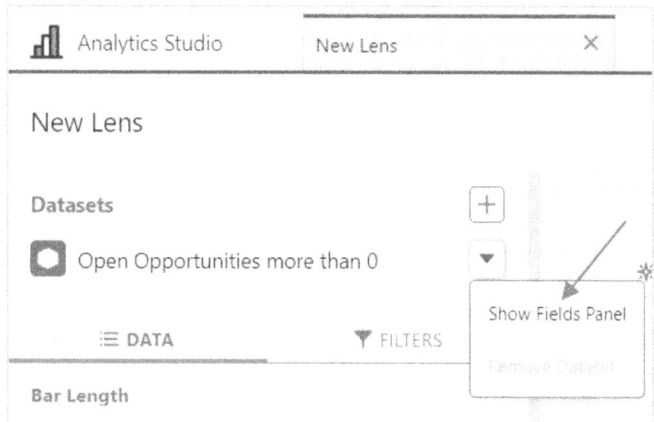

Figure 4-3. Click Show Fields Panel to configure the Dataset Metadata, see Figure 4-3

Then, you will be presented with a list of fields grouped by field type.

CHAPTER 4 DATASET

Rename the Field Label

To rename the field label, from the fields panel, hover your mouse over the field name, then click the pencil icon, see Figure 4-4; type in the new label, then click the Save button to save.

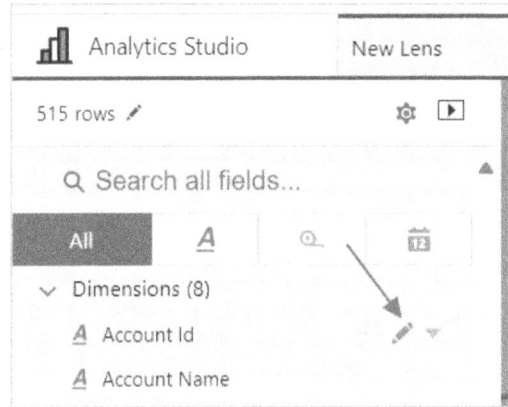

Figure 4-4. Rename the field label

Note Once saved, all existing labels in the dashboard or Lens using the field will be renamed with the new label.

Hide Fields

In a scenario where you need to hide fields that exist in a dataset, you can hide the fields from here. So, the user will not see the fields and will not be able to use them in the dashboard or Lens.

Similar to renaming a field, from the field panels, hover your mouse over the field, click the arrow icon, and select **Hide**, see Figure 4-5.

CHAPTER 4 DATASET

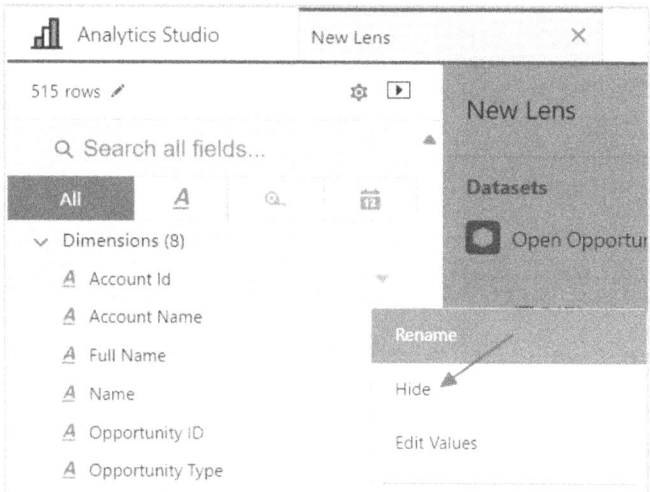

Figure 4-5. Hide fields

To show hidden fields, from the field panels, click the gear icon next to the number of rows, then select "Show Hidden Fields."

Note Once the field is set to be hidden, it will impact all existing dashboards and Lens. If the fields are used in the dashboards or Lens, this will cause errors in the dashboards or Lens.

Edit Values

This action only applies to the Dimension field; the purpose of this function is to change the field value; for example, instead of showing "Partner" in the Account Type field, let's change the value to "Channel." As previously mentioned, any changes here will impact all existing dashboards and Lens. You can also define the color of the selected field.

From the field panels, hover your mouse over the field, click the arrow icon, and select **Edit Values**, see Figure 4-6.

CHAPTER 4 DATASET

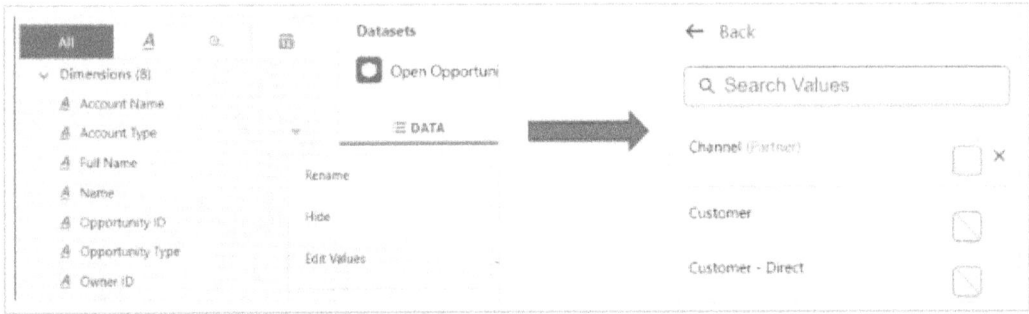

Figure 4-6. *Edit field values*

Note If you change two or more different values to the same value, CRM Analytics will not "combine" the data when you group it, even if the value is the same after editing.

Format Numbers

For the Measures field only, we can set the value shown in a specific format, such as percentage, currency, or custom format; this is very useful when you show the data in Table format or even in a chart. From the field panels, hover your mouse over the field, click the arrow icon, and select **Format Numbers**, see Figure 4-7.

Similar Format Numbers can be found in Dashboard widgets or Lens.

CHAPTER 4 DATASET

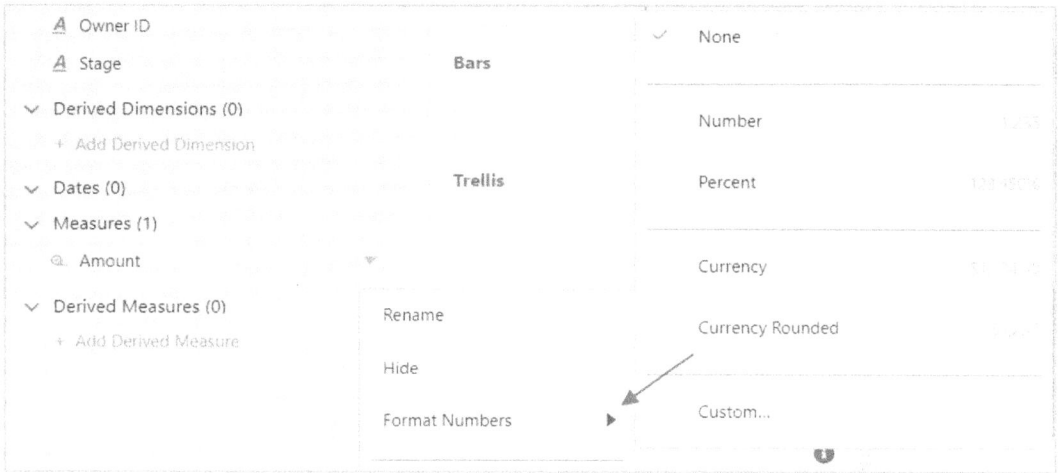

Figure 4-7. Format Numbers

Default Fields

When you explore a dataset, it will open as a new lens; if you change the chart to a **Values Table**, you will see a set of fields displayed. By default, it would be the first five dimension fields and the first five measure fields in alphabetical order.

You can set the default fields by clicking the gear icon and then selecting **Default Fields** in the field panels, see Figure 4-8.

73

CHAPTER 4   DATASET

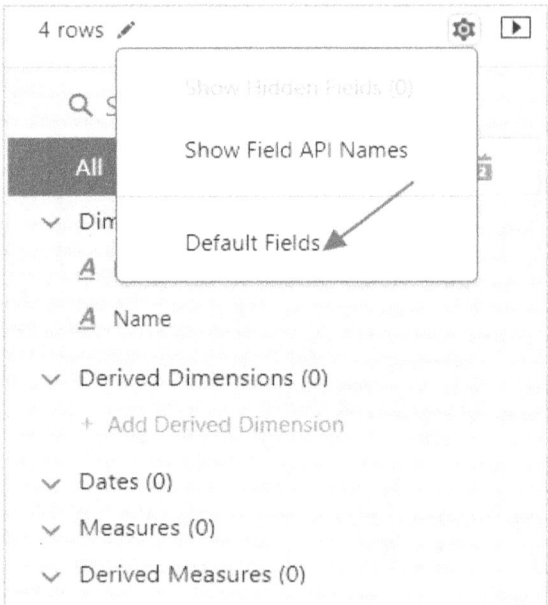

Figure 4-8. Set default fields

Specify the Dataset Grain Label

By default, each line of data will be called "Rows," but we can update the label of dataset grain to something else friendlier; look at the sample in Figure 4-9.

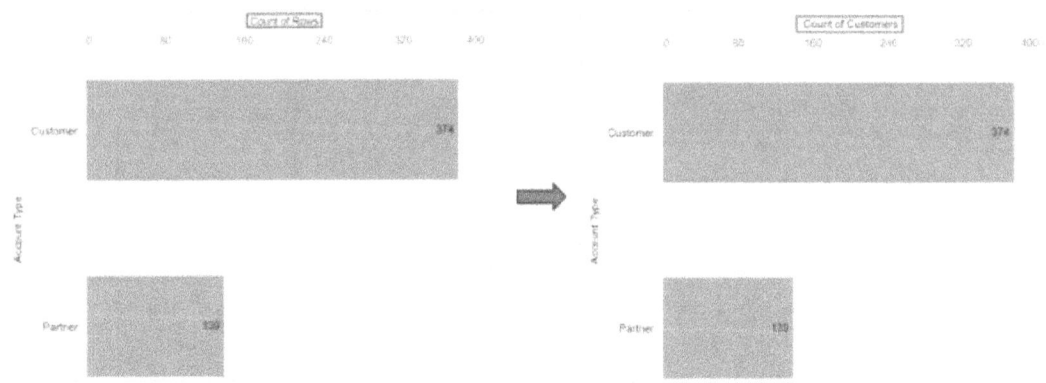

Figure 4-9. The grain label changed

To specify the Dataset Grain Label, from the fields panel, click the pencil icon next to the count of rows, see Figure 4-10, type in the new label, and then click Done.

CHAPTER 4 DATASET

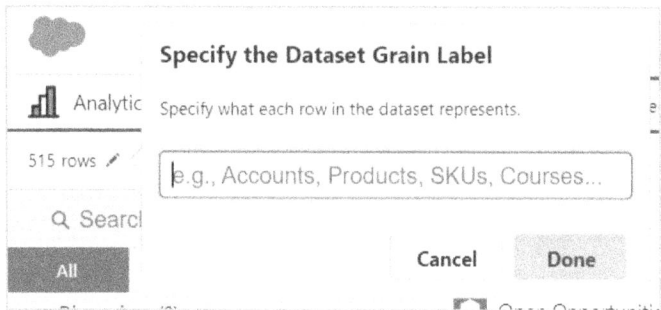

Figure 4-10. To change the grain label

Replace and Restore Dataset

CRM Analytics offers you options to replace and restore the existing Dataset; however, you cannot back up the Dataset manually online or offline.

A replacement dataset is usually only needed when the Dataset is manually loaded with a CSV file. To replace the Dataset, edit it and find the "Replace Data" icon in the top rows of the icon, see Figure 4-11. All existing data will be replaced; however, the extended metadata and security predicate (if any) will stay.

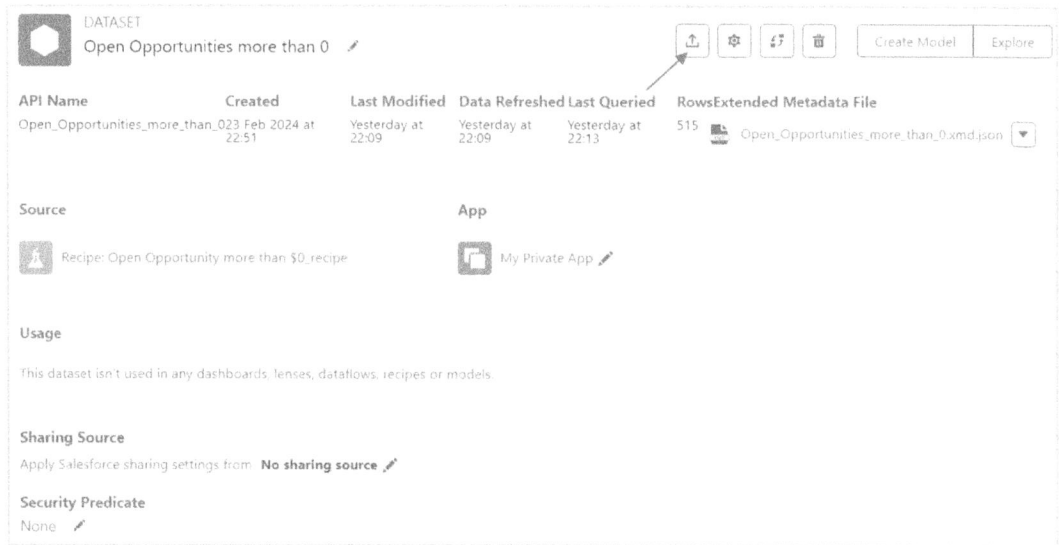

Figure 4-11. Replace Dataset

CHAPTER 4   DATASET

CRM Analytics also offers you the ability to restore the Dataset from the **last two versions**, whether the Dataset is overwritten manually using the Replace Dataset function or overwritten after a Recipe run. CRM Analytics automatically backs up the Dataset before overwriting it.

When you click the Restore Dataset icon, it will show two previous versions of the Dataset, including information on when the Dataset was created and the number of rows for that version. Select which version to restore, and then click the Restore button, see Figure 4-12.

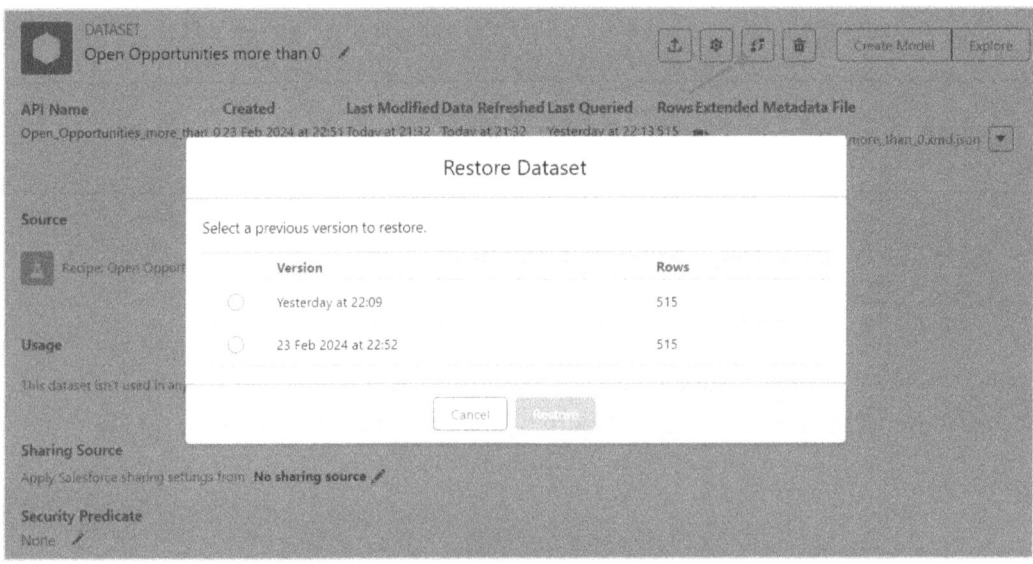

Figure 4-12.   Restore Dataset

Configure Actions for Dataset

An action is very useful for Datasets extracted from Salesforce, whether created using a Recipe or manually loaded from a CSV file of Salesforce data export, but you need to have the Salesforce record ID field in the Dataset. The data needs to be presented in a table or chart in a Dashboard or Lens, and then the user can select actions configured from a record.

Two types of actions can be configured:

1. **Open Salesforce Record**: With this action, the user can open the Salesforce record from the CRM Analytics dashboard or Lens. It could be in a table or chart widget.

2. **Perform Salesforce Actions**: You can choose whether to show all available actions or only selected actions, such as Email, Log a Call, etc., including custom actions created for the object.

To configure an action

- From the edit Dataset page, click the **Configure Actions** (gear) icon next to the Replace Data icon.
- Select the field to enable for action.
- Select the Record ID Field. This field must be the Salesforce record ID, and it is mandatory.
- Select Display Fields. This is not mandatory; however, this is useful when there are duplicate values of the field that are set for action. By adding other fields here, users will be able to differentiate which record they want to perform the action; we will see more in the following sample.

In Figure 4-13, we configure an action for the Name field. The Record ID Field is Opportunity ID, so when the user selects the action, it will act on that Opportunity ID. For Display Fields, let us select Name, Stage, and Opportunity Type; for Actions, let us select "Open Salesforce record."

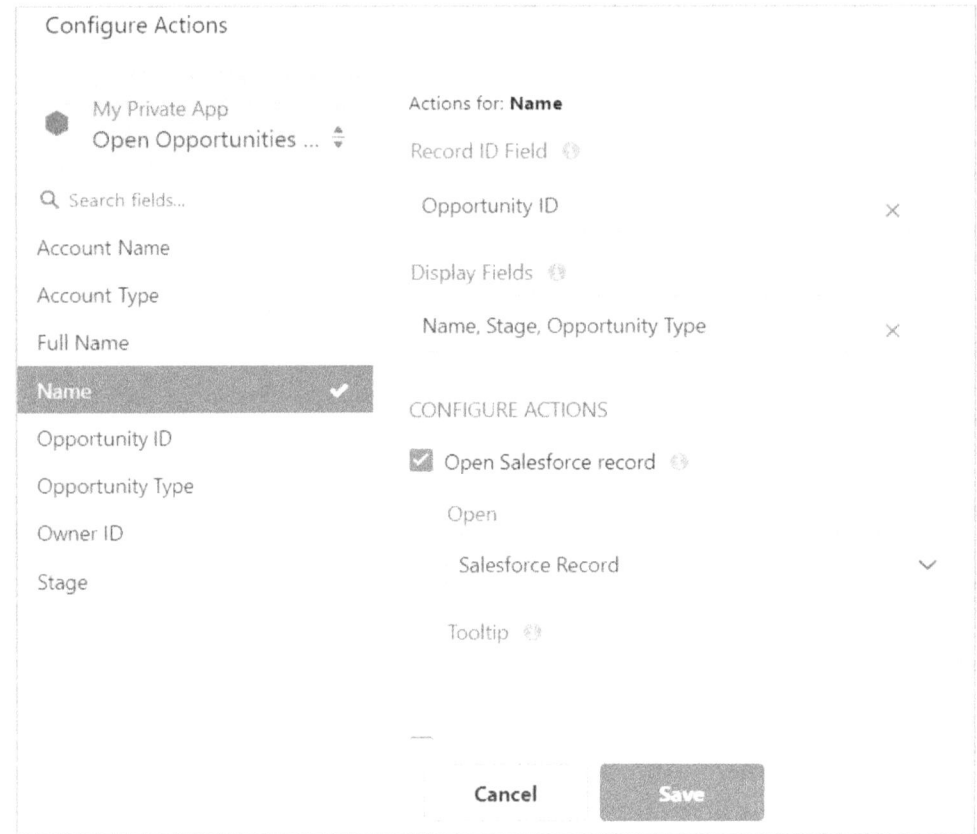

Figure 4-13. *Configure Actions*

Because we select the Open Salesforce record action, if there is no duplicate value of the Name, clicking the arrow next to Name in the table/chart will show the "Open Record" action.

Stage	Amount	Name ↑	Opportunity ID
Closed Won	2,016,250	Opportunity for Abbott1184	0065h00000PMnM1AAL
Closed Won	206,587	Opportunity for Abbott414	▼ 📤 Open Record
Closed Won	121,490	Opportunity for Abbott636	Salesforce Data Link
Closed Won	3,314,900	Opportunity for Aguilar1908	006...

Figure 4-14. *Open Record action*

However, if there are duplicate values for Name, the system will prompt users to select which record for the action. Because we select Display Fields = Name, Stage, and Opportunity Type, the screenshot in Figure 4-15 shows how the system will react when duplicate values are found; in this case, the Name "Opportunity for Abbott1184" exists twice in the Dataset, so the user needs to select a record to open the record in Salesforce. In short, configure "Display Fields" to help the user in selecting the correct record when there are duplicate values.

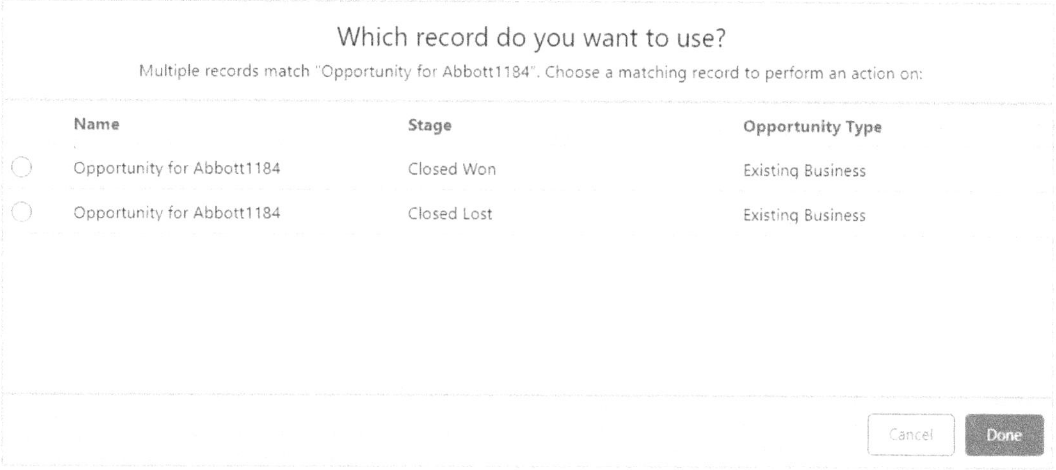

Figure 4-15. Display Fields in action

Note If there are no fields selected for "Display Fields" and any duplicate values are found, the system will show the Record ID for users to select.

You can quickly notice fields have been enabled for "action" by hovering the mouse over the field, and an arrow will appear right after the field value; see Figure 4-14.

For a Table widget, you can set up one-click actions from table properties, so clicking the field value will perform the action configured.

Summary

In this chapter, we discussed what can be done once a Dataset is created, whether it is manually loaded from a CSV file or created from a Recipe.

We started with dataset properties, which show the Dataset Created, Last Modified, Last Refreshed, Last Query, the Dataset usage, the Dataflow or Recipe that created the Dataset, the number of records in that Dataset, the security predicate defined, the dataset API Name, and the App name where the Dataset is located.

Also, on the Dataset properties page, we can perform multiple actions, such as changing the dataset label, replacing data, configuring Actions, restoring the Dataset, deleting the Dataset, exploring the Dataset to a Lens, downloading and replacing an extended metadata file, changing the app for the Dataset, and defining a security predicate.

We also discussed how easy it is to manipulate data and fields in the Dataset with extended metadata.

In the next chapter, we will discuss everything about Lens, how to create Lens, how to make use of a Lens in analyzing CRM Analytics data, how to use Lens to download and share data, and the types of chart and formatting available in Lens.

CHAPTER 5

Lens

When we explored the Dataset and played around with Extended Metadata in Chapter 4, without our awareness, we opened the Dataset as a new Lens. A lens is a view of a dataset or dashboard widget, and we can use it to explore the data and get insight. We have options to explore the data in a Lens as a chart or table, including using a query with SAQL or SQL. CRM Analytics provides many types of charts and table widgets for users to explore the data, including Conversational Exploration, which will be discussed later in this chapter.

If we compare Lens with Salesforce reports, there are similarities, but mainly differences. A dashboard in Salesforce requires reports as the data source, while a dashboard in CRM Analytics does not need Lens as the data source but directly retrieves data from the Dataset.

In this chapter, we will learn everything about Lens, including

- CRM Analytics App
- Explore Dataset with Chart, Table, SAQL, and SQL
- Explore Dataset with Conversational
- Clip Lens to Designer
- Download and share data

CRM Analytics App

In this chapter, we will discuss Lens; however, to store a Lens, you need an app, whether private or public. Let us discuss a bit on the App before starting our discussion on Lens.

You may have heard the term "app" earlier in the previous chapters of this book, so let us get the correct term for what App means in CRM Analytics. Apps provide containers for sets of related assets, such as dashboards, lenses, components, models, and datasets.

Similar to the Salesforce dashboard or report folder, there are three types of App in CRM Analytics:

- **My Private App**: This is similar to a private folder; all items in this folder are only accessible to you. If you create a dashboard to share with other users, make sure the Dataset is not stored in this App.

- **Shared App**: This is similar to a public folder; users who have a CRM Analytics license assigned will be able to access items stored in this App from the Dashboard, Lens, or Dataset.

- **Custom App**: Salesforce does not use this term, but this is the App that you can create for specific needs in CRM Analytics, where you can set who can access and edit existing assets stored or save new items to this App.

Apps also control user visibility and accessibility to the items within that App, whether as a manager, editor, or viewer. CRM Analytics allows a Dashboard or Lens to use the Dataset from different apps; this will cause errors when the user opens a Dashboard, but the Dashboard uses a Dataset that is stored in a different app, and the user has no access to the App.

Just to be clear, the App here has nothing to do with the CRM Analytics mobile app.

Creating App

From Analytics Studio, click the Create button, then select App, see Figure 5-1.

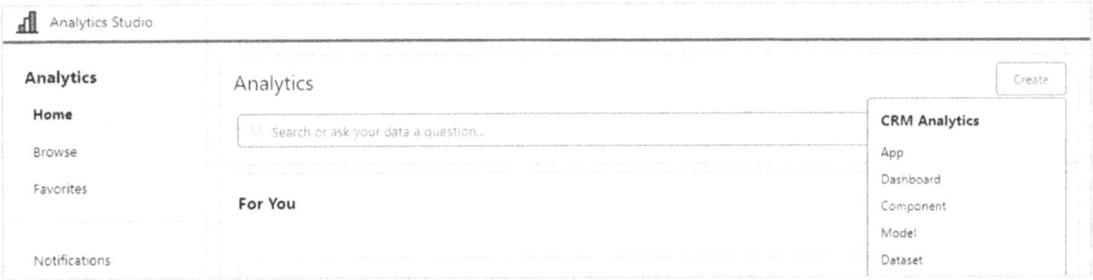

Figure 5-1. Create a new App

Depending on the CRM Analytics license that your organization purchased, you may ask if you want to create a Blank App or start with a template. For now, let us click the **Create Blank App** button, click the **Continue** button, and then name your App. I'll enter

CHAPTER 5 LENS

"Regional Sales," and we just have a brand-new app created. Figure 5-2 shows that within an app, we can store Dashboards, Components, Lenses, Models, and Datasets. Since this is a new app, we have nothing yet in that App.

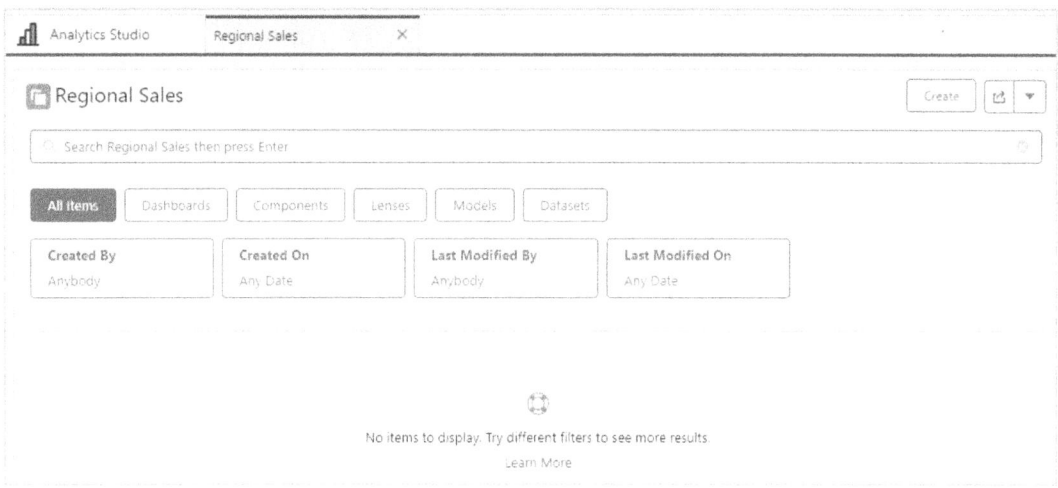

Figure 5-2. *A new App was created*

Run App

Open the App and notice the "Run App" button at the upper-right corner, or you can also search the App name in the Analytics Studio or Analytics tab; on the result, click the arrow at the end of the App name, then click "Run App."

Run App will open the Dashboard or Lens stored in that App; by default, it will be in alphabetical order; however, you can edit the list to hide or reorder the list, see Figure 5-3.

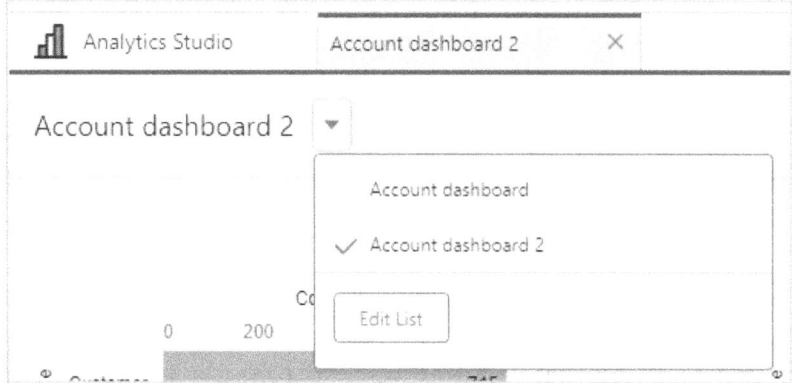

Figure 5-3. *Run App and the ability to edit a list*

83

CHAPTER 5 LENS

Share App

Sharing an App in CRM Analytics is simple; this is similar to sharing a dashboard folder in Salesforce. See Figure 5-2; click the **Share** icon (before the arrow icon) at the upper-right corner of the App or the drop-down menu when clicking the arrow after the App name in the Home or Browse page of Analytics Studio. You can share the App by **User**, **Group**, and **Role** (option to include Subordinates), see Figure 5-4 – this refers to User, Public Group, and Role in Salesforce.

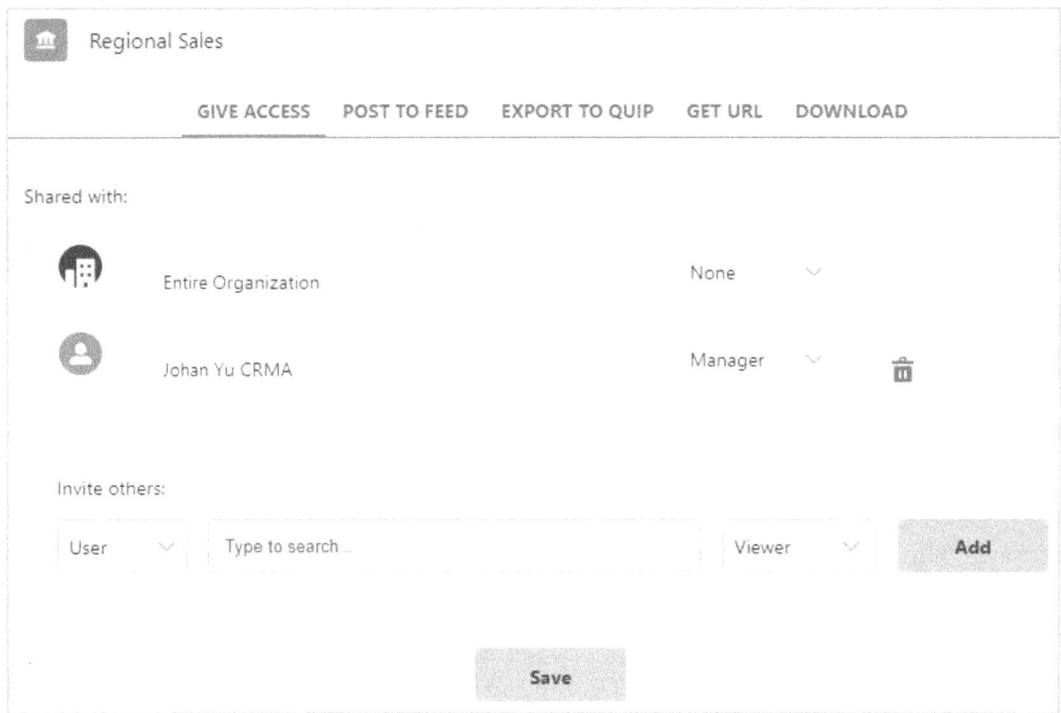

Figure 5-4. Give App access to other users

Exploring Dataset

Once we bring data into CRM Analytics, we should verify the data is correct based on data completeness, quantity, and quality. Completeness means the fields are complete as we expect, with no missing fields; otherwise, we need to re-upload the Dataset or modify and rerun the Recipe. Quantity means the number of rows is complete, with no missing rows. Quality means all the fields contain the right values with the correct data type.

CHAPTER 5 LENS

Using Chart in Lens

From a Dataset in the Home or Browse page or search result, click the dataset name; by default, the system will open the Dataset as a New Lens (see Figure 5-5) with a simple bar chart and contain the following setup:

- Bar chart.
- Bar length is the count of rows.
- No grouping.
- No filters.

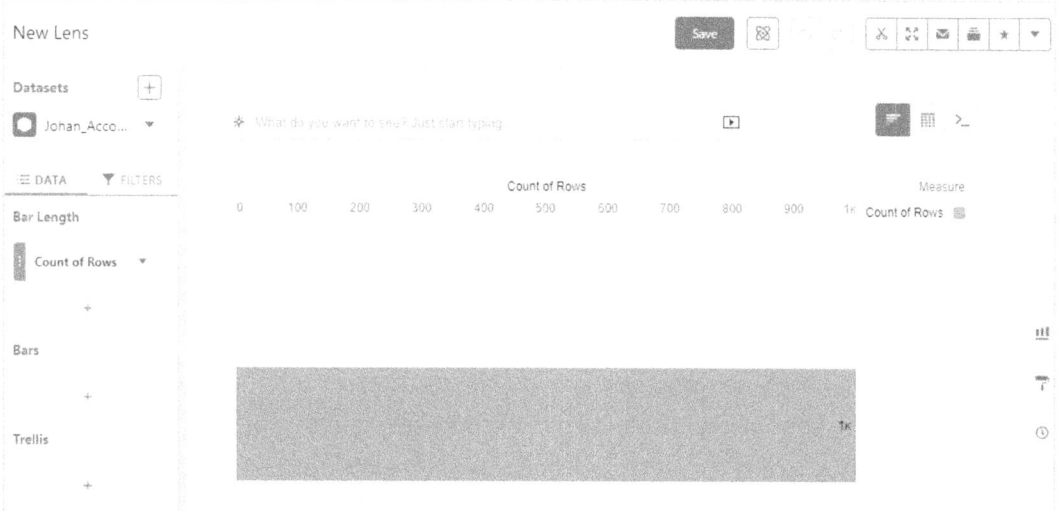

Figure 5-5. *New Lens*

With this simple chart, we can verify the data Quantity; from the chart, we see that the Dataset has 1K of rows; we can compare this from Dataset properties, as shown in Figure 4-2, and look for "Rows." However, we cannot verify if the Dataset contains complete fields, field type, and value of fields; we need to change the chart to Table Mode and select the **Values Table** to verify those items.

85

Before discussing Table Mode, let us explore the common things we can do in Chart mode and analyze data using Chart mode, see Figure 5-6:

- **Change Bar Length to Sum, Average, Maximum, Minimum, Unique, Median, First, Last, Stddev, Stddevp, Var, and Varp**: All of them are only applicable to the Measures field, with the exception of Unique, which can be used in any type of field. I am not going to explain each of the functions, but it is good to familiarize each of them.

- **Add Additional Bar Length**: With this, you can analyze multiple measurements at a glance, such as the Count of Rows and the Sum of Annual Revenue.

- **Add Bars**: This means that we are going to have a new grouping in the chart.

- **Add Filters**: We can add multiple filters for multiple fields, and we can apply filter logic OR and AND here.

- **Change Chart Type**: CRM Analytics offers more than 30 chart types for us to use, but remember that each chart type has its own properties, so your existing selection may be removed if the new chart type does not have such properties or move as other properties. If you are confused about which chart is best suited to you, click "Suggested Chart" to let CRM Analytics offer a few options based on the data and selection.

- **Apply Chart Formatting**: You can set the chart title, font size, show axis, show legend, etc.

CHAPTER 5   LENS

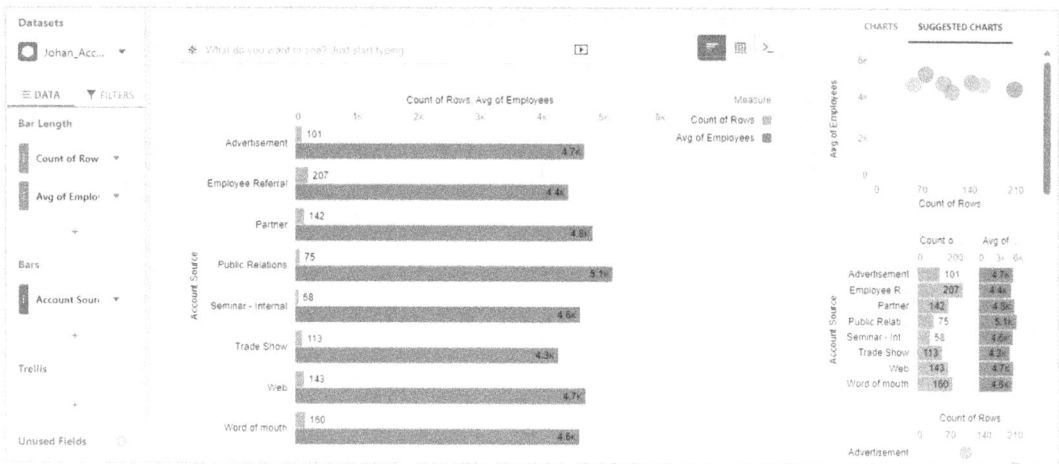

Figure 5-6. *Analyze data with a chart*

Using Table in Lens

Let us switch to the table mode by clicking the "Chart Mode" icon and then selecting the "Values Table", see Figure 5-7.

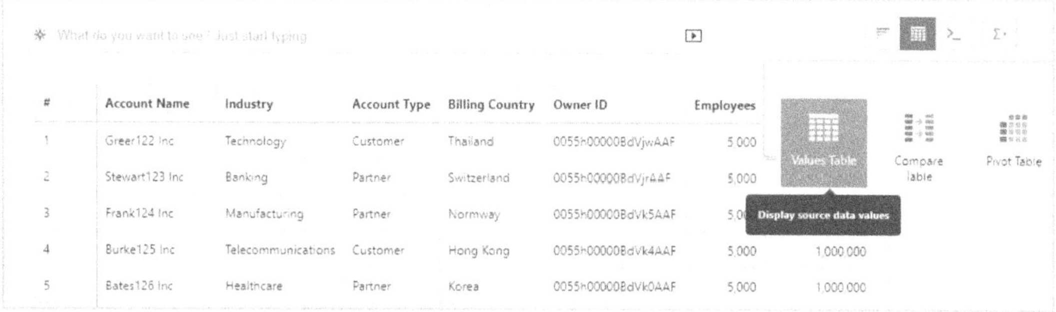

Figure 5-7. *Switch to the Values Table*

If you remember, in Chapter 4, we discussed Extended Metadata; we can set default fields for a dataset. If default fields for the Dataset have been configured, switching to Table mode will give us those default fields in the table columns.

Actions that have been set when in Extended Metadata will be applied, including renaming field labels, editing values, formatting numbers, etc.

87

CHAPTER 5 LENS

Here are a few things you can configure on the table, see Figure 5-8:

- At the bottom of the left panel, look for "Query Limit"; by default, it will show only 100 rows; you can edit to set the query limit to a maximum of 25,000 rows, although the suggestion is a maximum of 2000 rows for better performance.

- Add or remove fields easily by clicking the pencil icon at the left panel; you are also able to reorder fields by dragging and dropping the fields accordingly.

- Click the "Formatting" icon at the right to format the table with spacing, color, header, etc.

- Click the table header to sort the table ascending or descending by a specific field.

- Click the arrow next to the field name and select "Freeze Columns Up to Here"; all the fields from the selected field and fields on the left will always be visible if you have a lot of fields added and you scroll to see fields at the right.

Figure 5-8. Values Table

88

Using the Values Table, we will be able to verify if the Dataset contains all the fields that we need to build a dashboard and if all fields contain correct values, which we cannot verify in Chart mode. However, chart mode allows us to group data and sort it quickly, so we can analyze the data on the fly, get percentages of each group, or get data trends over a timeline.

Additionally, in the Table mode, we can switch to **Compare Table**, where we can group the table based on fields, and **Pivot Table**, where we can organize and summarize data grouped by rows and columns.

Saving Lens

After the Dataset opens as a new lens, hit the **Save** button on the upper-right corner to save the configured Lens so that you or your team member can reuse it in the future. You can store it in "My Private App" if you do not want anyone else to touch it, in the "Shared App" to let everyone in the organization access it, or in a Custom App if you need to share it with your team or other users. Enter the Lens Name, Description (optional), and Version History (optional).

When saving a Lens, all items within the Lens will be saved, from the table or chart type, including all the filters, fields, grouping, sorting, conditional formatting, etc. If you have edited the chart or table with the custom query SAQL or SQL, this will be saved as well.

If you save an existing Lens to a different App, CRM Analytics will **move** it to the new App, so it is **not** a **Save As**. If you need to save the Lens as a new Lens, you should clone it, click the arrow at the corner, and select "Clone in New Tab", see Figure 5-9.

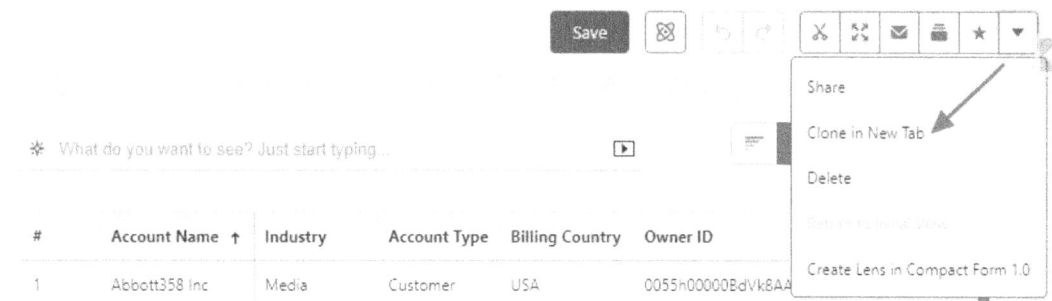

Figure 5-9. *Clone Lens*

CHAPTER 5 LENS

Present Lens

There is an icon called **Present** at the Lens. The purpose of Present Lens is to show the Lens on the web browser at full screen. If you are using the Google Chrome or Microsoft Edge web browser, this is similar to hitting the F11 key. Press the F11 key again to exit from the full-screen mode.

The Present mode is useful when you need to present the Lens and not be disturbed by other things or when you need to analyze the Dataset with more real estate.

Clip Lens to Designer

The scissors icon before the Present icon is called Clip to Designer. The purpose of this function is to add the Lens to a dashboard. CRM Analytics will add the Lens as a new **Query** to all dashboards that are currently open. If there is no dashboard open, CRM Analytics will create a new dashboard, then add the Lens as a new Query to the new Dashboard created.

When clicking this icon, CRM Analytics will ask for a Query Label; click the **Clip to Designer** button to apply. Notice that Clip to Designer will not add a chart or table widget to the Dashboard, but a Query, see Figure 5-10; you can drag the Query added to the Dashboard Designer to get it added as a widget in the Dashboard. Furthermore, you can change the chart type or formatting in the Dashboard.

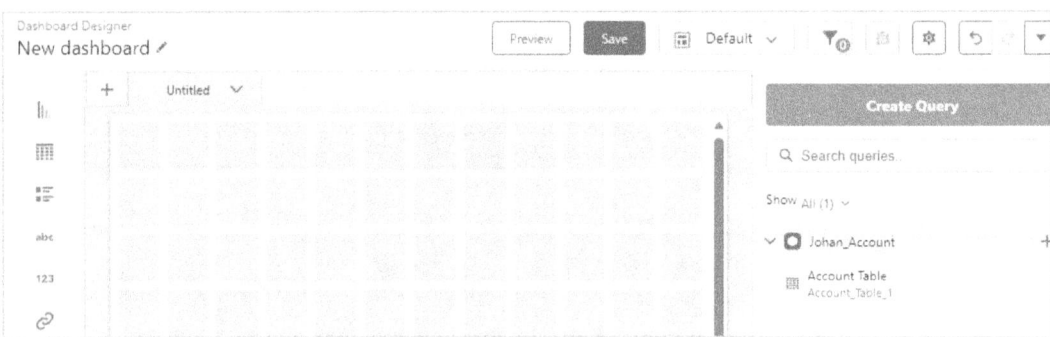

Figure 5-10. Clip a lens to the Dashboard

Once a lens is clipped to a dashboard, the Lens is copied to the Dashboard; this means the Query created in the Dashboard does not relate to the original Lens; they are completely independent. Any changes in the Lens will not impact the Dashboard, and any changes in the Dashboard will not impact the Lens either. We will discuss the Dashboard in Chapter 6, so you do not need to worry about it for now.

Share and Download Lens

Sharing Lens with your team or the whole company is easy; as discussed in Chapter 1, the permission to access CRM Analytics assets is controlled by the App, including Lens and other assets such as the Dataset and Dashboard. So, before sharing a Lens, make sure the Lens is stored in the App accessible by the users and the Dataset used for that Lens is also stored in an app accessible by the users.

> **Note** You can have the Lens and Dataset stored in different apps.

Get URL

Instead of manually copying and pasting the URL to your colleague, click the arrow icon at the far right of the Lens, then click **Share**. Click the Get URL tab, and you will see two options: open the link in the Analytics Tab or Analytics Studio. So, which one should we get? Ideally, if your colleague needs to edit the Lens, get the URL for **Analytics Studio**, but if they just need to explore the Lens, get the URL for **Analytics Tab**, see Figure 5-11.

CHAPTER 5 LENS

Figure 5-11. Get the URL to share a Lens

Post to Feed

With this feature, you can easily share the Lens to a User Chatter feed or a Group Chatter feed. Posting this will add the chart or table as an image and will be visible to all users in the group or users who follow the user. Even if users do not have a CRM Analytics license, they will be able to see the feed posted as an image.

Download

Does your team ask how to download data from a dataset? The answer is that CRM Analytics does not give options to download directly from the Dataset to an Excel or CSV file. However, they can explore a Dataset as a table and then download the data into an Excel or CSV file, making sure all the fields needed to download are added to the table.

If you notice, I mentioned fields added to the table; this means that you should not use the Chart lens if you would like to download the raw data. Downloading from chart lens will only give you a summary number based on the chart configured.

CRM Analytics also gives you the option to download the Lens as an image. The image will be in PNG format and will be similar to the one in Post to Feed.

> **Tip** If you do not see the Download option, check with your Salesforce admin to enable the "Download CRM Analytics Data" permission on your CRM Analytics permission set.

Add Lens to Subscriptions

We will discuss Subscription in Chapter 9, but in short, Subscription is a feature that allows you to receive lenses, dashboard widgets, and collections to your email on a schedule.

You can add a Lens to your Subscription by clicking the **Show Subscriptions** (envelope icon). As per the Spring '24 release, you can only subscribe to a Lens that has been converted to SAQL by clicking the Query Mode icon and saving the Lens.

If you have already created the Subscription, the system will ask you for the Title; otherwise, you need to create the Subscription by selecting the Frequency and Time for the email to be delivered, then click the Subscribe button to confirm.

Now, go back to Analytics Studio and click the **Subscriptions** tab; you will see that the Lens has been added to your Subscription, see Figure 5-12.

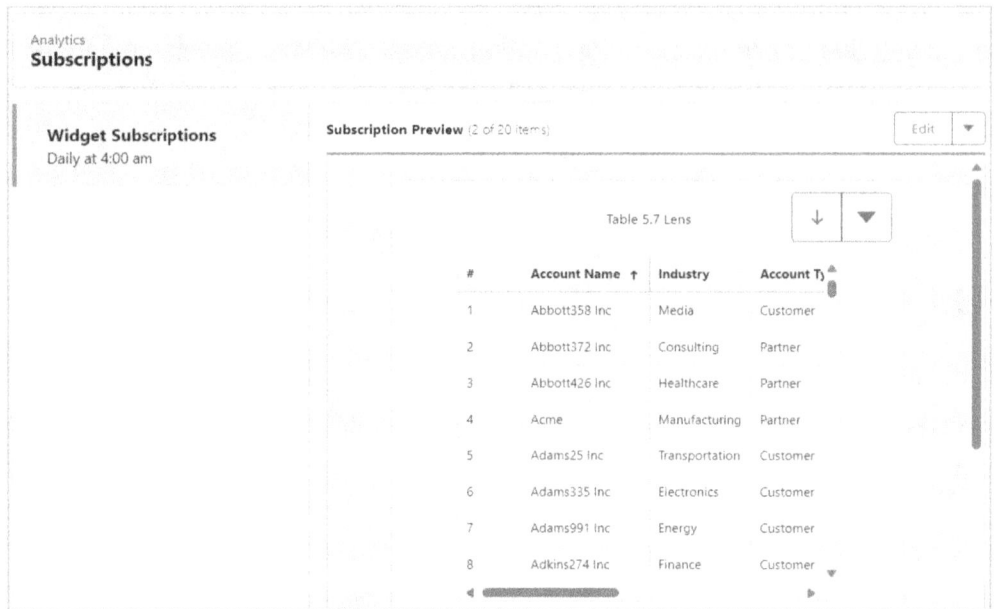

Figure 5-12. CRM Analytics Subscription

Note When the Lens is updated, the Subscription will be updated too; the email will deliver the latest Lens saved.

Add Lens to Collection

The purpose of the Collection is to organize CRM Analytics assets into a collection, such as the Dashboard, Component, and Lens. With the Collection, you and your team are able to access the related assets easily, regardless of whether they are stored in different apps.

You can add Lens to an existing Collection or create a new Collection; click the **Add to Collection** icon next to the "Show Subscriptions" icon, see Figure 5-13.

CHAPTER 5   LENS

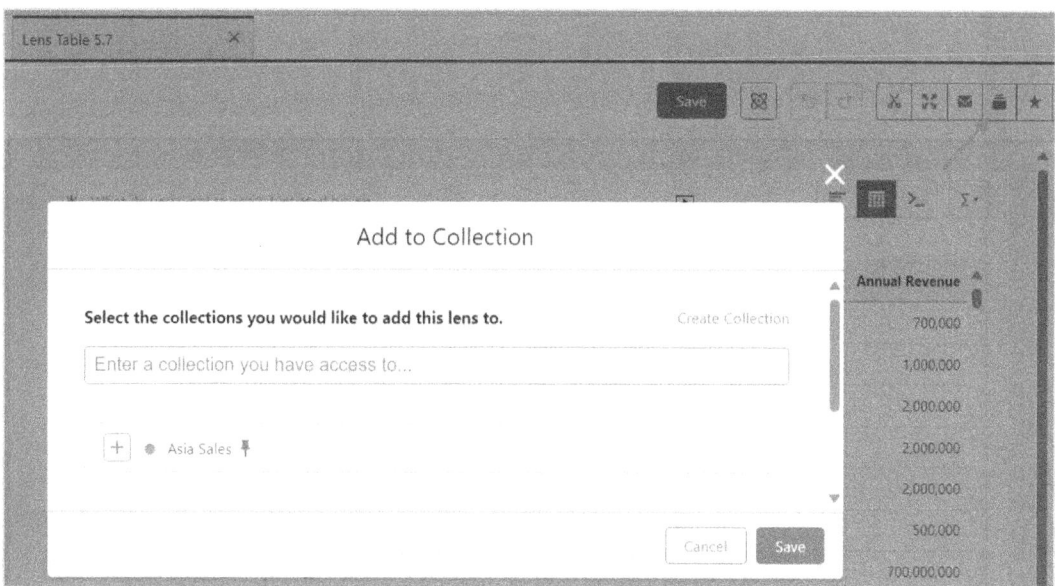

Figure 5-13. *Add Lens to a Collection*

Add Lens As Favorite

Suppose you have used Salesforce for some time; you may be aware of the Favorite feature, where you can access Salesforce assets, such as records, list views, and reports/dashboards, that have been marked as favorite, so that you can access them from anywhere in Salesforce via the Favorite icon.

The same applies to Favorite in CRM Analytics, where you can add CRM Analytics assets such as Apps, Lens, and Dashboards as Favorites. Even better, the CRM Analytics assets that are added as favorites will be shown in Salesforce's Favorites icon, see Figure 5-14.

CHAPTER 5   LENS

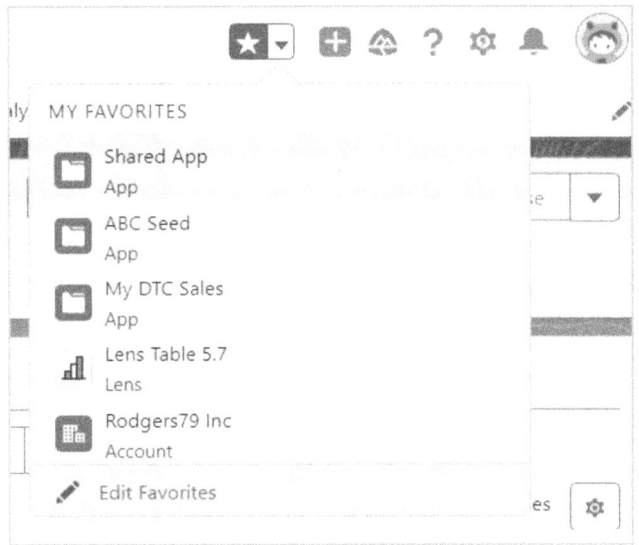

Figure 5-14. Accessing Favorites from Salesforce

You can access CRM Analytics assets added as favorites from Analytics Studio as well, see Figure 5-15; however, this will not include Salesforce assets here.

Figure 5-15. Accessing Favorites from Analytics Studio

CHAPTER 5   LENS

Explore with Conversational

When you explore Lens with Chart mode or Table mode, you may notice there is a text box above the chart or table with the following sentences: "What do you want to see? Just start typing…." If you do not see this box, reach out to the CRM Analytics admin to make sure "Conversational Exploration" has been enabled; navigate to the setup menu, type Analytics in the Quick Find box, and then click Settings, see Figure 5-16.

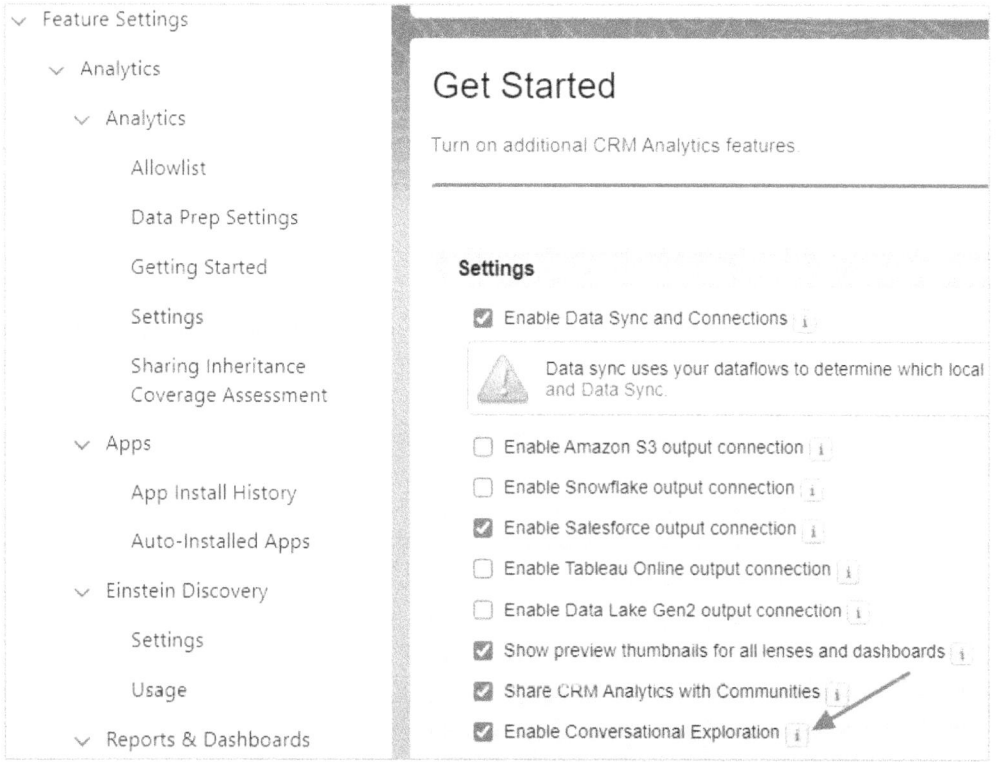

Figure 5-16. *Enable Conversational Exploration*

Let's go back to open a Lens or explore from a Dataset. Conversational Exploration means asking questions about the Dataset using nontechnical language and getting a quick answer as a chart; this is useful when you need to analyze a Dataset quickly.

How could we interact with the Dataset using this method? Click the Conversational Exploration text box; you will get a few suggestions on what you can ask. A conversation can begin with "show me" or "what is," with a dimension like "industry," or with a measure like "amount," "top x," etc. It is even better that you can include filters in the conversation to narrow the result area.

Chapter 5 Lens

Here are a few sample questions you can ask based on fields in the Dataset:

- Top two annual revenue by account type
- Show count of rows by account type
- Show me sum annual revenue by owner ID
- Show me average employees by account type
- What is annual revenue for previous year

Ideally, the question should contain a measure field for CRM Analytics to build the chart. All parameters or filters will be automatically entered based on the questions, and you will also be able to modify the parameters and filters manually as needed, see Figure 5-17 and notice the conversation submitted.

Figure 5-17. *Converse with data in Lens*

Summary

In this chapter, we discussed everything about Lens. Usually, we use Lens to explore a dataset, both from the Dataset or from a Dashboard widget. So far, we have not discussed the Dashboard yet, but in the next chapter, we will build a dashboard from scratch.

CHAPTER 5   LENS

We had a hands-on experience exploring the Dataset into a new lens, including both chart mode and table mode, and then we learned about saving and cloning lens. We also discussed Clip Lens to Designer which offers to copy Lens into an existing dashboard or to a new dashboard. We also mentioned that Lens is not related to a dashboard; anything added to the Dashboard will not impact the Lens or Dashboard anymore; they are entirely independent, just sharing the same Dataset.

We discussed how to share Lens with your team or the whole company; we can also post a Lens chart or table into someone's Chatter feed or Group feed, and with Lens, we are able to download raw data from CRM Analytics. Subscriptions, Collections, and Favorites are additional CRM Analytics features that can be added from Lenses.

We ended the chapter with a discussion on how to explore Lens with conversational language, so instead of manually selecting and adding fields and grouping, Conversational Exploration will do the job for us.

CHAPTER 6

Building Dashboard

After discussing the Recipe, Dataset, and Lens in previous chapters, we are going to start building a dashboard in this chapter. Let us start with the permission, layouts, dashboard template, widget, query, page, facet, and using multiple datasets in a dashboard; you will use most of those items when building a dashboard, although it is not a must to have all of them in a dashboard.

What can we expect from a CRM Analytics dashboard? With CRM Analytics, we can build a dashboard that shows numerous key metrics for our business with specific needs, from sales, support, marketing, adoption, etc. When building a dashboard, you can easily add dashboard filters using any fields available in the dataset, so your users are able to analyze data, including using facets.

For users on the road, CRM Analytics also comes with a mobile app that can be downloaded from the App Store or Google Play Store. By default, all CRM Analytics dashboards will work in the mobile app; however, the layout will not be friendly when it opens on the mobile device until you create a layout that is optimized for mobile.

In this chapter, we will learn the following topics related to creating a dashboard:

- Permission
- Layout
- Template
- Widgets
- Query
- Pages
- Faceting and global filter
- Using multiple datasets

Permission

We discussed the "App" in Chapter 1; the App controlled user permission to access items within that App, whether as a viewer, an editor, or a manager. Only users with editor or manager access (defined in each App) will be able to save dashboards into the App; otherwise, they will not see the App when saving a dashboard.

On top of permission on the app, to create dashboards, the user also needs to have a "Create and Edit CRM Analytics Dashboards" permission in their Salesforce user via Permission Set assignment.

Layout

When we create a new dashboard, the default layout is called "Default," and it is optimized for viewing the dashboard with a web browser from a computer, not from the mobile app. The CRM Analytics dashboard allows you to create multiple layouts for a dashboard, which are optimized for web browsers, tablets, and mobile devices.

Let's start creating a new dashboard:

1. Log in to Salesforce and open Analytics Studio.

2. Click the "Create" button, then select "Dashboard."

3. Select "Create Blank Dashboard"; this will bring you to the Dashboard Designer with a blank canvas.

4. By default, there will be 12 columns; on the right, notice the Layout panel with multiple properties, starting from General, Device, and Background Image. If you can't find the Layout panel, click the gear icon (Dashboard Properties) at the upper-right corner; see Figure 6-1.

CHAPTER 6 BUILDING DASHBOARD

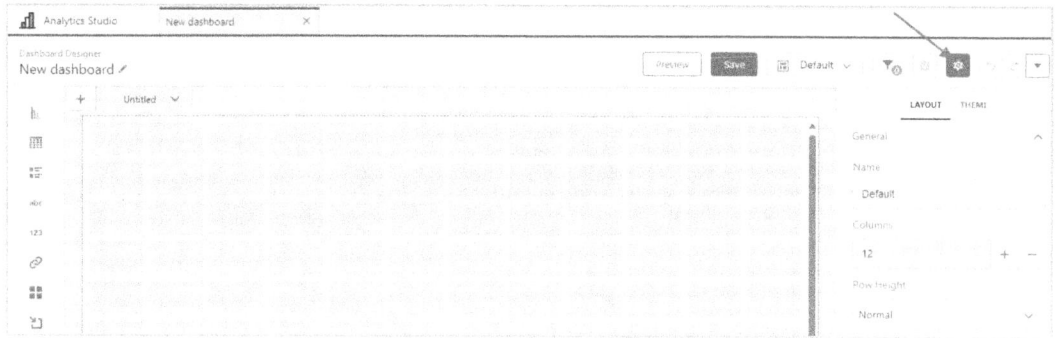

Figure 6-1. *Dashboard Designer without widgets added*

5. From this panel, we can change the layout name and other layout properties, such as column, row height, cell spacing, background color, etc. From this panel, let us change the layout name from default to "Web Browser" and columns to 18.

6. At the left bar below the default dashboard name, *New dashboard*, there is a + icon and an *Untitled* tab with an arrow. When you create a dashboard, it will start with one page only and is called "Untitled"; we can rename this by clicking the arrow and selecting Rename. Another option is Hide from Navigation and Clone; for now, let us rename the page to "Page-1" and click the Apply button.

7. A CRM Analytics dashboard can have multiple pages; click the + icon to create a new page and enter the name; for now, let's stick with one page. Later in this chapter, we'll discuss the dashboard with multiple pages.

8. Let us rename the dashboard accordingly from the default "New dashboard" to "Global Accounts" by clicking the pencil icon next to the dashboard name, see Figure 6-2.

CHAPTER 6 BUILDING DASHBOARD

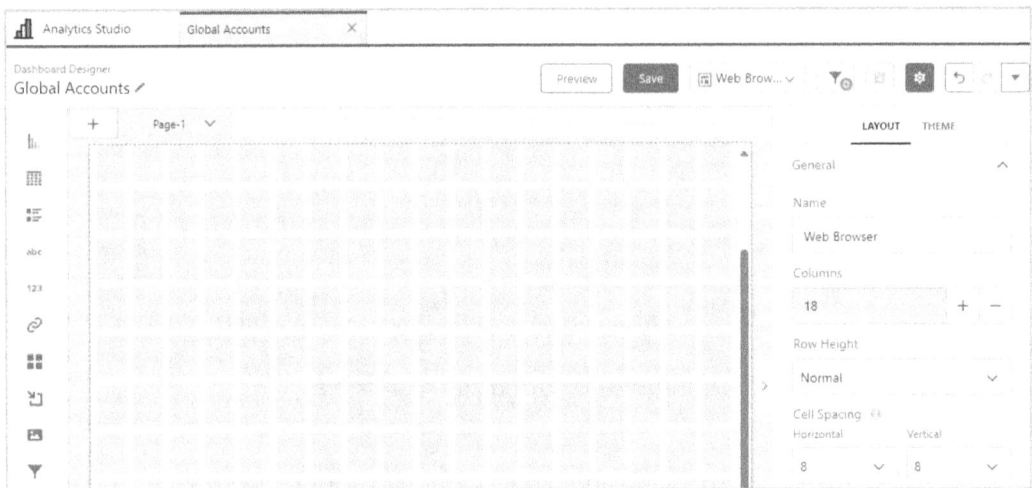

Figure 6-2. *Change in the layout name, columns, page name, and dashboard name*

To manage layouts, click the arrow in the layout drop-down; in our case, remember that we renamed it "Web Browser" and then click **Manage Layouts**. From here, we can rename the layout and see all the layouts that are available for the dashboard. If multiple layouts have been created, you can delete them, except the current layout.

9. If you create a layout with the Mobile layout type, this template will be auto-selected when the user opens the dashboard from the mobile app. We also have the option to copy all content from the current layout to the new layout and also to enable **Sync** widgets across pages, see Figure 6-3.

10. Let us save the dashboard by clicking the Save icon at the upper right; the dashboard name by default will follow the dashboard title, **Global Accounts**; save it to **My Private App**.

CHAPTER 6   BUILDING DASHBOARD

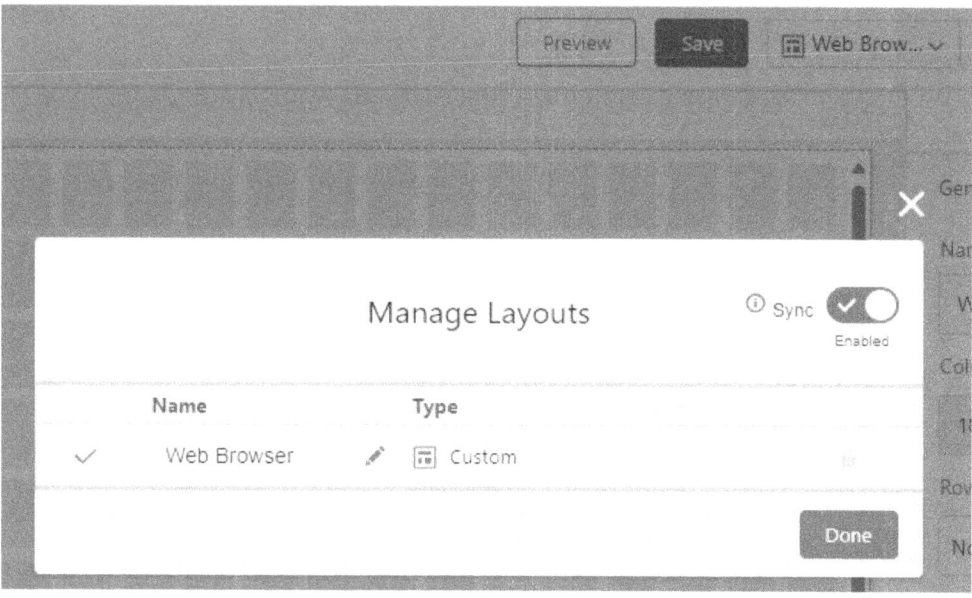

Figure 6-3. Manage Layouts to see and rename layouts

Template

When you create a new dashboard, CRM Analytics will ask if you would like to create it from a blank dashboard or a dashboard template. If you select to create from a template, you can choose from ten templates available:

- Comparison Dashboard
- Details Dashboard
- GMT Blank Dashboard
- Metric Trend
- Performance Summary
- Summary Dashboard
- Table Expansion
- Three-Columns Dashboard
- Tile Dashboard
- Time Series

105

Using a dashboard template, you can speed up the development process in creating a new dashboard; the new dashboard will have widgets and layouts based on the selected template but still give you the flexibility to move, add, and delete widgets. Some templates come with filters, containers, main charts, supporting charts, tables, and key metrics.

While some of them, such as Metric Trend, Performance Summary, Table Expansion, and Time Series, will ask you a few questions, each of these templates will ask for different questions, but the dataset will always be asked.

Table 6-1. Questions for the Dashboard Template

	Metric Trend	Performance Summary	Table Expansion	Time Series
Choose a dataset	✓	✓	✓	✓
Choose a metric	✓	✓		
Choose a date	✓	✓	✓	✓
Choose groupings	✓			
Choose filters		✓		
Choose dimensions			✓	✓
Choose measures			✓	✓
Choose a confidence interval				✓
Indicate if seasonality impacts your data				✓

Some of the templates are also marked as "smart," which means the dashboard requires little to no additional configuration; for example, in the Time Series template, the dashboard visualizes how metrics change over time and predicts future metric trends based on historical data.

We will not discuss each template in this book, but let us create a new dashboard using the Time Series template (which is marked as smart); make sure the dataset has a date field and a measure field.

CHAPTER 6 BUILDING DASHBOARD

1. Log in to Salesforce and open Analytics Studio.

2. Click the "Create" button, then select "Dashboard."

3. Select the "Create Dashboard from Template" button.

4. Select the "Time Series" template and click the Continue button.

5. You need to select a dataset and fields for a few questions, then click "Looks good, next.", see Figure 6-4.

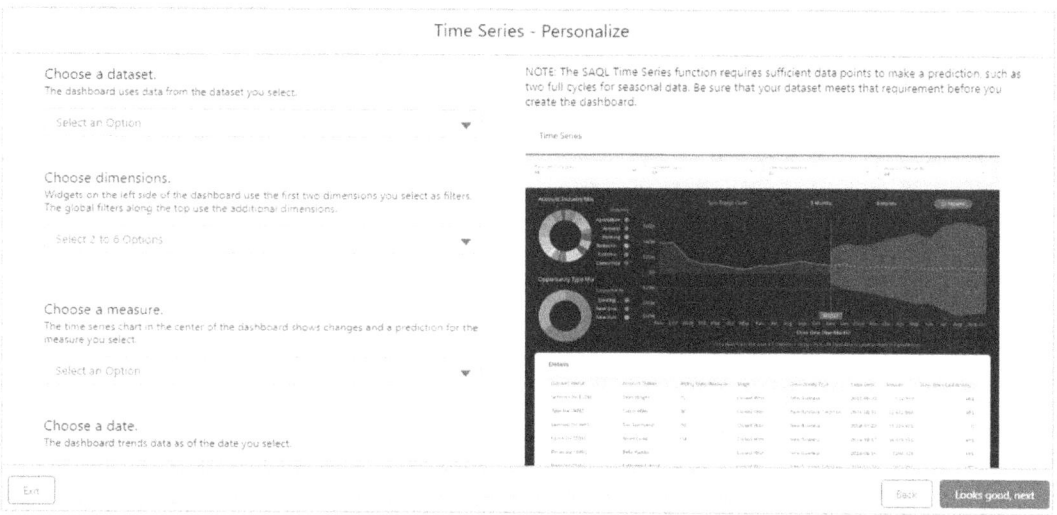

Figure 6-4. *Create a dashboard with the Time Series template*

6. Enter the dashboard name as "Time Series" and save it in "Shared App."

7. A Time Series dashboard is created with filters; the main chart is a timeline chart with trends over months; supporting charts and tables are added to the dashboard based on fields selected in the wizard. The timeline chart shows the prediction of future metrics based on historical data, see Figure 6-5.

107

CHAPTER 6   BUILDING DASHBOARD

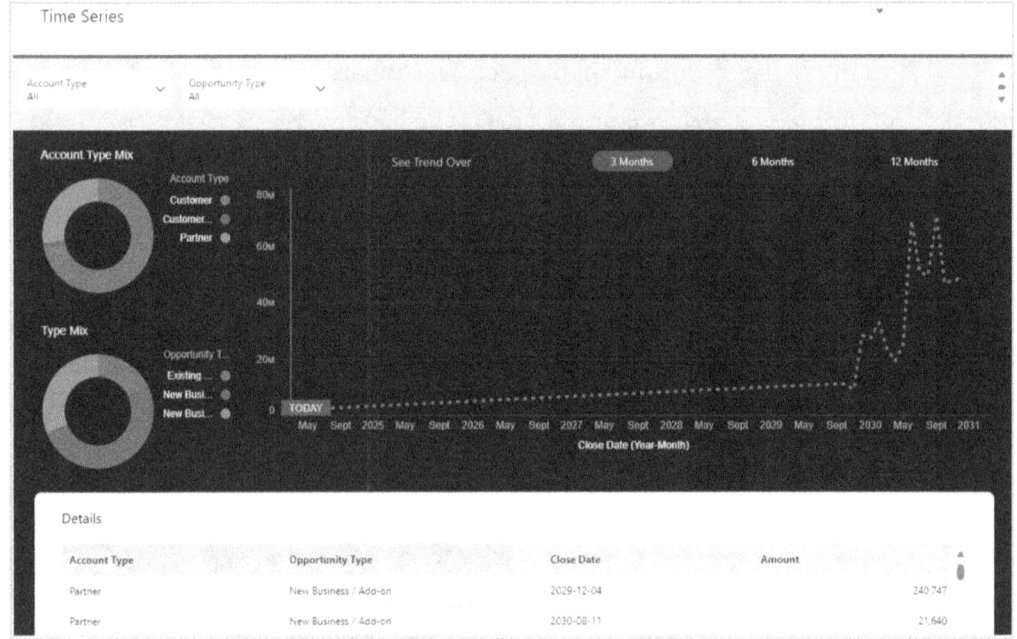

Figure 6-5. *A Time Series dashboard*

However, not all dashboard templates may be suitable for our business needs, so we may find ourselves creating blank dashboards more often.

Widgets

When you create a new blank dashboard, you will see a blank canvas with 12 column boxes and a list of icons at the left panel; see the blank dashboard that we created earlier, "Global Accounts," as in Figure 6-2, each icon represents a widget that can be used in the dashboard designer for different purposes. Let us walk through some of them and learn to use them.

Chart

The chart is the first icon from the top and is the most commonly used widget in every dashboard. Use the chart widget to show data as a chart in the dashboard. There are more than 30 types of charts provided by CRM Analytics. Let us do a quick hands-on exercise to use this widget:

CHAPTER 6 BUILDING DASHBOARD

1. Open the Global Accounts dashboard created earlier and click the Edit button.

2. Drag the chart widget to the dashboard designer.

3. Click the "Chart" icon at the center of the widget added.

4. You will be asked to select a dataset; find the "Open Opportunities more than 0" dataset created in Chapter 3. Once a dataset is selected, by default, you will get

    - Bar chart
    - Bar length, which is the count of rows
    - Without filter
    - Without grouping

    The chart looks similar when we explore the dataset by creating a new lens, with the difference at the top-left corner, "Untitled Query," instead of "New Lens," and the additional Back and Done buttons at the bottom. Clicking the Back allows you to select a different Dataset.

5. Change "Untitled Query" to "Step No of Rows."

6. Click the Done button and Save icon to save the dashboard.

7. Notice that a query is created at the right panel of the dashboard designer; this panel will show all queries created for the dashboard; we can also create the query manually here, see Figure 6-6. We'll discuss "query" later in this chapter.

Figure 6-6. *Blank dashboard with a widget and query*

109

Table

Use this widget to display the record values table, compare table, and pivot table. Similar to the chart widget, let us continue the Global Accounts dashboard:

1. Assume the Global Accounts dashboard has been opened; if not, open it and switch to edit mode by clicking the Edit icon at the upper right.

2. Drag the table icon into the dashboard designer below the chart widget.

3. Click the "Table" icon at the center of the widget added. You may notice that the system no longer asks you to provide a dataset; this is because CRM Analytics remembers that you have selected a dataset earlier and will be using the same dataset; however, if you need to select a different dataset, click the "Back" button.

4. Even if this is a table widget, by default, we'll get a bar chart with a count of the number of rows; if you do not change the chart to table mode, you will get only the number of rows in the table. To get record details in the table, change the table by selecting **Table Mode**, then **Values Table**.

5. Select fields that we would like to show in the dashboard.

6. Change the query title to "Query Record Detail."

7. Click the Done button.

8. To get better visibility of the table content, you can move and resize the widget accordingly, see Figure 6-7.

9. Click the Save icon.

CHAPTER 6 BUILDING DASHBOARD

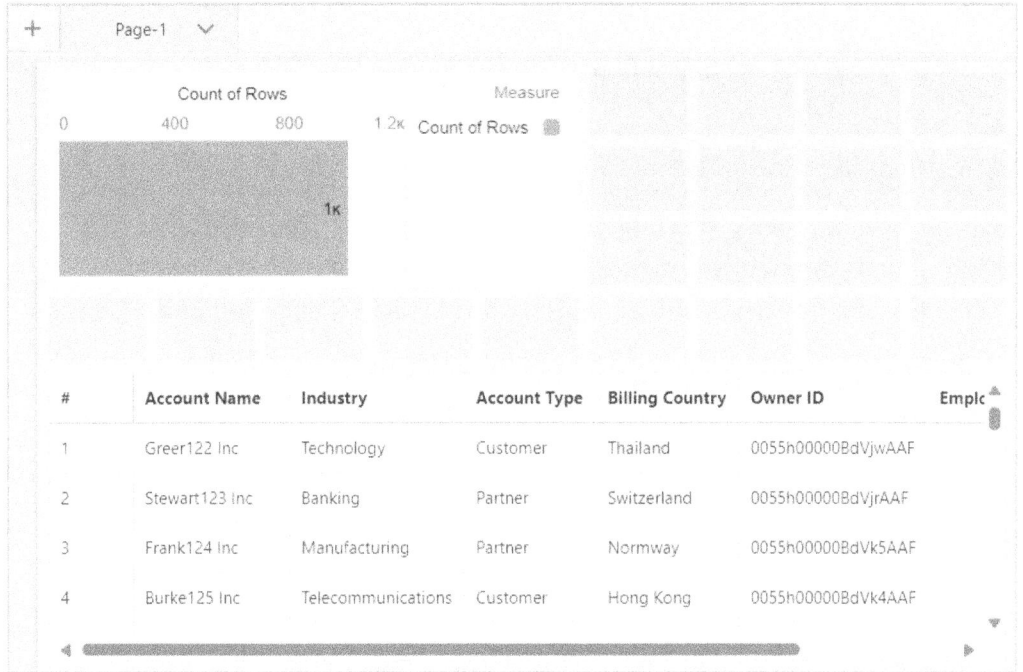

Figure 6-7. A dashboard with chart and table widgets

Tip To have columns occupy the whole table width, from the widget properties at the right, find the Spacing section, then set Column Width = Fit to Widget; with this setting, the width of the columns will be auto-adjusted when the web browser size changes.

Filter

Use this widget to make a global filter of the data displayed in the dashboard. You can select to have a single or multiple global filters. Let's do a hands-on exercise to use this widget:

1. Open the Global Accounts dashboard, then switch to edit mode.

2. Drag the filter widget into the dashboard designer.

3. Select the "Single Global Filter" under widget properties on the right panel.

111

CHAPTER 6   BUILDING DASHBOARD

4. Click the "Filter" icon at the center of the filter widget added.

5. Select the same dataset used earlier, then select a field from the selected dataset.

6. Click the "Create" button.

7. Click the "Preview" button at the top panel to test if the added filter is working correctly, see Figure 6-8; notice that the dashboard is no longer in edit mode (there are no blocks in the background).

8. To edit the dashboard again, click the Edit icon.

9. Click the Save icon to save the dashboard.

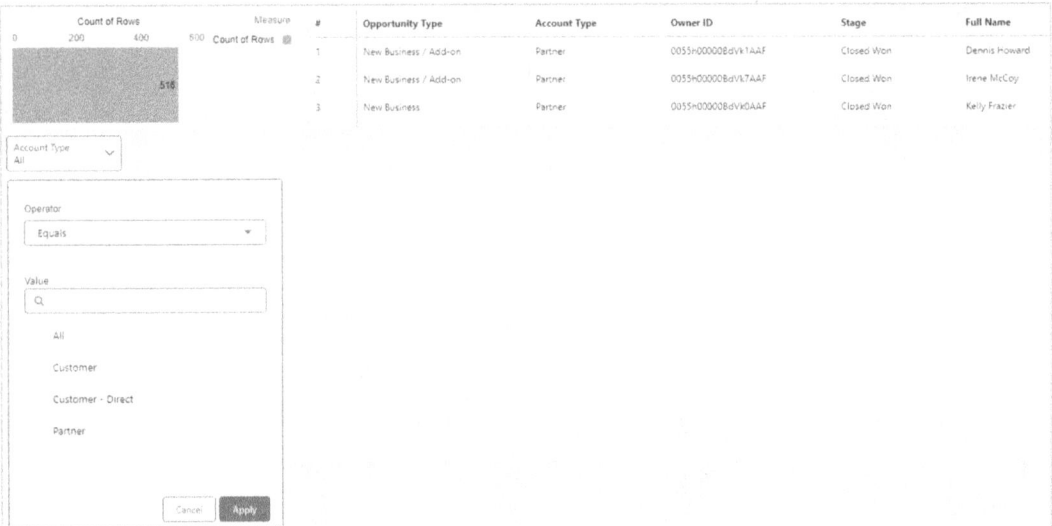

Figure 6-8. Dashboard with a global filter

Tip   You can simply hit the "e" key to switch to edit mode, hit the "e" key again to go back to preview mode, and hit the "s" key to save the dashboard.

Container

The container widget is useful for grouping a few widgets into a container, so you can move them easily. You can also set the background or border color to group multiple widgets with the same purpose.

112

CHAPTER 6 BUILDING DASHBOARD

1. Open the Global Accounts dashboard and switch to edit mode.

2. Drag the Container widget to the dashboard designer.

3. Resize the widget to be wider and occupy the whole width of the dashboard.

4. Drag the chart and table created into the container.

5. Change the container widget background color to dark green; you can do this by selecting the container widget, then looking for Widget Style on the right panel, clicking the arrow under Background Color, and selecting dark green, see Figure 6-9.

6. Hit the "e" and then the "s" key to exit from edit mode and save the dashboard.

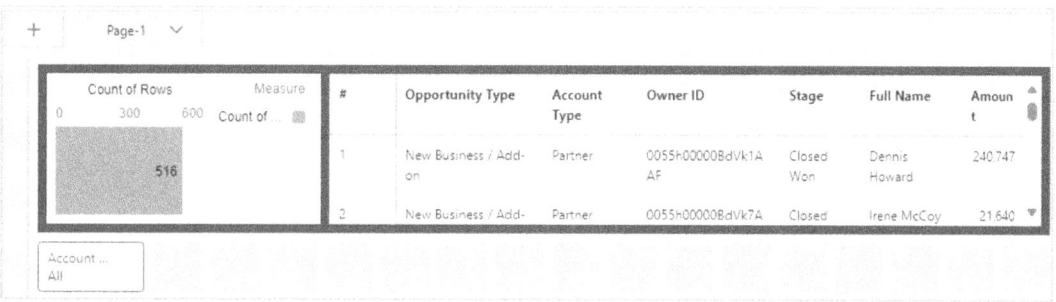

Figure 6-9. Dashboard with a container

Date

Use the calendar widget to add a date field as a filter. You can only select a date field for this widget.

1. Open the Global Accounts dashboard and switch to edit mode.

2. Drag the Date widget to the dashboard designer.

3. Click the "Date" icon at the center of the widget.

4. Select a date field; only date fields will be available here.

5. Click the "Create" button.

113

CHAPTER 6 BUILDING DASHBOARD

6. Select the widget from the right panel for widget properties, change the widget title to "Date," and enable "Update instantly."

7. Click the Query tab; few things to notice here:

    - **Apply Global Filters**: Enable this to implement the value selected in the Global Filter widget discussed earlier.

    - **Faceting**: When the user clicks a selection from a chart widget, and the widget is set to broadcast to other widgets, enabling this will filter available dates based on the selection; you can select All, Include, Exclude, and None.

    - **Selection Type**: Configure if the selection is required and as a single or multiple selection.

    - **Broadcast Selection As Facets**: When a user selects a value of dates, this selection will broadcast to other widgets; this is related to faceting.

    For now, do not change the preceding items, and use the default values.

8. Move and resize the widget accordingly. I'll move this widget to the top-left corner, above the container created earlier, and the filter widget next to it.

9. Click the Preview button (or hit the "e" key) to verify the Date filter is working correctly, see Figure 6-10.

10. Hit the "s" key to save the dashboard.

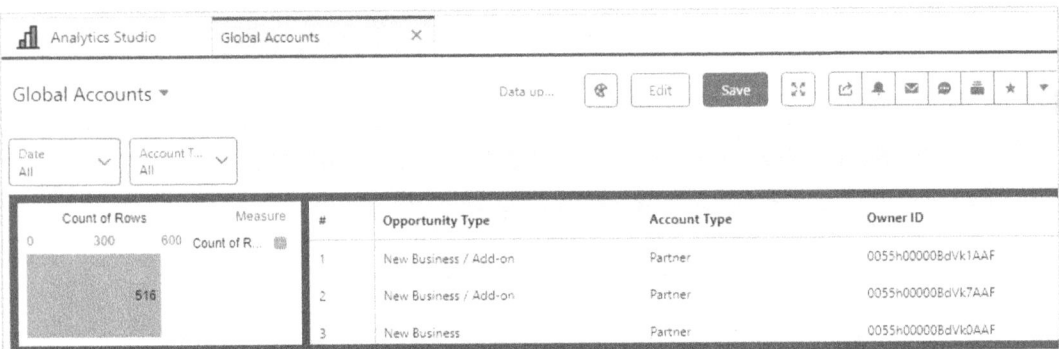

Figure 6-10. Dashboard with a date filter

Link

Use this widget to navigate the user to

- **Saved Lens**: Open an existing lens.
- **Saved Dashboard**: Open an existing dashboard.
- **New Lens**: Create a new lens based on the existing query.
- **URL**: Open any URL into a new tab.
- **Page in Component**: Open an existing component.
- **Page in Layout**: Only available if there are multiple pages in the dashboard.

Even the widget name is "Link," it will appear as a button in the dashboard. Let us continue with the hands-on exercise:

1. Continue with the Global Accounts dashboard and switch to edit mode.
2. Drag the Link widget to the container and drop it at the top-right corner.
3. Change the Text to "Search with Google."
4. Set "Link To" to URL.
5. Destination = http://www.google.com.
6. Link Tooltip = "Click to open Google."
7. Hit the "e" key to preview and then the "s" key to save.
8. Click the "Search with Google" link; it should open the Google website as a new tab, see Figure 6-11.

CHAPTER 6   BUILDING DASHBOARD

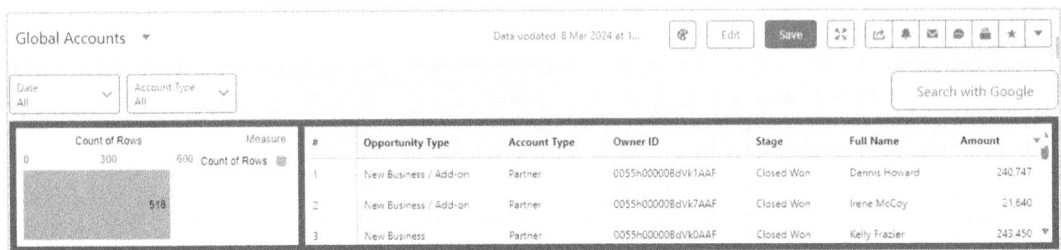

Figure 6-11.   Dashboard link at the top right

Tip   To get round corners for the link button, click the widget from the widget properties, look for the Widget Style section, then set the border radius to 8 or 16. You also can change the background color and border color.

Image

As the name suggests, this widget is used to add an image to the dashboard. It can be for a logo or other images to be embedded in the dashboard. Let's do a hands-on exercise:

1. Open the Global Accounts dashboard and switch to edit mode.

2. Move the Date widget to the right so we have space in the upper-left corner for the image widget.

3. Drag the image widget to the upper-left corner.

4. Click the Image icon within the widget.

5. Click the Browse Files button and select the image for a logo from your computer; image format supported gif, bmp, jpeg, jpg, png, and svg.

6. From widget properties, change the Image Scale to Fit Width or Fit Height, arrange Image Alignment, and you also can resize the widget, see Figure 6-12.

7. Hit the "e" and then the "s" key.

CHAPTER 6 BUILDING DASHBOARD

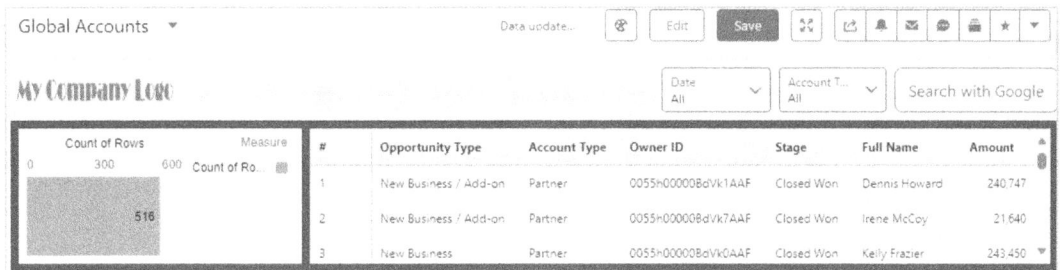

Figure 6-12. *Adding the image widget to the dashboard*

List

The list widget is another most commonly used widget, and its purpose is to filter data shown in the chart or table. List values will be automatically populated as a unique value from a selected field. Let's do a hands-on exercise:

1. Open the Global Accounts dashboard and switch to edit mode.

2. Drag the List widget after the Date widget.

3. Resize the widget height to occupy two blocks.

4. Click the List icon in the widget.

5. Select a field, and choose Account Type, then click the Create button.

6. Hit the "e" and then the "s" key.

7. Click the Account Type drop-down; in my case, I'll see three options with the radio button – you can only select one value, and there is a number at the right, meaning the number of records for each value, see Figure 6-13.

    You can compare the visualization with the Filter widget using the same Account Type field. Although they do similar things, the experience is a bit different.

117

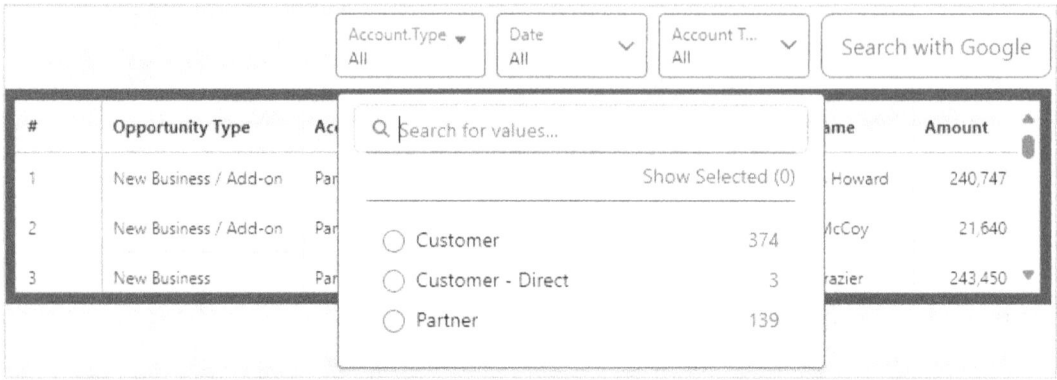

Figure 6-13. Adding a List widget

8. Let us edit the dashboard again; from the list widget properties, click the Query tab and change Selection Type to "Multiple selections." Now, the radio button has changed to a checkbox, which means you can select multiple values.

Number

In some cases, you would like to show numbers in the dashboard; this is good for catching user attention, such as the total amount, the number of open cases, etc. Let's do a hands-on exercise:

1. Open the Global Accounts dashboard and switch to edit mode.

2. Resize the container bigger, move the table to the bottom, and chart to the right so we'll have space under the logo.

3. Drag the Number widget below the logo.

4. Resize the widget height to occupy three blocks' width and three blocks' height.

5. Click the Number icon in the widget.

6. Let's use the default value, which is the Count of Rows, and click the Done button.

CHAPTER 6 BUILDING DASHBOARD

7. From the Number widget properties, look for the Text Style section, change Number Size to 48, and Alignment to Center, see Figure 6-14.

8. Hit the "e" and then the "s" key.

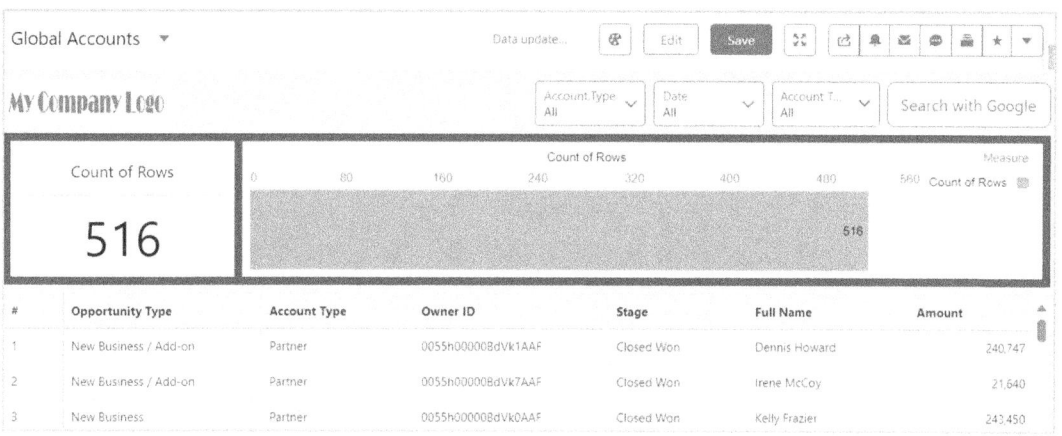

Figure 6-14. Adding a Number widget

Range

Use this widget and link it to a Measure field to filter dashboard data. This widget allows users to filter data by entering from and to values or slide the slider provided; the number will be adjusted as the user adjusts the slider.

1. Open the Global Accounts dashboard and switch to edit mode.

2. Drag the Range widget to a space at the top in the dashboard designer.

3. Click the Range icon in the widget.

4. Select a Measure field and click the Create button.

5. Hit the "e" and then the "s" key, see Figure 6-15.

119

CHAPTER 6 BUILDING DASHBOARD

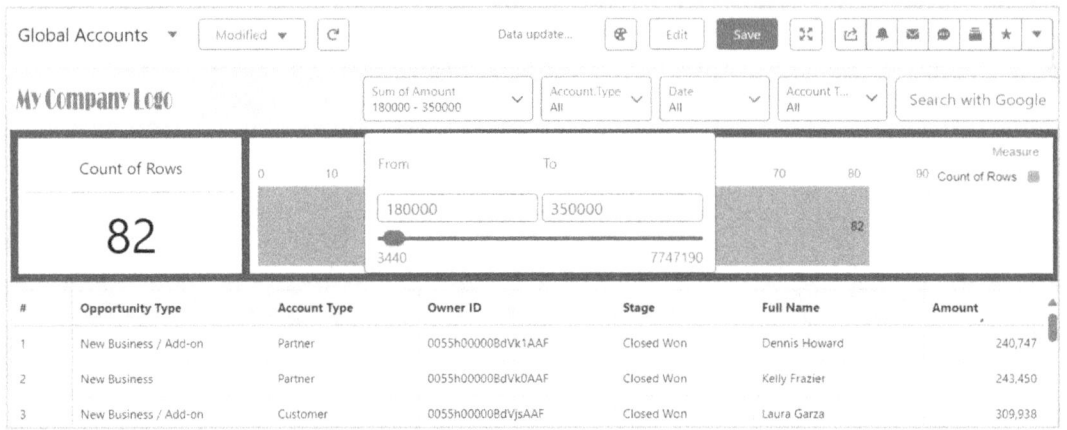

Figure 6-15. *Adding a Range widget*

Text

In many cases, we need to inform the user about a chart added to the dashboard; we can use a Text widget to add that information as a label; we can also use this widget to inform the dashboard in general, including as a dashboard title or subtitle. Apply text style and widget style to make the widget attractive.

1. Open the Global Accounts dashboard and switch to edit mode.

2. Drag the Text widget to the empty space in the dashboard designer.

3. Look at widget properties on the right panel and modify the text to "this dashboard contains global data"; you can change the font format, color, and size, see Figure 6-16.

4. You will see the changes immediately as you work.

5. Hit the "e" and then the "s" key.

CHAPTER 6   BUILDING DASHBOARD

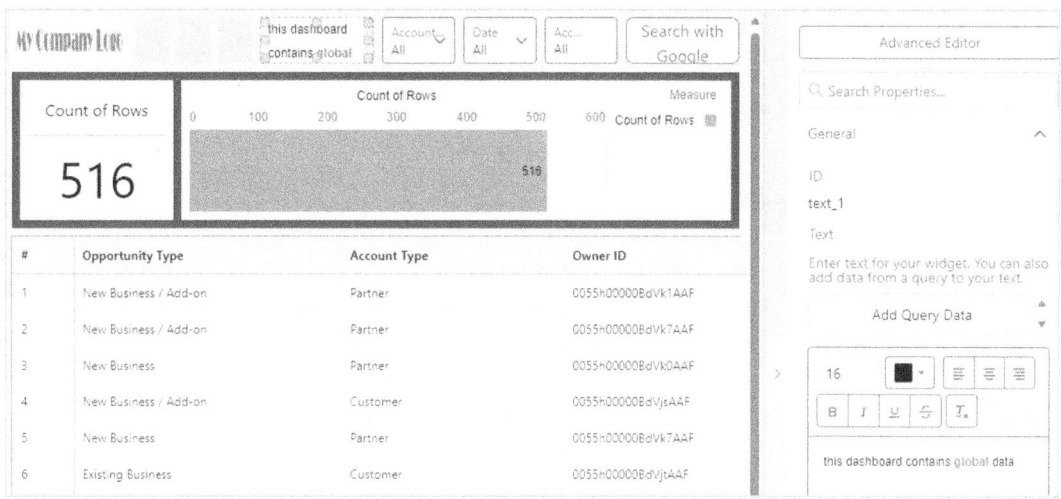

Figure 6-16. *Adding a Text widget as a dashboard title*

Toggle

Adding a toggle widget will allow our users to filter data easily with one click. Only data that exists in the dashboard will appear in the toggle, for example, you have Account Types Customer, Prospect, and Alumni, but within a period, there is only Prospect and Customer, so your user will not see the Alumni in the toggle. However, we can use a static step to handle this; we will discuss a static step in the last chapter.

1. Open the Global Accounts dashboard and switch to edit mode.

2. Drag the Toggle widget to an empty space in the dashboard designer.

3. Click the Toggle icon in the widget.

4. Select Account Type to use for the toggle.

5. Click the Create button to continue.

6. Adjust the widget size as necessary, ideally making all values visible; otherwise, the user will need to scroll.

7. Click the Query tab and change Selection Type to "Multiple selections"; this is to allow the user to select multiple values.

8. Hit the "e" and then the "s" key.

121

Figure 6-17 shows a toggle with two values selected (background in blue).

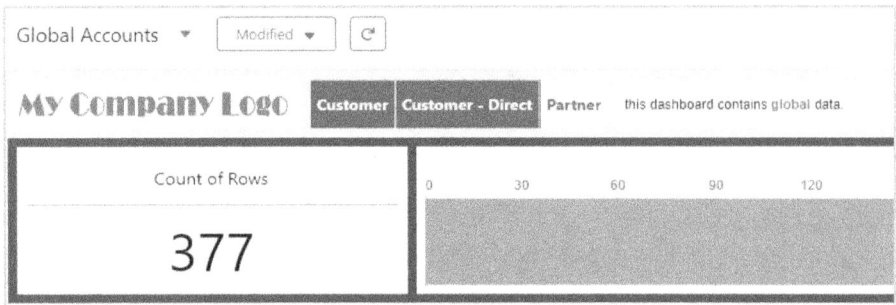

Figure 6-17. *Adding a Text widget as a dashboard title*

Navigation

Before adding this widget, let us add a new page to the dashboard. Remember that we can have multiple pages in a dashboard; we will discuss pages in the next section.

1. Open the Global Accounts dashboard and switch to edit mode.

2. Click the + icon under the dashboard name.

3. Enter the page name; I will enter "Page-2" and click the Add button.

4. Now, we have a blank dashboard designer, and the Page-2 tab is selected.

5. Click the Page-1 tab, and now you will see all widgets added previously.

CHAPTER 6 BUILDING DASHBOARD

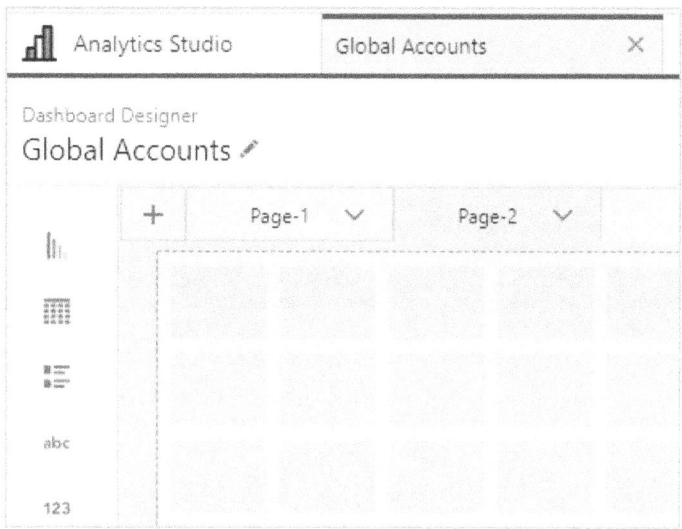

Figure 6-18. *Adding a Text widget as a dashboard title*

6. Drag the Navigation widget to the bottom of the dashboard designer.

7. By default, it will show Page-1 and Page-2 as available pages; you can update the color and style of the widget.

8. Step 6 will add the Navigation widget to Page-1 only, not Page-2, so select the widget:

    a. Select "Add to Page" at the bottom left.

    b. Click "Page-2."

    c. Click the "Apply" button.

9. Now the widget is copied to Page-2

10. Hit the "e" and then the "s" key.

Play around by navigating to page 2 and back to page 1.

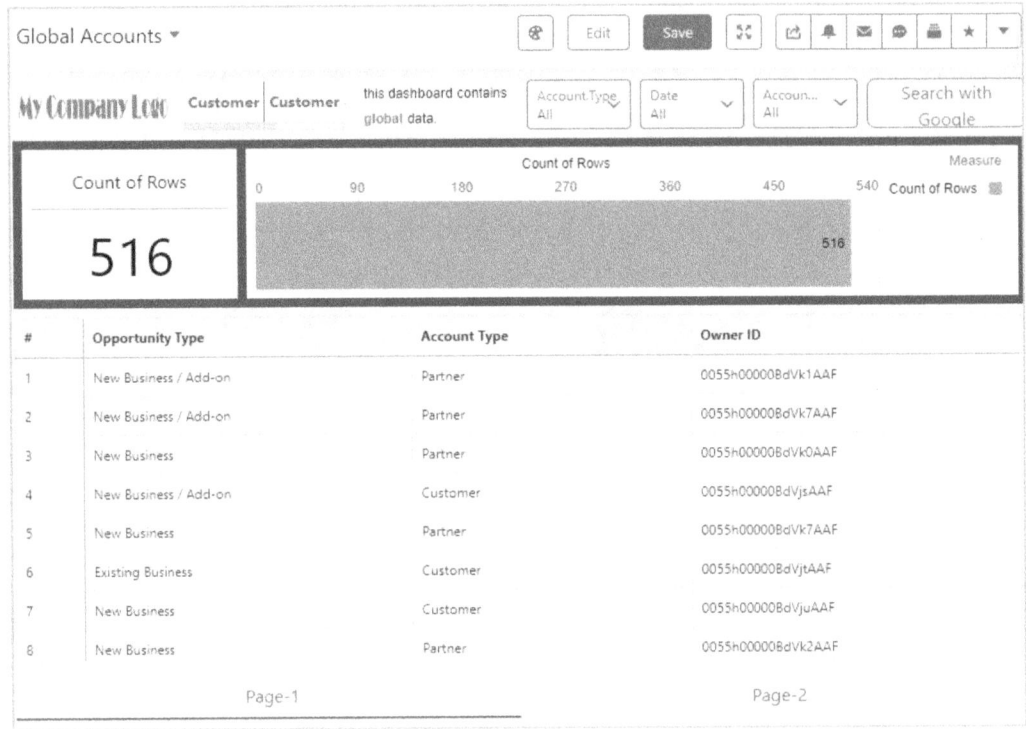

Figure 6-19. Dashboard with a Navigation widget at the bottom

Page

As mentioned earlier, a dashboard can have multiple pages. For admins, this is good in terms of maintaining dashboards; instead of showing many dashboards in Analytics Studio, a dashboard with multiple pages will be shown only as one dashboard. From the user perspective, this offers a better experience as the user will not open the wrong or many dashboards; for example, if we have a "main" dashboard with multiple "child" dashboards, the system will open a new tab when clicking a link which will confuse by having many web browser tabs opened.

However, it depends on the needs; sometimes, we must use multiple dashboards instead of one dashboard with multiple pages. Let us go through each use case, including when we need to use multiple pages in a dashboard or when using multiple dashboards. We will have no hands-on exercise in this section, but you can refer to the hands-on exercises in Figures 6-18 and 6-19 when we discussed the Navigation widget.

Sharing Widget

A multipage dashboard will offer the ability to share widgets across pages. When you add a widget to other pages, they will share the same widget style, meaning changing the widget style on a page will impact the widget style shown on other pages; however, you still can shift the widget in the dashboard designer, and this will not impact the location of the widget in other pages.

CRM Analytics also offers the ability to unlink the widget from other pages; select the widget and click the Unlink link above the widget to unlink it, see Figure 6-20.

Figure 6-20. Unlink a widget used in multiple pages

Dataset Filter

When you use a dataset across pages, and if there are filters set, the filter selected on one page will also filter the result on other pages; this includes faceting from other charts too. If you totally need to separate them, you must use multiple dashboards or multiple datasets.

Dashboard Tab

One of the benefits of using multiple pages is transparency for users; the user will not know if they are opening multiple pages because the tab and URL are not changed, and it also does not open a new tab when users switch across pages. Using the link widget will open the new dashboard as a new tab so that multiple tabs will be opened.

Performance

Because the dataset was loaded when opening the dashboard, a dashboard with multiple pages will offer better performance compared to opening multiple dashboards.

Adoption and Maintenance

Using a dashboard with multiple pages will allow the admin to monitor the usage and adoption of a dashboard more easily; the admin just needs to monitor a dashboard instead of monitoring multiple dashboards. Dashboards with multiple pages will only show once in Analytics Studio; this is also cleaner for maintaining overall dashboards.

Faceting

Faceting, which is enabled by default, is one of the most useful features in CRM Analytics for a user to drill down and analyze data. For a dashboard using a dataset, when the user clicks a group in a widget, the whole dashboard will be filtered based on the selection on the widget; for example, clicking a product in a widget will filter the whole dataset to the specific product clicked, so other widgets using the same dataset will be automatically filtered.

Let's go back to the Global Accounts dashboard created earlier, edit the dashboard, click a chart, and then click the **Query** tab. Notice there are two checkboxes related to faceting:

a) Apply filters from faceting.

b) Broadcast selections as facets.

Both options are enabled by default. The first option is to accept filters when other widgets broadcast faceting, and the second option is to broadcast selection as facets to other widgets, see Figure 6-21, so if other widgets have "Apply filters from faceting" enabled, the widget data will be filtered based on the selection in the selected widget. You can have more than one widget that broadcasts a facet; all selections will filter the dataset, for example, the product is A and the region is US. However, you cannot have more than one selection in a widget; this is different from using a List as a filter.

CHAPTER 6   BUILDING DASHBOARD

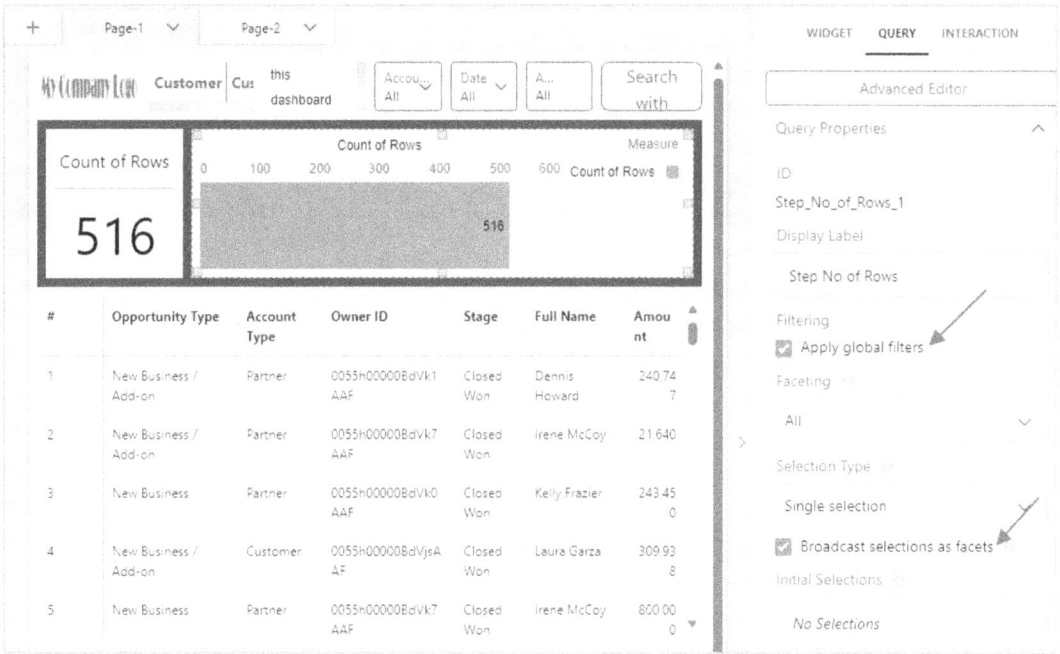

Figure 6-21. *Faceting options in the query*

Global Filter

When you need to use partial data from a dataset based on some criteria, adding a global filter widget is the easiest option, rather than recreating a new dataset using a dataflow or recipe, which will give us, as admins, another item to maintain. Also, this option will save the number of rows used by CRM Analytics because we do not create a new Dataset. This method is also simpler than applying filters to each widget in the dashboard.

To achieve partial data usage, we should make the filter locked so our users will see only related data in the dashboard, for example, we need to build a Customer dashboard, but our dataset is combined between Customer and Prospect, so we can add a global filter to filter only customers, then lock the filter.

When the dashboard is added with the filter widget, in the dashboard edit mode, notice the number in the filter icon is no longer zero (located at the upper right, next to the layout drop-down), but tell us how many filters were added, see Figure 6-22. You can add multiple filters into a global filter panel as explained in the hands-on exercise earlier; check out Figure 6-8.

127

CHAPTER 6　BUILDING DASHBOARD

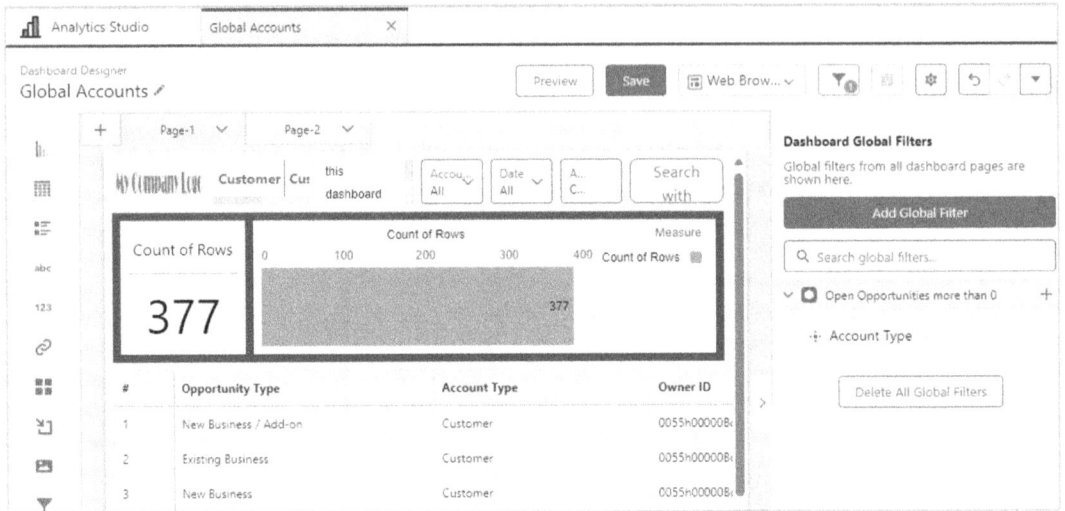

Figure 6-22. *Dashboard with global filter and filter properties*

Tip　To lock a filter widget, click the filter icon next to the layout drop-down, click the pencil icon after the field name, enable "Locked" properties, see Figure 6-23, and click the Apply button. Once the filter is locked, notice the keypad icon in the filter widget.

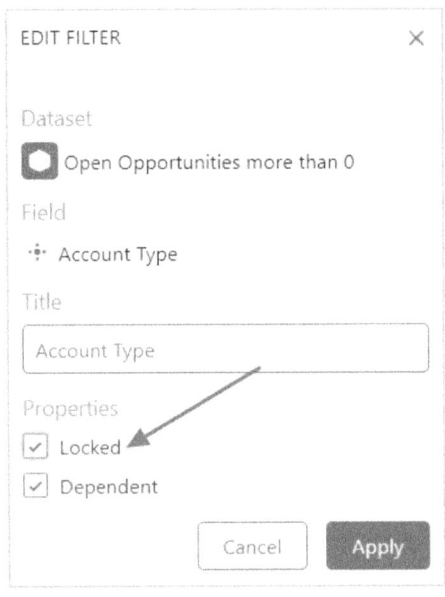

Figure 6-23. *Locked a filter widget*

Tip To add values to the filter widget, make sure the field is not locked in the Global Dashboard Filters. In dashboard edit mode, click the arrow button at the upper-right corner and select Pick Initial Values, select the filter widget, select values to filter, click the Apply button, click the Done button, and then lock the field.

Using Multiple Datasets

So far, we have discussed using only one dataset in a dashboard; however, we can use multiple datasets in a dashboard. When you add the widget from a different dataset, filtering and faceting will not work across widgets that use different Datasets.

However, we can link them using a common value, for example, we have a dataset called "Order" for actual sales and another dataset called "Target," so when we select a name from a widget, we would like to show Target only for the sales rep selected; in this case, we will use the "User Name" to connect both datasets. Let's have a quick hands-on exercise:

1. Prepare the data for a new dataset; for this, I'll sample using Microsoft Excel.

   Table 6-2. *Target Dataset*

Name	Target
Dennis Howard	10
Irene McCoy	20
Kelly Frazier	15

2. Create a new Dataset using the CSV file upload.

3. Open the Global Accounts dashboard and switch to edit mode.

4. Drag a list widget to the dashboard designer.

5. Click the "List" icon in the widget.

CHAPTER 6   BUILDING DASHBOARD

6. By default, it will auto-select the last dataset used; since we are going to use a new dataset, click Change Data Source at the top right of the window.

7. Select the Target Dataset just created and select a field; for this scenario, select Name.

8. Click the Create button and change the widget title to Target.

9. Add the Number widget next to the List widget added.

10. Change the bar length to Sum of Target and click the Done button.

11. Now, let us connect the dataset; click the arrow button at the upper-right corner and select Connected Data Sources.

12. Click the New Connection button.

13. Enter Connection Name = Sales Name and select a field for both data sources – Data Source 1: User.Name; Data Source 2: Target:Name, see Figure 6-24.

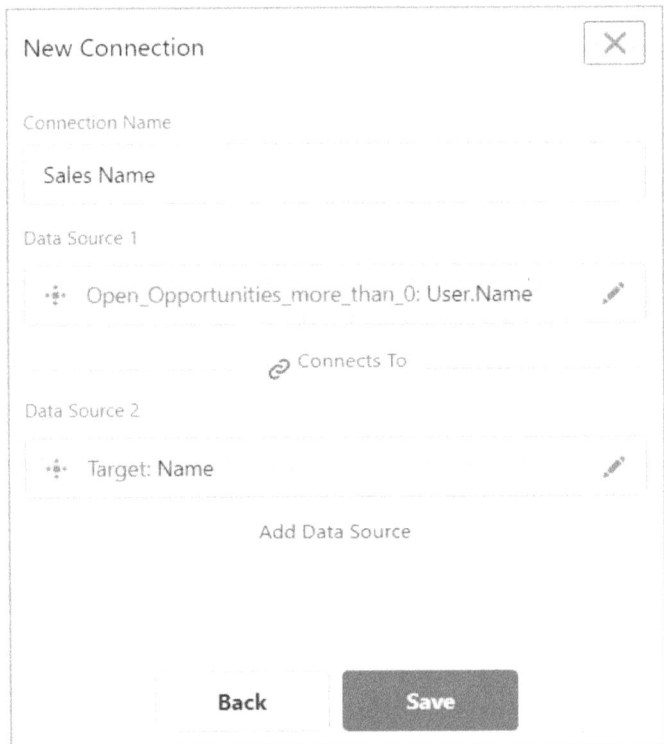

Figure 6-24. Build data source connection

130

14. Click the Save button, then the Close button.

15. Done, and now let us try.

16. Exit from edit mode by hitting the "e" key.

17. When selecting a Name from the Account owner widget, the Target will be updated as in the Target dataset, see Figure 6-25.

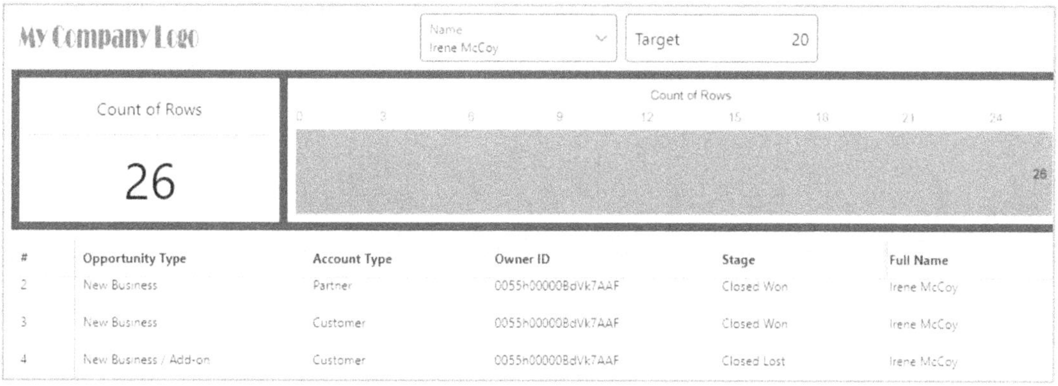

Figure 6-25. Dashboard with connected datasets

Summary

In this chapter, we discussed everything a dashboard builder needs to know to build a dashboard from scratch in CRM Analytics. We started with the permissions needed for the user to build a dashboard. Layouts and templates are something that a dashboard builder should know and make use of when building a good dashboard.

We discussed widgets available in CRM Analytics, including hands-on exercises for most of the widgets. Then, we looked into building a dashboard with multiple pages, and we explained the benefits of using multiple pages in a dashboard.

We discussed how faceting works across widgets, and faceting is one of the most frequently used features in analyzing data in the dashboard. Then, we shared how to use global filters in a dashboard; with global filters, we can use only partial data of the dataset and lock it according to the dashboard's purpose.

We ended with a hands-on exercise to use and connect multiple datasets in a dashboard. In the next chapter, we'll discuss how to explore and make use of a dashboard to analyze data.

CHAPTER 7

Exploring Dashboard

If you have a Salesforce background, CRM Analytics offers a more advanced and interactive dashboard compared to Salesforce's standard dashboard. Faceting in the CRM Analytics dashboard offers your users the ability to analyze and drill down data easily and quickly.

In addition to having chart widgets, adding a table widget to the dashboard to show record-level details is very useful for users exploring data. Data in the chart and table will automatically be filtered when a selection is made on other charts. The user can make selections on multiple charts, and this will filter the whole dashboard further, but only one selection can be made from each chart. When users select a chart segment, by default, it will broadcast as a filter to other widgets. "AND" is the filter logic when multiple charts are selected. We will see the sample later in this chapter.

Before exploring dashboards, as admins, we should look into how to inspect the dashboard for better performance; this will include detailed information for each query in the dashboard and advice on how to improve it.

In this chapter, we will learn the following topics:

- Dashboard inspector
- Set notifications on the widget
- Make annotations on the dashboard
- Share widget
- Embed a dashboard to the Lightning page

Chapter 7 Exploring Dashboard

Dashboard Inspector

Once a dashboard is built, ideally, a dashboard builder should evaluate if the dashboard is designed for optimal performance. The good thing is CRM Analytics comes with a feature called "Dashboard Inspector" to analyze dashboard performance. Let's have a quick hands-on exercise for this:

1. Open **Analytics Studio** and open the Global Accounts dashboard built in the previous chapter.

2. Click the arrow icon at the upper-right corner.

3. Select "Dashboard Inspector"; it depends on the dashboard wizards and queries; this process should only take a few seconds, see Figure 7-1.

4. Dashboard Inspector will show the

    - Total Query Time
    - # Queries
    - Performance Bottlenecks and Query Details

5. Performance Bottlenecks will show all issues and recommendations to increase dashboard performance; for example, a dashboard page has too many queries, queries that fire multiple times, and redundant queries. With this info, we can fix the query to improve dashboard performance. You can edit the dashboard JSON to update the query.

CHAPTER 7   EXPLORING DASHBOARD

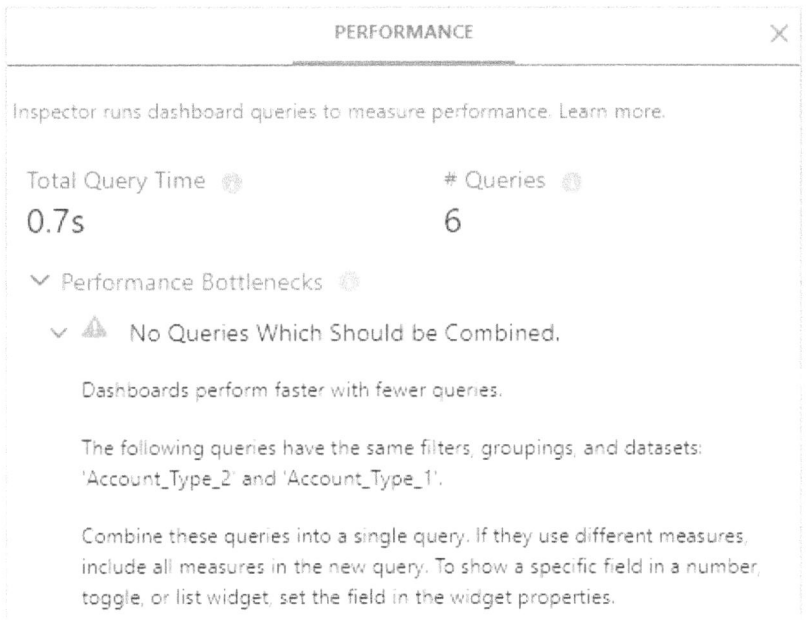

Figure 7-1. Performance Bottlenecks in Dashboard Inspector

6. Query Details will show all queries and the time needed for each query on the current dashboard page. You can sort the table by clicking the Header and clicking each query to get the details:

   - **Datasets**: Dataset used for query and when the last data refresh.
   - **Filters**: All filters impacted that query, including broadcast from other widgets and Global Filter.
   - **Dimensions**: All fields used related to the query.
   - **Measures**: All fields used and the aggregation, such as sum, count, etc.
   - **Last Run Metrics (ms)**: This includes metadata, waiting, and query in milliseconds.

If you add a filter to the dashboard, the preceding value will be updated immediately. The information here is similar to selecting "Show Details" from a widget.

CHAPTER 7 EXPLORING DASHBOARD

Additionally, there are two more icons on the upper right, see Figure 7-2:

- **View Performance Details**: This will tell the dashboard builder if any data manipulation is not optimal.

- **View More Details**: Use this feature if you need to debug the query.
  - Original Query
  - Final Query
  - Result

In this window, we see how a compact form query is translated into SAQL and what the result from the query is.

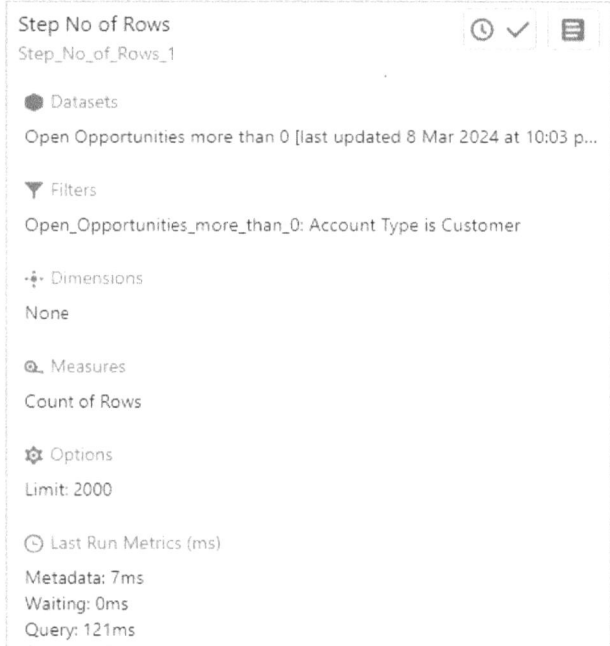

Figure 7-2. *Query Details in Dashboard Inspector*

Set Notifications

This function helps the user be notified when specific criteria in the widgets are met. With notifications, you can get CRM Analytics to work for you, select a widget and define the criteria, set if the notification should notify you only once or continuously, and then set when the schedule for the notification will run.

Each user can set up to ten notifications; because of the limit, you should set notifications only for items essential for you and delete notifications that are no longer needed. You can see the notifications in Analytics Studio, Lightning Experience notification, Analytics mobile app for iOS, and email.

Users can set notifications from the Chart, Table, and Number widgets. Make sure "Show widget actions" is enabled for the widget; otherwise, the arrow handler will not be available. You can only set notifications in view mode, not when you build/edit the dashboard.

When exploring a dashboard, click the "bell" (Show Notifications) icon next to the Share icon to show all notifications that have been set for the dashboard. You can also check all notifications added from all CRM Analytics dashboards from Analytics Studio or the Analytics tab and then click the **Notifications** menu on the left panel, see Figure 7-3.

Let's have a quick hands-on exercise for this feature:

1. Open Analytics Studio and open the Global Accounts dashboard built in the previous chapter.

2. Edit the Global Accounts dashboard, click a number or chart widget under Widget properties at the right panel, and make sure the "Show widget actions" checkbox is enabled.

3. Save the dashboard and exit from edit mode.

4. Hover your mouse over the widget edited in step 2, click the arrow icon, then click "Set Notification."

5. Depending on the operator used for that widget, for example, count, sum, average, etc., it will be used as the criteria, then select the operator and value threshold.

6. Next, you should be notified only once if the threshold value is met or every time when the schedule runs.

CHAPTER 7   EXPLORING DASHBOARD

7. Schedule when the notification should run, from weekday, daily, weekly, and time.

8. Click the Save and Run button.

9. Once added, notice a number in a blue square appears when you have the Notifications panel open.

Figure 7-3. *Set Notification in a number widget*

10. The notification details from status, last modified, and criteria will be shown in that panel.

11. Now go to the Analytics Studio main page and click the Notifications tab; you will see all notifications that you have set up from all dashboards and the status of whether the criteria have been met, see Figure 7-4.

CHAPTER 7 EXPLORING DASHBOARD

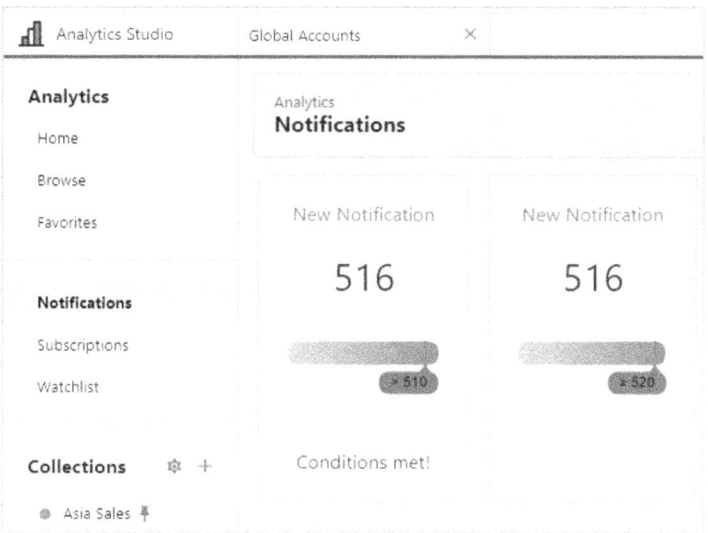

Figure 7-4. Monitor all notifications

12. Once the conditions are met, the user will get the notifications in the Lightning bell notification (see Figure 7-5), as well as email and the Salesforce mobile app.

Note If the query is built on the binding for a dynamic chart, you cannot set a notification for that widget. For Notification on the value table, you can select any Measure column added to the table.

CHAPTER 7　EXPLORING DASHBOARD

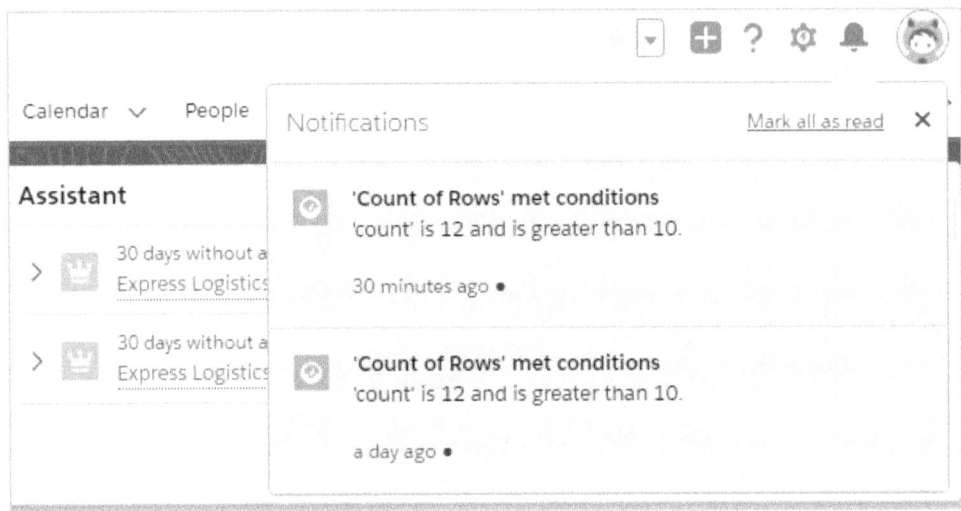

Figure 7-5. Notifications in Lightning

Annotations

With the annotation feature, you can annotate dashboard widgets with comments posted in the dashboard and Chatter. You can hold conversations about the widget, including posting a screenshot of the whole dashboard. Similar to Chatter, you can mention someone's name or a Chatter group name to get their attention on the post, and other users can comment on the Annotation.

Different from notifications, Annotations are available on more widgets, such as Toggle and Text widgets. You must enable "Show widget actions"; otherwise, the arrow menu will not be available when your users hover the mouse over the widget.

Once the post is considered done, you can select Resolve in the annotation post, and the Annotation will be moved under the Resolved tab. Also, you can reopen the annotations when needed. You can add as many annotations as you need in a widget.

Following Annotations

Notice the Annotations icon on the CRM Analytics dashboard, see Figure 7-6. Click this icon to show all Open and Resolved annotations for a dashboard. Clicking the **+ Follow** button will allow you to receive all posts on the dashboard. Similar to Chatter in a record, when you follow a dashboard, you will get a notification if someone annotates the dashboard.

140

CHAPTER 7   EXPLORING DASHBOARD

Figure 7-6. Annotations in a dashboard

Hands-On Annotations

1. Open Analytics Studio and open the Global Accounts dashboard built in the previous chapter.

2. Edit the Global Accounts dashboard, click a number or chart widget, and under Widget properties at the right panel, make sure the "Show widget actions" is enabled.

3. Save the dashboard and exit from the dashboard designer.

4. Hover your mouse over the widget edited in step 2, click the arrow icon, then select "Annotate."

5. Share an update; you can mention someone's name starting with @.

6. Select "Attach current screenshot."

7. Click the Share button.

8. Verify the Annotation is created under the Open tab and also in the mentioned user's Chatter feed, see Figure 7-7.

141

CHAPTER 7   EXPLORING DASHBOARD

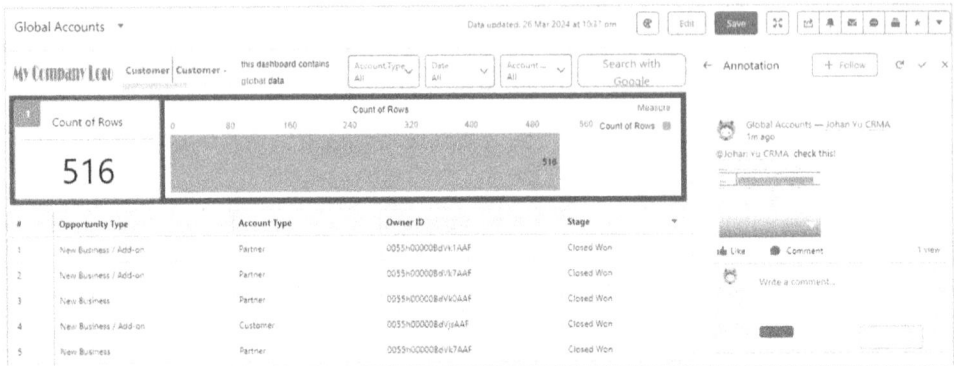

Figure 7-7. Adding an annotation to the widget

9. Click the arrow and select Resolve to move the Annotation from the Open to Resolved tab.

Share Widget

When exploring a dashboard, users can share the Chart, Table, and Number widgets. Hover the mouse over the widget and click the arrow drop-down, see Figure 7-8.

Note The arrow drop-down is only available for the widget when "Show widget actions" is enabled.

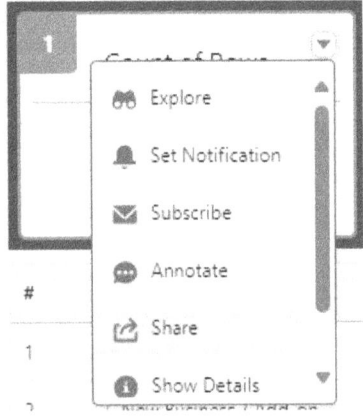

Figure 7-8. Share action from a widget

142

There are three tabs under the Share action: Post to Feed, Export to Quip, and Download, see Figure 7-9.

1. **Post to Feed**

    Post the widget as an image to the Chatter feed:

    - Users can share the widget as a Chatter post to a user feed or a Chatter group.
    - Add comment for the post (this is optional).
    - The widget will be shared as an image.

    Because this is a chatter feed, the image will be visible to all users who have access to it.

2. **Export to Quip**

    If your organization is using Quip, you can publish the widget as a Quip document.

3. **Download**

    From here, users can download the widget as

    - Image (PNG format)
    - Excel format
    - Excel format with metadata: This one will include the dashboard title, timestamp, generated by, filtered by, grouped by, etc.
    - CSV format: This is useful when you need to get the raw data for a table widget.

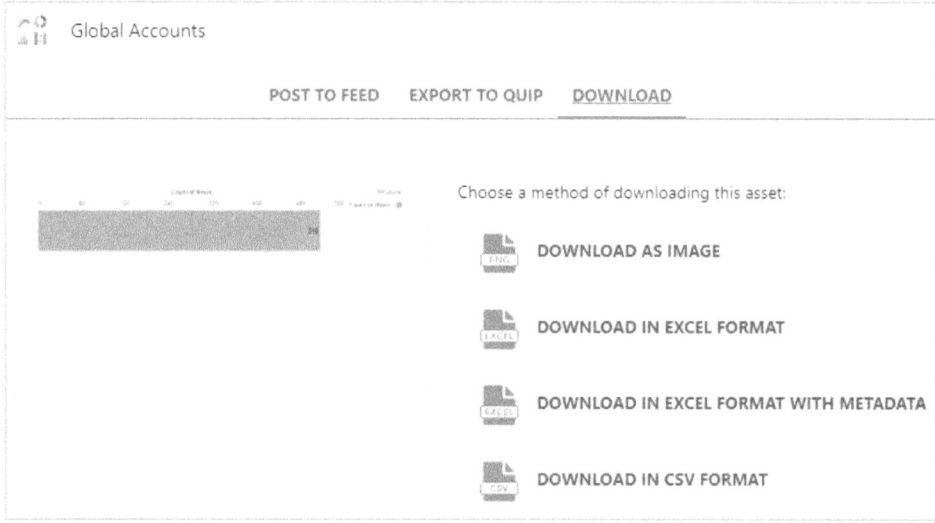

Figure 7-9. Share the widget as a feed, Quip, or download

Show Details

From a widget dropdown menu, the Show Details action will show detailed info of a widget, such as the dataset used, filters applied, dimensions and measures field, and last run metrics (ms). Show Details is similar to Dashboard Inspector, where it shows all the queries available on the page; click a query, and the details will be shown.

While the Show Details action shows the same information as if we click a query from Dashboard Inspector, sometimes we do not know easily which query is related to a widget. So, clicking "Show Details" from a widget will guide us precisely to the query name that powers the widget, including all information related to the widget, see Figure 7-10.

This action is most useful for dashboard explorers to analyze data shown in the widget, including dashboard builder, to make sure the widget shows the correct data, for example, not using the wrong dataset, wrong filters, etc.

CHAPTER 7 EXPLORING DASHBOARD

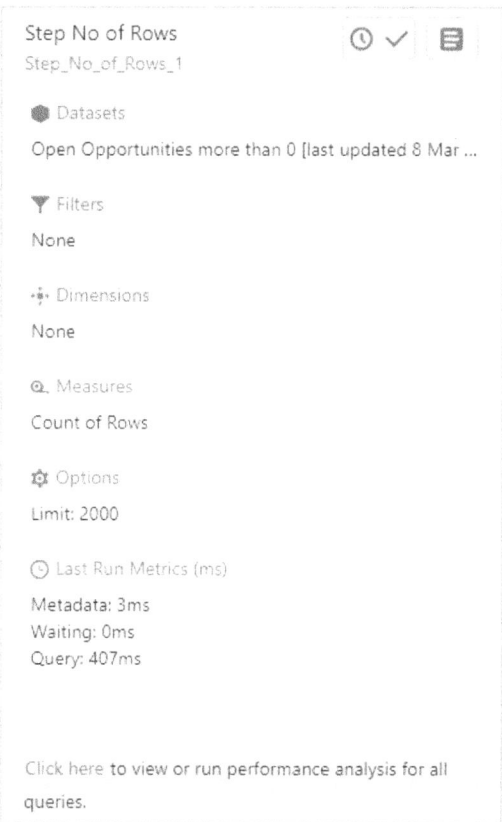

Figure 7-10. *Information from Show Details of a widget*

Explore

Similar to previous actions, the Explore action is only available for the Chart, Table, and Number widgets. In addition to enabling the "Show widget action," the "Show explore action" must also be enabled. But in some scenarios, you may need to turn off the Explore action, so users will not be able to explore and download the data.

When exploring a widget, CRM Analytics will create a new lens, and the user can analyze it from the Lens, including changing chart type, changing table mode, adding filters, and editing with SAQL. If users need to store the modified Lens, they can store it in their private app or public app when the user has editor or manager permission for the app. However, unlike standard Salesforce reporting, the Lens created here will not impact the dashboard or widget in the dashboard.

CHAPTER 7   EXPLORING DASHBOARD

Hands-On Explore Widget

1. Open Analytics Studio and open the Global Accounts dashboard built in the previous chapter.

2. Edit the Global Accounts dashboard, click a number or chart widget, and under Widget properties at the right panel, make sure the "Show widget action" and "Show explore action" are enabled.

3. Save the dashboard and exit from edit mode.

4. Hover your mouse over the widget edited in step 2, click the arrow icon, and then click "Explore.", see Figure 7-11.

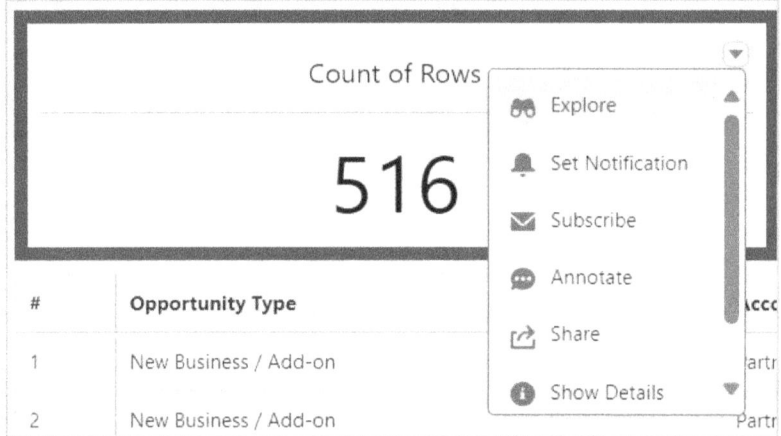

Figure 7-11. *Exploring a widget*

5. The widget will be opened as a new lens. By default, it would be the same chart type or table as the widget, except for the Number widget, which would be a bar chart without grouping. The filters from the widget will be applied to the new Lens.

6. If it is a bar chart, you can change the grouping by changing the fields under Bar, or you can add another level of grouping.

7. Optionally, you can save the Lens to your private app or to a public app to share with your team.

8. You can perform all features offered by Lens, such as Clip to Designer, present, save, share, and clone. We have discussed this in Chapter 5.

CHAPTER 7 EXPLORING DASHBOARD

In case you need to export data in the widget to an Excel or CSV file, you can use the same method as shared in Chapter 5: open the widget as Lens, change the format to the table (if necessary), click Share and then Download, then select to download as Excel or CSV format.

Widget Built with SAQL

For widgets built with SAQL, users will not be able to update the Lens with clicks, so users must use SAQL to update. To check if a widget is powered by a query build using SAQL:

- For the dashboard builder, edit the dashboard, select a widget, and click the pencil icon "Edit Query and Widget" at the bottom; you will find that you cannot edit the values such as Bar Length, Filter, Query Limit, etc. See Figure 7-12.

- For the dashboard user, click the "Show Details" action, then the "View more details" icon at the right, and select the "Original Query" tab. The SAQL-powered query will show SAQL here, while a non-SAQL query will show a JSON format compact form.

CHAPTER 7   EXPLORING DASHBOARD

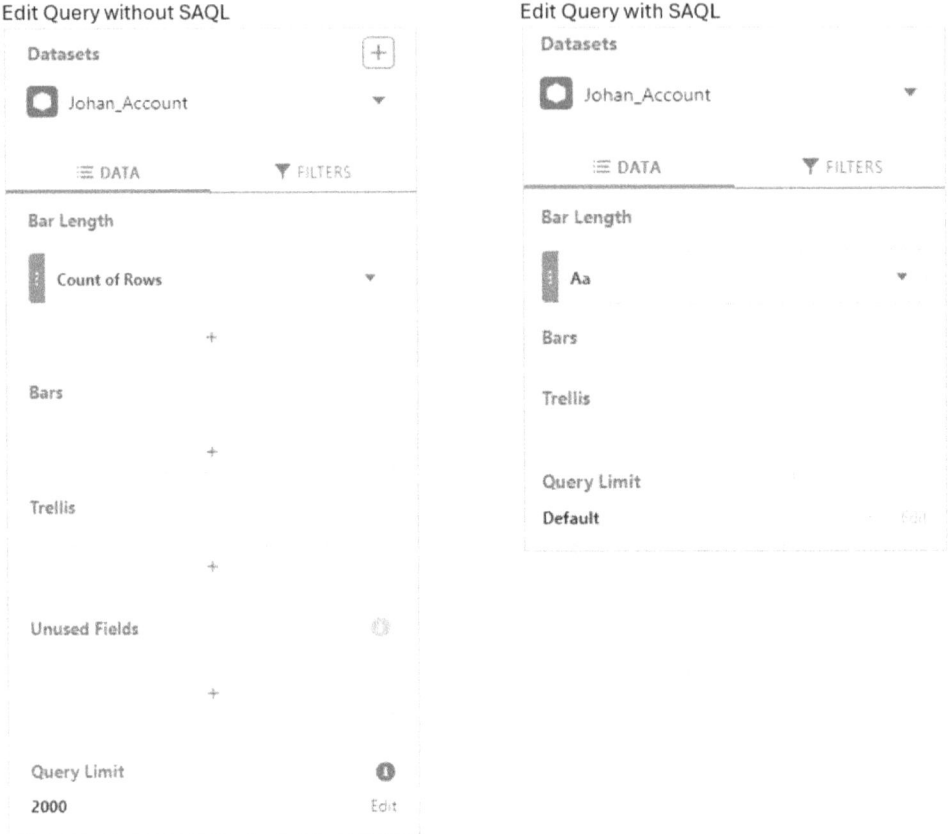

Figure 7-12. *Comparison edit query for SAQL and standard query without SAQL*

Embedding CRM Analytics Dashboard to Salesforce Lightning Page

As discussed in the previous chapter, to explore the CRM Analytics dashboard from Salesforce, users need to open the Analytics tab and find the dashboard to explore. However, for some scenarios, it would be great if a user is able to access the dashboard on the Lightning record page, app page, and Home page.

Similar to accessing the dashboard from the Analytics tab or Analytics Studio, the user needs to have a CRM Analytics license to view the dashboard from the Lightning page.

When you embed a dashboard, the whole dashboard will be shown; you cannot just show a widget. To enable the dashboard sharing from Lightning, the CRM Analytics component must have a minimum height of 612 pixels. For widgets with the Explore action enabled, users will be able to explore the widget from Lightning. Explore will open Analytics Studio and create a new lens. Faceting and filtering will work as normal.

To add a CRM Analytics dashboard to a Lightning page, your Salesforce system admin just needs to drag the "CRM Analytics Dashboard" component to the Lightning page. Once added, there are a few options that can be configured:

- **Dashboard Name**: Select a CRM Analytics dashboard that has been prepared, and make sure the dashboard and dataset are stored in the app that is accessible to the users.

- **Height**: This is the component height in pixels.

- **Filter**: This is optional but most useful when we need to auto-filter the dashboard based on the record ID.

- **Show Sharing Icon**: This can only be enabled when the component height minimum is 612 pixels.

- **Show Tile**: To show/hide the dashboard title.

- **Show Header**: To show/hide the header, which includes the title, dataset last refresh, and Analytics Studio icon.

- **Open Links in New Windows**: If there is a link in the dashboard, clicking this will open the target as a new window.

- **Hide on Error**: To show/hide if an error occurred in the dashboard.

- **Enable Notifications**: If this is enabled, clicking the arrow at the widget will have the Set Notification option.

- **Enable Subscriptions**: If this is enabled, clicking the arrow at the number widget will give you the Subscribe option.

- **Set Component Visibility**: This is a standard Lightning component feature if we want to show the component just for a group of users, such as profile or record values.

CHAPTER 7   EXPLORING DASHBOARD

Hands-On Adding Dashboard to Lightning Home Page

Scenario: Add an interactive dashboard using CRM Analytics to show all open and closed Opportunities for the current quarter and next quarter on the Lightning Home page.

The assumption is that you already have a dataset created from a recipe. Make sure the following fields are added to the recipe: Account ID, Account Name, Account Type, Account Number, Opportunity ID, Opportunity Name, Opportunity Stage, Opportunity Amount, Opportunity Close Date, Opportunity Owner Name, Is Closed, and Is Won.

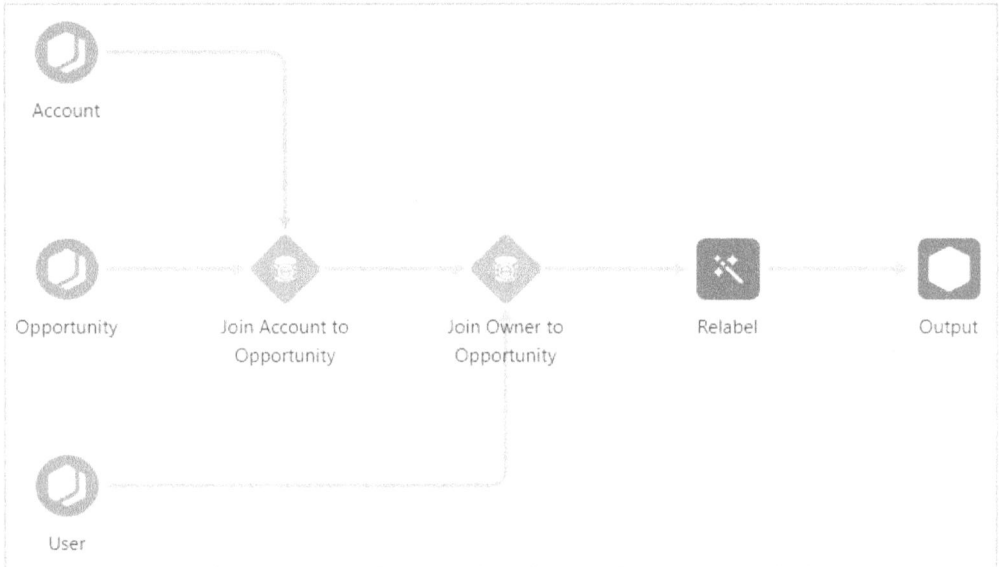

Figure 7-13. *A recipe pulls data from Account, Opportunity, and User objects*

1. Open Analytics Studio.

2. Create a new Recipe, as in Figure 7-13, and a new dashboard to use the dataset that outputs from the recipe.

3. We'll not go through the steps of creating the recipe and dashboard, as we already covered them in previous chapters. Check Figure 7-14 for a sample of the dashboard; you can create your own Opportunity dashboard, but make sure the fields mentioned earlier are included in the recipe. Let's name the dashboard "Current & Next Quarter Opportunities."

CHAPTER 7   EXPLORING DASHBOARD

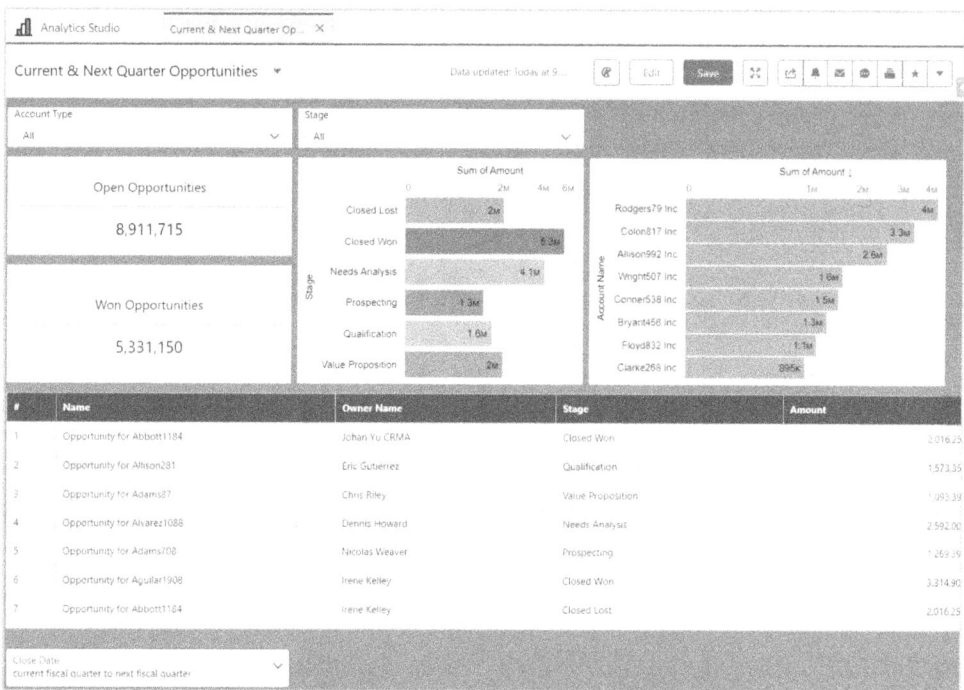

Figure 7-14. *A dashboard shows Current and Next Quarter Opportunities*

4. Let's embed the dashboard into the Lightning Home page. Navigate to the Lightning Home page and click "Edit Page" under the gear icon on the upper-right screen.

5. Drag the "CRM Analytics Dashboard" component in the Lightning App Builder.

6. Select the component and enter the following in the properties:

   - Dashboard: Current & Next Quarter Opportunity

   - Height: 612

   - Leave the rest as default

7. Click the Save button, then the Back button; if this is your first time editing the Home page, you need to click the Activate button, then Assign as Organization default.

CHAPTER 7   EXPLORING DASHBOARD

8. You should be able to filter and facet the dashboard as you open it from the Analytics tab, but note that the Share and Annotate actions are not available here. Figure 7-15 show Lightning Home page with a CRM Analytics dashboard embedded.

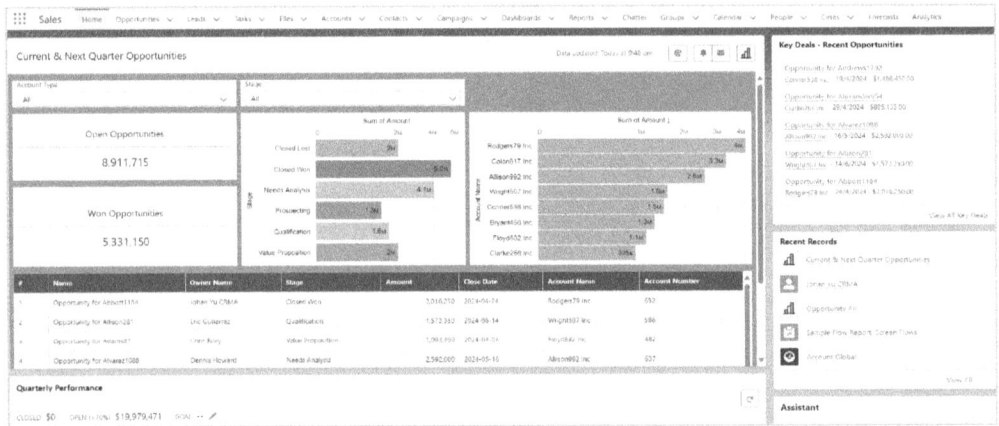

Figure 7-15. CRM Analytics dashboard embedded as a Lightning Home page

Hands-On Adding Dashboard to the Record Page

Scenario: Add an interactive dashboard using CRM Analytics to the account record to show all opportunities related to that Account.

Let us clone the "Current & Next Quarter Opportunities" dashboard as "Opportunities of Account." We can use the same dataset, and nothing needs to change in the recipe.

1. Open Analytics Studio.

2. Clone the "Current & Next Quarter Opportunity" dashboard as "Opportunities of Account."

3. Modify the dashboard accordingly; for this dashboard, let us remove all the filters, as the dashboard should show all opportunities for the Account, see Figure 7-16.

152

CHAPTER 7   EXPLORING DASHBOARD

Figure 7-16. *Modified dashboard without filters*

4. Open an Account record where you want to embed the dashboard, then click "Edit Page" under the gear icon at the upper-right screen.

5. Drag the "CRM Analytics Dashboard" component to the upper right in the Lightning App Builder.

6. Select the component and enter the following in the properties:

    - Dashboard: "Opportunities of Account"

    - Height: 400

    - Untick all checkboxes

7. Make sure "Filter Builder" is selected, then click the "+ Add Dashboard Filter" button.

    - Select the dataset

    - Dataset Source Field: Account ID

    - Operator: Equals

    - Object Field: Account > Id

153

CHAPTER 7 EXPLORING DASHBOARD

8. Click the OK button, click the Save button, then the Back button; if this is your first time editing the Account Lightning page, you need to click the Activate button, then Assign as Organization default. Figure 7-17 show a Lightning Account page with a CRM Analytics dashboard embedded and filtered by the Account opened.

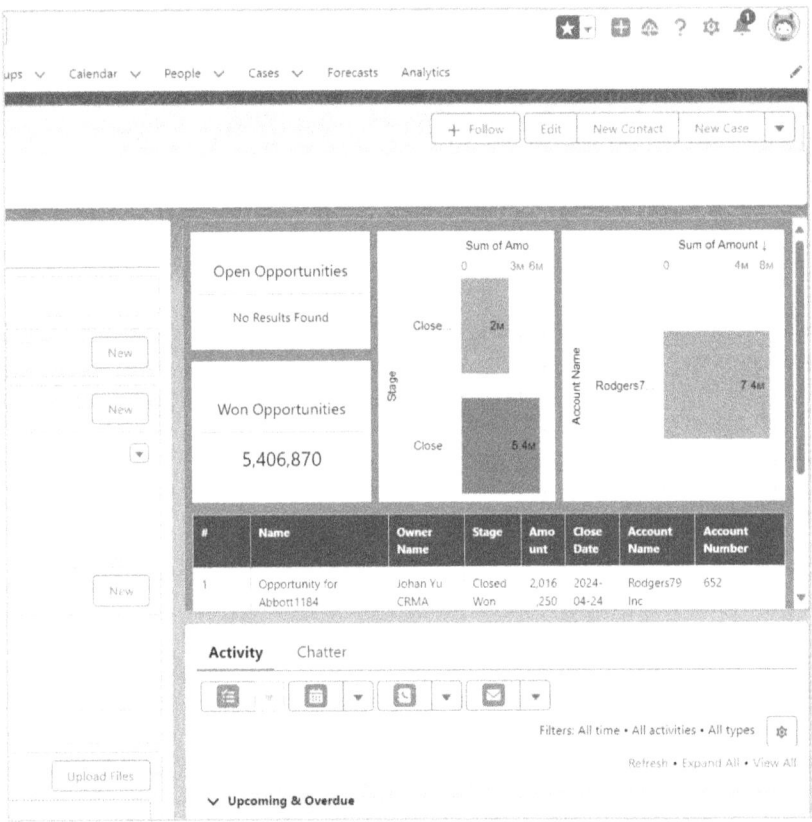

Figure 7-17. Account Lightning page embedded with the CRM Analytics dashboard

In the same way, you can embed the CRM Analytics dashboard into any other Lightning pages without the need to write any script.

You can also embed a CRM Analytics dashboard into the Lightning app page, where the app page can be used in both web browsers and mobile apps.

Summary

In this chapter, we discussed everything about exploring a dashboard. We started with Dashboard Inspector; dashboard explorers can use this tool to understand the widgets, and dashboard builders can use this tool to debug dashboard widgets, analyze queries, and optimize dashboard performance.

Next, we learned how to set notifications on widgets; this notification is personal and will not impact other users; we'll get notifications once all the criteria defined are met. Annotation is the following action; we can use it to collaborate with our team in discussing business metrics shown in a widget. Annotation directly integrates with Chatter; users can set the Annotation as resolved so it will not appear as an Open tab.

We discussed the Share action, which is sharing the widget as a Chatter feed or downloading the widget as an image, Excel file, or CSV file. The Explore action, as it is named, is very useful for users to explore the widget as a lens; all existing filters from the dashboard will be automatically added to the Lens.

Embedding CRM Analytics dashboards to the Salesforce Lightning page is another great feature, so the dashboard can easily be accessed by Salesforce users from Lightning Home, record, and app pages or show data related to a record.

Next, in Chapter 8, we will learn how to set security to the dashboard and the data, so stay tuned!

CHAPTER 8

Applying Security

This chapter will discuss all aspects of security that can be implemented in CRM Analytics. Same as other reporting tools, you always need to secure access from multiple points of view, for example, hide a particular dashboard from all users and only make it visible to a specific group of users, or make the dashboard visible to users but not allow them to edit it. In CRM Analytics, we can use Apps to control dashboard visibility.

For a more advanced technique, you can show the dashboard result based on who the user is, so everyone will not see the same result in a dashboard; this is controlled in the Dataset.

But before looking at Apps and Dataset security, we can also control the basic permissions for the user, which are things that a user can do in CRM Analytics in general. Hence, this is a blanket permission given for that particular user. For example, users are not allowed to download data from CRM Analytics or upload external data to CRM Analytics. This permission is controlled under the Permission Set.

In this chapter, we will learn the following topics:

- Permission Set Assignment
- Apps Level Sharing
- Security Predicate
- Sharing Inheritance

Permission Set Assignment

This setting is configured in Salesforce user detail, not in CRM Analytics. If you know how Salesforce users are assigned extra permission using the Permission Set, this is precisely the same.

Depending on the CRM Analytics licenses purchased, you will get two additional permission sets added to your Salesforce organization:

- CRM Analytics Platform Admin and CRM Analytics Platform User for CRM Analytics Growth license

- CRM Analytics Plus Admin and CRM Analytics Plus User for CRM Analytics Plus license

As these are default permission sets, you cannot edit or delete them, but the Salesforce admin will be able to clone and adjust the cloned system permissions.

We will not discuss each of the system permissions as in Figure 8-1, but if you look at the permission name and description, some of them are pretty obvious, for example, "Create and Edit CRM Analytics Dashboards" permission; without this permission, the user will not be able to create or edit any CRM Analytics dashboards; for "Upload External Data to Analytics," this permission gives the user the ability to upload a CSV file as a dataset in CRM Analytics.

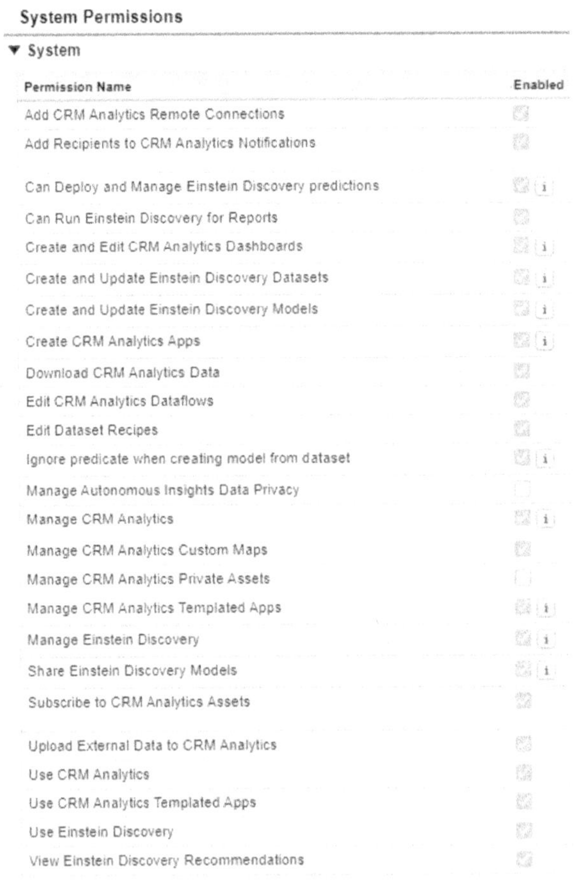

System Permissions	
▼ System	
Permission Name	Enabled
Add CRM Analytics Remote Connections	☑
Add Recipients to CRM Analytics Notifications	☑
Can Deploy and Manage Einstein Discovery predictions	☑ i
Can Run Einstein Discovery for Reports	☑
Create and Edit CRM Analytics Dashboards	☑ i
Create and Update Einstein Discovery Datasets	☑ i
Create and Update Einstein Discovery Models	☑ i
Create CRM Analytics Apps	☑ i
Download CRM Analytics Data	☑
Edit CRM Analytics Dataflows	☑
Edit Dataset Recipes	☑
Ignore predicate when creating model from dataset	☑ i
Manage Autonomous Insights Data Privacy	☐
Manage CRM Analytics	☑ i
Manage CRM Analytics Custom Maps	☑
Manage CRM Analytics Private Assets	☐
Manage CRM Analytics Templated Apps	☑ i
Manage Einstein Discovery	☑ i
Share Einstein Discovery Models	☑ i
Subscribe to CRM Analytics Assets	☑
Upload External Data to CRM Analytics	☑
Use CRM Analytics	☑
Use CRM Analytics Templated Apps	☑
Use Einstein Discovery	☑
View Einstein Discovery Recommendations	☑

Figure 8-1. System Permissions for CRM Analytics

As per the Salesforce permission set model, the Salesforce admin can clone the standard permission set to many permission sets, and each permission set can have different permissions enabled; a user can be assigned with many permission sets.

Apps Level Sharing

We discussed Apps in Chapter 5; when we start creating Lens, we can share an App by

- User Name
- Public Group
- Role

With access as a Manager, Editor, and Viewer

- Users with **Manager** access have the highest level of access; in addition to Editor access, these users will be able to share and delete the App.

- Users with **Editor** access will be able to edit and save dashboards and Lens in the App.

- The **Viewer** users are only able to view the dashboard, Lens, and Dataset stored in the App, but even if the user only has viewer access in an App, the user will be able to save the Lens or dashboard into their Private Apps.

Users with **Manage CRM Analytics** permissions will be able to access all dashboards and Lens stored in public Apps, including access to the Data Manager. Users with a CRM Analytics license and **Modify All Data** or **View All Data** permission in Salesforce will be able to see all Apps. Manage CRM Analytics should only be given to CRM Analytics admin users.

CHAPTER 8   APPLYING SECURITY

Security Predicate

A security predicate is a filter condition that defines row-level access for users to a dataset, and it is defined in the Dataset. Every time users access a dataset (including those from the Dashboard or Lens), the system checks the running user details to compare them with the security predicate defined in the Dataset. You can use any fields in the Salesforce user object, such as Profile Name, Role ID, User ID, and Department, or you can also create custom fields.

The security predicate is not configured in Salesforce, so it will also work for datasets that do not originate from Salesforce. The security predicate will check running user detail with the Dataset; in some cases, we may need to add additional columns in the Dataset, for example, as an exception to let a profile have visibility to all data in the Dataset, no matter what the Profile is – in this case, the Profile is defined in the security predicate.

Syntax

The following syntax is fixed; you cannot put the dataset column after the operator; it will not work.

`<dataset column> <operator> <value>`

Example valid security predicate: 'ProfileId' == "$User.ProfileId"

- 'ProfileId' is the API field name in the Dataset.
- == is the operator.
- "$User.ProfileId" is the running user profile ID in Salesforce.

Please note the difference in " and ' syntax used.

You can use || as OR and && as AND and use () to set the order of operators if needed in the security predicate. In the following sample, we are going to give the visibility of all rows to all users with a Marketing profile, while other users are only allowed to see data in their region:

`'Region' == "$User.Region__c" || 'View_All' == "$User.ProfileId"`

160

In the preceding security predicate

- Region and View_All are the field API Names in the Dataset.
- We use a custom field called Region__c in the User object in Salesforce.
- View_All should contain the Profile ID of "Marketing" for each row in the Dataset.

> **Note** The security predicate does not support using IN or comma, for example, if you have multiple profiles that need to see all rows, you need to have multiple fields for each Profile, for example, 'Region' == "$User.Region__c" || 'View_All_1' == "$User.ProfileId" || 'View_All_2' == "$User.ProfileId" .

Hands-On Security Predicate

In this hands-on, you will see the use of a security predicate to limit record visibility. We will use the Department field in the Salesforce user detail to set record visibility:

1. Open Analytics Studio.
2. Create the Dataset from CSV files; you must change the View_All value in Table 8-1 to a valid Profile Id in your Salesforce organization. If you are unsure about the Profile Id, check with your Salesforce administrator; the ID should have prefix 00e.

Table 8-1. *Load This Table As a New Dataset and Name It "Top Account"*

Department	Account Name	View_All
Sales	Data Inc	00eB0000000KmquIAC
Sales	Manager Inc	00eB0000000KmquIAC
Support	Workflow Inc	00eB0000000KmquIAC
Sales	Process Inc	00eB0000000KmquIAC
Support	System Inc	00eB0000000KmquIAC
Support	Business Inc	00eB0000000KmquIAC

Note: You must use 18 characters instead of 15 characters for the ID.

CHAPTER 8   APPLYING SECURITY

3. Find the Dataset created, click the Dataset to open it, and verify that the data loaded is correct; you should see six records.

4. Back to the Analytics Studio, find the same Dataset, click the arrow at the far right, and select Edit.

5. Click the pencil icon under the Security Predicate, and enter 'Department' == "$User.Department" || 'View_All' == "$User.ProfileId"; click out from the box to exit and then click the "Got It" button from the pop-up window.

6. When you click the mouse out of the Security Predicate box, the system will auto-check and reject if the security predicate syntax is invalid, such as "$User.Department" == 'Department' (wrong order), and if the field does not exist, such as 'Department == "$User.UserDepartment" (the UserDepartment field does not exist in the User object). However, the system will not validate and not reject if the column name in the Dataset does not exist, such as 'UserDepartment' == "$User.Department" (the UserDepartment field does not exist in the Dataset).

7. If the syntax check is passed, the security predicate will be saved automatically.

8. Change your Department in your Salesforce user detail to Sales, see the result in Figure 8-2.

9. Back to Analytics Studio and open the Top Account dataset again; now, you should only see three records.

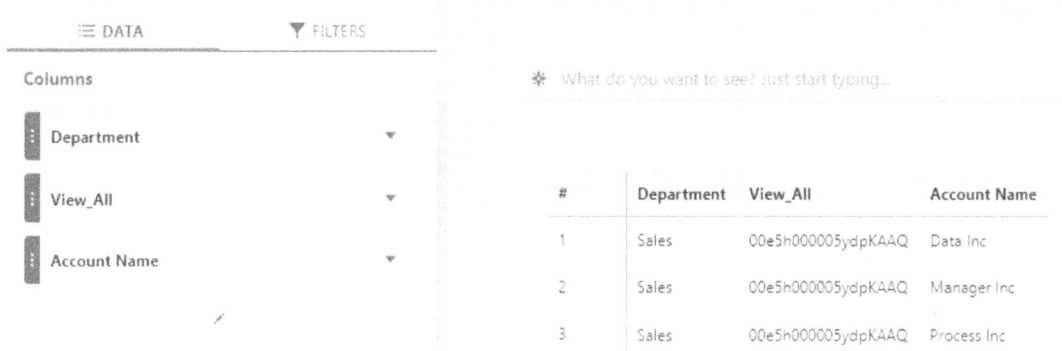

Figure 8-2. *Security Predicate filter row Department = Sales*

10. Edit the Dataset and move it to the Shared App.

11. Now, log in as a user with the Profile as in step 2, and open the Dataset again; it should show six records because we made the Profile ID the exception, see Figure 8-3.

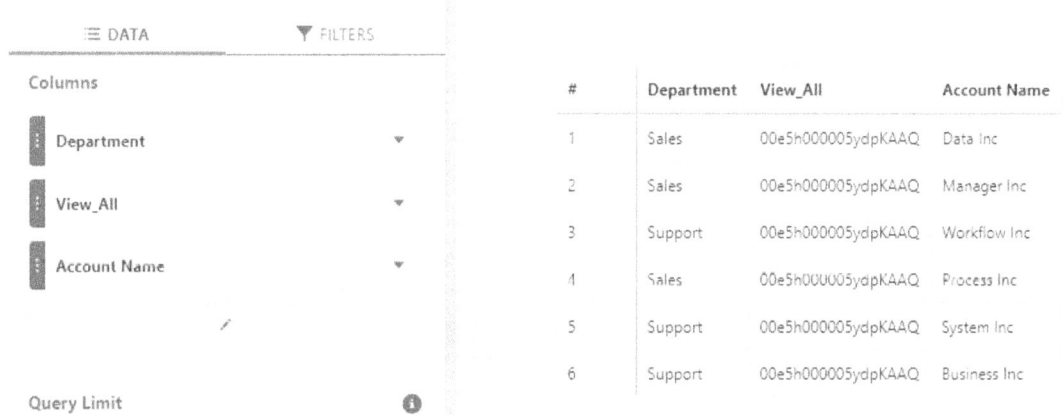

Figure 8-3. *Security Predicate filter with exception*

Role Hierarchy Access

As you see from the preceding hands-on, the security predicate supports the filter on a specific ID or word; furthermore, if we combine with the "flatten" transformation to flat all Role Id in the Recipe, we can use the security predicate to let users in the higher role hierarchy access data visible by users in the lower role hierarchy.

163

CHAPTER 8 APPLYING SECURITY

Check out Figure 8-4 for a sample of the Recipe with flattening nodes.

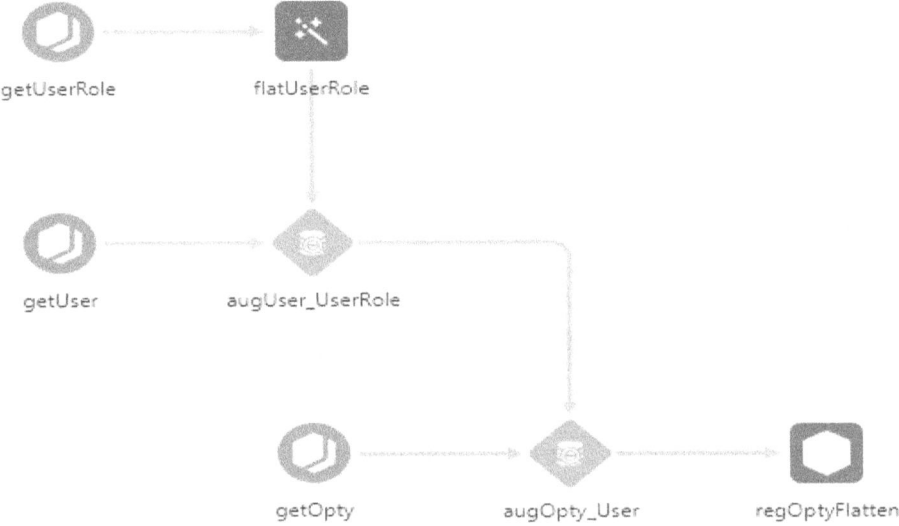

Figure 8-4. *Recipe with the flatten transform*

Check out Figure 8-5 to set parameters in the flatten transform.

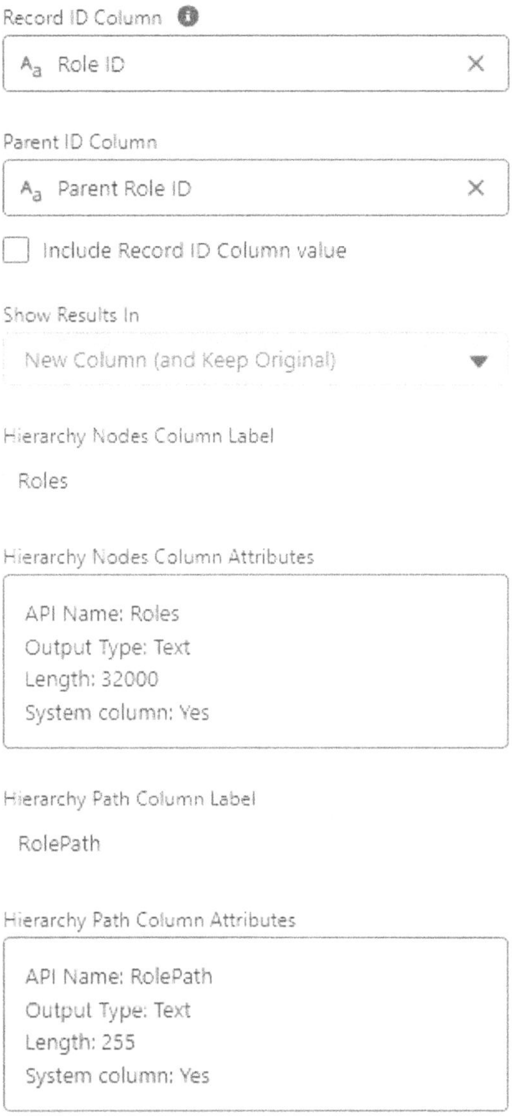

CHAPTER 8   APPLYING SECURITY

Record ID Column
[Aa Role ID   ×]

Parent ID Column
[Aa Parent Role ID   ×]

☐ Include Record ID Column value

Show Results In
[New Column (and Keep Original)   ▼]

Hierarchy Nodes Column Label
Roles

Hierarchy Nodes Column Attributes
```
API Name: Roles
Output Type: Text
Length: 32000
System column: Yes
```

Hierarchy Path Column Label
RolePath

Hierarchy Path Column Attributes
```
API Name: RolePath
Output Type: Text
Length: 255
System column: Yes
```

Figure 8-5. Flatten node properties

You will see fields added from Flatten nodes in the Recipe but not in the Dataset. See Figure 8-6 and notice the fields in the Dataset.

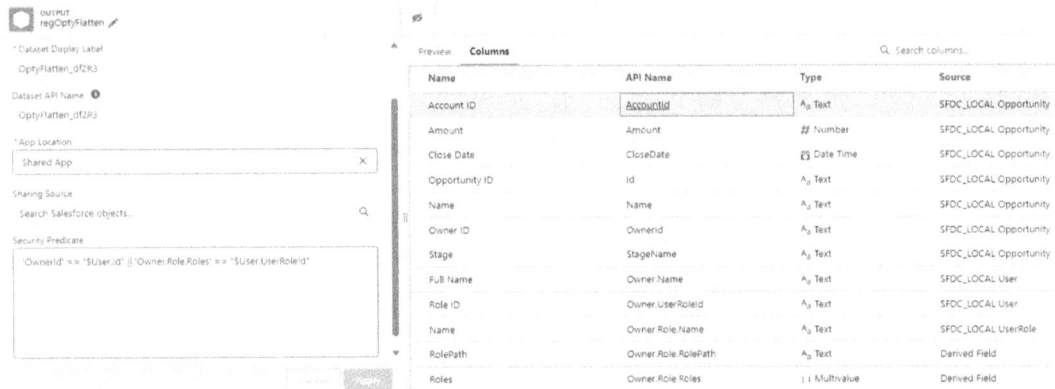

Figure 8-6. Output to the Dataset with fields from the flatten transform

Here is the security predicate for the role hierarchy access:

```
'OwnerId' == "$User.Id" || 'Owner.Role.Roles' == "$User.UserRoleId"
```

> **Note** This is only to give access to specific Datasets based on the Salesforce role hierarchy, no matter how the security setting for the objects in Salesforce, and it also does not relate if you have any additional sharing rules in Salesforce.

Sharing Inheritance

As you see in the security predicate, we defined row-level security based on criteria we defined in CRM Analytics, and this has no relationship with Salesforce record security. Sharing Inheritance will give us the ability to use the same row-level security defined in Salesforce; this includes object sharing, role hierarchy, manual sharing, team sharing, and sharing rules added for the object.

Sharing Inheritance sounds perfect for Salesforce customers to set data visibility as defined in Salesforce; however, Sharing Inheritance has limitations; it only works for five standard objects:

- Account
- Case

CHAPTER 8 APPLYING SECURITY

- Contact
- Lead
- Opportunity

Additionally, if the record access is granted by more than 3000 sharing descriptors, Sharing Inheritance will not work, and the backup security predicate will take effect. But users with the "View All Data" permission will be covered by Sharing Inheritance. You can use "Sharing Inheritance Coverage Assessment" from the Salesforce setup menu to evaluate the user's eligibility to use Sharing Inheritance.

Sharing Inheritance is defined in the Recipe on the output node when creating a Dataset.

Enable Sharing Inheritance

From the Salesforce setup menu, in the Quick Find box, type **Analytics**, and then click **Settings**; look for **Inherit sharing from Salesforce** and enable it.

Configure Recipe

Let us create a very straightforward Recipe with two nodes, see Figure 8-7:

1. **Input**: This is to get data from an object.
2. **Output**: This is to store the data in a dataset.

Figure 8-7. *A simple recipe to get data from Salesforce and store it in a Dataset*

To enable security inheritance, we need to define the object that will be used as the sharing source in the Output node. For this sample, because we only have one input node, which is from Opportunity, the option is only to use Opportunity as the Sharing Source in the output node, see Figure 8-8.

167

CHAPTER 8   APPLYING SECURITY

Figure 8-8. Configuring Output node with Sharing Source

Sharing Inheritance Coverage Assessment

To access if you can use Sharing Inheritance for a Salesforce object

1. Navigate to the Salesforce setup menu.

2. Look for "Sharing Inheritance Coverage Assessment."

3. Select the object.

4. Click the **View Assessment** button.

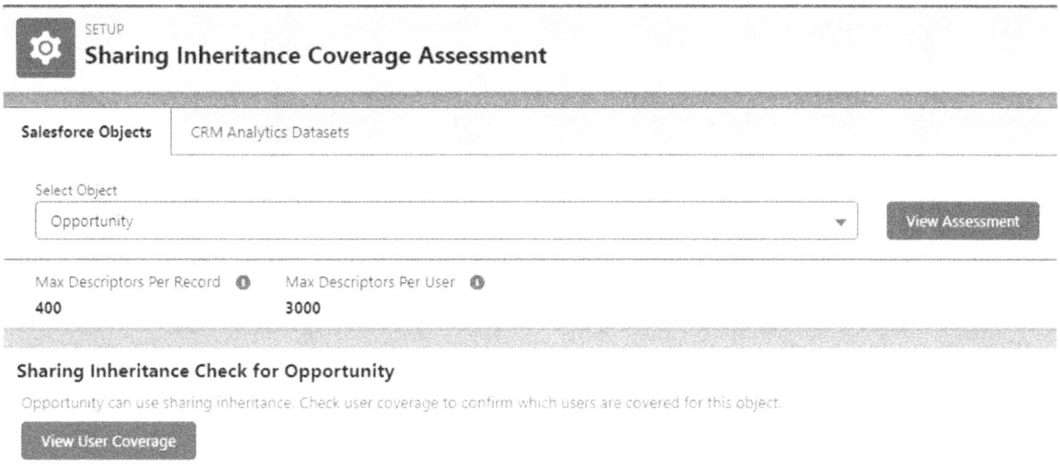

CHAPTER 8 APPLYING SECURITY

Figure 8-9. Sharing Inheritance Coverage Assessment

igure 8-9 shows the Opportunity object (as my example) can use the Sharing Inheritance. However, it does not mean that it can cover all CRM Analytics users.

To evaluate user coverage, click the **View User Coverage** button; depending on the number of CRM Analytics users that you have, the process can take some time, see sample result in Figure 8-10.

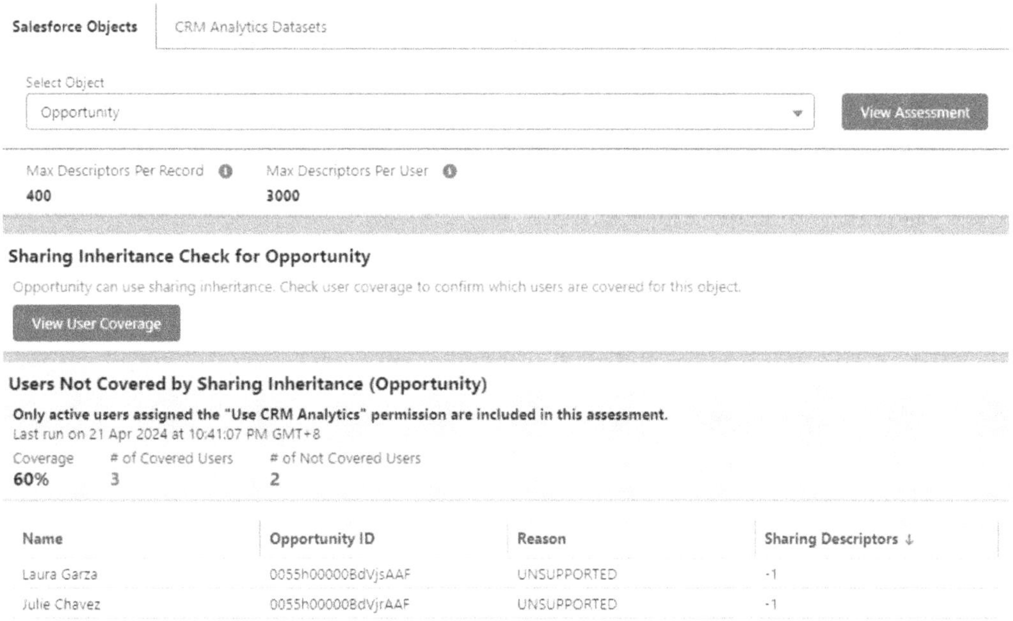

Figure 8-10. Sharing Inheritance user coverage result

169

CHAPTER 8   APPLYING SECURITY

Summary

In this chapter, we discussed every aspect of security that can be implemented in CRM Analytics. We started with basic permissions for what a user can do in CRM Analytics, which are defined in the Permission Set and can be assigned to each user.

Next, we discussed App security. We can share Apps with users based on User Name, Role (including subordinates or not), and Public Group. As you can see, all these sharings are related to the Salesforce setup. Then, similar to the Salesforce report or dashboard folder, the App manager can define the level of access for each user, Role, or Group as a Manager, Editor, and Viewer.

With the Security Predicate, we can define row-level security; the system will compare user details with data in the Dataset. You can set exceptions for particular users based on Role, Profile, or custom fields. We can also use the flatten transformation node in the Dataflow to give row-level access based on the Salesforce role hierarchy.

The last security aspect that can be implemented in CRM Analytics is Sharing Inheritance; this is pretty nice when you can inherit all security measures as defined in Salesforce; however, a user is limited to particular standard objects only and also max descriptors per record and per user; otherwise, it will not be used. We can use the Sharing Inheritance Coverage Assessment to evaluate if we can apply Sharing Inheritance to the object and user coverage.

In the next chapter, which is the last chapter of this book, we will discuss advanced topics related to CRM Analytics. We will learn advanced transformation nodes in the Recipe and real-time data access from Salesforce, SAQL, JSON, Custom Query, and Binding.

CHAPTER 9

Advanced Topics

Congratulations, you've reached the last chapter of this book. By now, you know what a Dataset is, how to import data into CRM Analytics, enable data sync with Salesforce, work with dataset, explore dataset with lens, how to build a dashboard from scratch, create a simple recipe, explore the dashboard with features offered, and also learned on security implementation.

In this chapter, we will learn a few techniques that we may face when creating a dashboard in CRM Analytics:

- Edit Attributes, Drop Columns, Custom Formula, and Filter
- Augment node with multiple value lookup
- Real-time data pull from Salesforce with SOQL (Salesforce Object Query Language)
- JSON
- SAQL (Salesforce Analytics Query Language)
- Binding

Recipe Nodes

In Chapters 3 and 7, we have hands-on building simple recipes with nodes:

- Input
- Output
- Transformation
- Join

CHAPTER 9   ADVANCED TOPICS

We have also discussed each node in Chapter 3, section "Data Transformation in Recipe," so we will not repeat them here. But let us see a few features and scenarios that can be performed in the Transform node.

Edit Attributes

Scenario: Create a recipe with join nodes for Opportunity, Account, and User, which gets an Opportunity owner and Account owner (Figure 9-1).

Figure 9-1. *Recipe with input nodes of Opportunity, Account, and User*

If you look at the dataset label result, there are duplicate field names, such as Owner ID, Account ID, User ID, and Full Name (Figure 9-2).

CHAPTER 9 ADVANCED TOPICS

Name	API Name	Type	Source
Owner ID	OwnerId	A₀ Text	SFDC_LOCAL Opportunity
Opportunity ID	Id	A₀ Text	SFDC_LOCAL Opportunity
Account ID	AccountId	A₀ Text	SFDC_LOCAL Opportunity
Name	Name	A₀ Text	SFDC_LOCAL Opportunity
User ID	Owner.Id	A₀ Text	SFDC_LOCAL User
Full Name	Owner.Name	A₀ Text	SFDC_LOCAL User
Owner ID	Account.OwnerId	A₀ Text	SFDC_LOCAL Account
Account ID	Account.Id	A₀ Text	SFDC_LOCAL Account
Account Name	Account.Name	A₀ Text	SFDC_LOCAL Account
Account Type	Account.Type	A₀ Text	SFDC_LOCAL Account
User ID	Account.Owner.Id	A₀ Text	SFDC_LOCAL User
Full Name	Account.Owner.Name	A₀ Text	SFDC_LOCAL User

Figure 9-2. Recipe with duplicate names

As a dashboard builder or data analyst, it is never good to have duplicate field labels. For this scenario, we can add a Transform node using Edit Attributes to change the field name; let us do a quick hands-on exercise:

- From the last node before Output, add the Transform node.

- Click the new node added, then from the Preview or Columns tab, click the field that we want to relabel, then click the "Edit Attributes" icon.

- Change the label, for example, from Owner ID to Opportunity Owner ID, and click the Apply button.

- Perform the same for other fields so it is clear without duplicate labels. See Figure 9-3 after the field name updated with Edit Attributes.

CHAPTER 9   ADVANCED TOPICS

Name	API Name	Type	Source
Opportuntiy Owner ID	Ownerid	A_a Text	SFDC_LOCAL Opportunity
Opportunity ID	Id	A_a Text	SFDC_LOCAL Opportunity
Opportunity Account ID	AccountId	A_a Text	SFDC_LOCAL Opportunity
Opportunity Name	Name	A_a Text	SFDC_LOCAL Opportunity
Opportunity Owner ID	Owner.Id	A_a Text	SFDC_LOCAL User
Opportunity Owner Name	Owner.Name	A_a Text	SFDC_LOCAL User
Account Owner ID	Account.OwnerId	A_a Text	SFDC_LOCAL Account
Account ID	Account.Id	A_a Text	SFDC_LOCAL Account
Account Name	Account.Name	A_a Text	SFDC_LOCAL Account
Account Type	Account.Type	A_a Text	SFDC_LOCAL Account
Account Owner ID	Account.Owner.Id	A_a Text	SFDC_LOCAL User
Account Owner Name	Account.Owner.Name	A_a Text	SFDC_LOCAL User

Figure 9-3. *Clean duplicate with Edit Attributes*

Update the recipe by adding a Transform node to edit the attributes, see Figure 9-4.

Figure 9-4. *Recipe with a Transform node*

Drop Columns

Let us continue with the preceding recipe if you notice that we still have duplicate labels: the Account Owner ID and Opportunity Owner ID. The API Names are different, which explains how the data is transformed. However, do we need both similar fields? It is always a best practice to remove unnecessary items to keep the dataset clean.

For some scenarios, you may want to keep the field, but for this exercise, let us remove the Account.Owner.Id and Owner.Id fields.

Using the same recipe, let us add Drop Columns transformation in the same Transform node; we can rename the node to "Transform" since the node is not only Edit Attributes.

- Click the Transform node.

- Switch to the Columns tab and look for Owner.Id, then click the "Drop Columns" icon, which is next to the Edit Attributes icon. Leave Drop selected and click the Apply button.

- Repeat the same for Account.Owner.Id.

Here is the updated result of our dataset, see Figure 9-5; nothing has changed in the recipe layout.

Name	API Name	Type	Source
Opportuntiy Owner ID	OwnerId	Text	SFDC_LOCAL Opportunity
Opportunity ID	Id	Text	SFDC_LOCAL Opportunity
Opportunity Account ID	AccountId	Text	SFDC_LOCAL Opportunity
Opportunity Name	Name	Text	SFDC_LOCAL Opportunity
Opportunity Owner Name	Owner.Name	Text	SFDC_LOCAL User
Account ID	Account.Id	Text	SFDC_LOCAL Account
Account Name	Account.Name	Text	SFDC_LOCAL Account
Account Type	Account.Type	Text	SFDC_LOCAL Account
Account Owner ID	Account.Owner.Id	Text	SFDC_LOCAL User
Account Owner Name	Account.Owner.Name	Text	SFDC_LOCAL User

Figure 9-5. *Remove unnecessary fields with Drop Columns*

Custom Formula

I want to say this is the most essential item in a recipe. With the Custom Formula in a recipe, you can create new calculated fields in the dataset based on some logic, including from existing fields, without the need to change the data source. It would be a good practice to standardize new fields created using a Custom Formula, as we may have many fields created using this method.

Scenario 1: For Accounts with Billing Country = USA or Canada and Type <> Customer, show them as "Yes," and the rest as "No."

Let's do a quick hands-on exercise:

- From the Account input node, click the "Change columns" button and add the Billing Country field.

- Click the Transform node and look for the formula (*fx*) icon; select Custom Formula from the drop-down.

CHAPTER 9 ADVANCED TOPICS

- Enter the following formula, see Figure 9-6:

  case when "Account.BillingCountry" in ('USA','Canada') and "Account.Type" != 'Customer' then 'Yes' else 'No' end

- At the left panel, scroll down and change the Column Label and API Name to "Target."

- In Output Type, select Text, and click the Apply button.

Figure 9-6. *Formula editor*

Scenario 2: Look for the latest opportunity created for each Account and mark it with Latest Opportunity = Yes. In this scenario, the formula will scan data across many records with the same partition value defined.

Use the same recipe:

- From the Opportunity input node, click the "Change columns" button and add the Created Date field.

- Click the Transform node and look for the formula (*fx*) icon; select Custom Formula from the drop-down.

CHAPTER 9 ADVANCED TOPICS

- Enable the "Multiple row formula" switch at the upper right of the transformation panel.

- Enter the following formula:

  ```
  case when row_number() = 1 then 'Y' else 'N' end
  ```

- In Partition By, select "Account ID."
- In Order By, select "Created Date."
- In Sort Direction, select "Descending."
- In Output Type, select Text.
- Column Label = "Latest Opportunity" and API Name = "Latest_Opportunity.", see Figure 9-7.
- Click the Apply button.

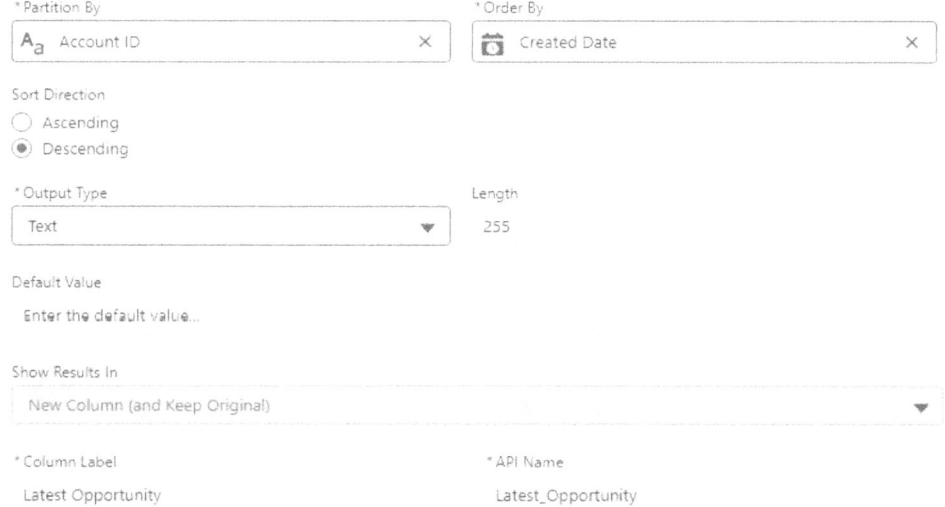

Figure 9-7. Options for the multiple row formula

Filter Node

In Chapter 3, we discussed the Filter node, where we can use a simple filter, add filter logic, and use Custom Expression.

177

CHAPTER 9   ADVANCED TOPICS

Let us have a quick hands-on exercise using Custom Expression to filter:

- Hover over the Transform node, click the small icon at the right, and select filter from the drop-down menu.

- Click the arrow at the upper right of the Filter panel and select "Add Custom Expression."

- Now, you should see an editor where you can type in criteria for data to be selected; data that does not match the criteria here will be filtered out.

- We can use "fields" created in the Transform node in the section "Custom Formula"; let us enter `Latest_Opportunity = 'Y'`.

- Click the Apply button.

Now, we need to break the link between the Transform and Output nodes; click the arrow between these two nodes, and select Delete (the last option), see Figure 9-8.

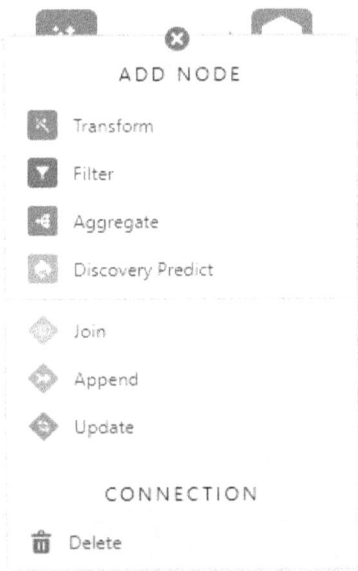

Figure 9-8. Deleting links between nodes

To link the Filter node to the Output node, simply drag from the plus icon next to the Filter node to the Output node and select Connect Nodes, see Figure 9-9. You must delete the link earlier before you are able to link the node.

CHAPTER 9 ADVANCED TOPICS

Figure 9-9. Connecting nodes

Append Node

Use Append to combine data from two nodes; you can map the fields between the first and second nodes; if the fields are different, the fields in the second node will be removed.

Another option is to enable "Allow disjoint schema." Prior to enabling "Allow disjoint schema," the "Map all column" option must be enabled; otherwise, you will not see the option for "Allow disjoint schema." CRM Analytics will auto-match the fields with the same name and add new fields if no matching field is found. The fields with no matching will have null values for unmatched nodes; see the example in Figure 9-10.

Data-1

No	Name	Sales
1	Mike	500
2	Lee	800
3	Steve	900

Data-2

No	Name	Amount
11	John	800
12	Henry	700
13	Jenny	850

Data-Append

No	Name	Sales	Amount
1	Mike	500	-
2	Lee	800	-
3	Steve	900	-
11	John	-	800
12	Henry	-	700
13	Jenny	-	850

Figure 9-10. Append result with "Allow disjoint schema" enabled

179

CHAPTER 9   ADVANCED TOPICS

Join with Multiple Value Lookup

So far, in all our samples, we are joining nodes without enabling "Look Up Multiple Values," which means if there are many matches in the child records, the system will randomly select a matched child record. But if we enable "Look Up Multiple Values" in the join node, the system will pull all matched child records into a field with multiple values.

Let's create a new recipe to see how this works.

Figure 9-11. Join with Look Up Multiple Values

From Figure 9-11, the Account is the granular record, and Opportunity is the child. An Account may have zero, one, or multiple opportunities. Because we enable "Look Up Multiple Values," CRM Analytics will pull all opportunities and store them into a field so that the Opportunity ID may have multiple values; see the last row in the figure.

Note   Even if the multivalues look separated with a comma in the Recipe preview, they are actually stored as multivalue, which means each value is independent; you can filter/select by each value.

CHAPTER 9 ADVANCED TOPICS

Salesforce Direct Data Queries

So far, we have discussed building CRM Analytics dashboards using datasets stored in the CRM Analytics platform. All the data shown in the dashboard or lens is not real time; it will only be updated when the recipe runs by schedule for minutes, hourly, daily, or weekly.

However, in some scenarios, we need the dashboard to show real-time data from Salesforce, and it's great that CRM Analytics supports this; since the data is pulled directly from Salesforce, there is no data transformation as we can do using a recipe.

Hands-On

In this scenario, we need to show open opportunities from Salesforce, group by Stage:

1. Open Analytics Studio.
2. Create a new Dashboard; select Blank Dashboard.
3. Drag a Chart widget to Dashboard Designer and click the Chart icon at the center.
4. Click the Salesforce Object tab, then find Opportunity and select it.
5. In the query, click + under Bars, select Stage, and add filter Closed = false.
6. Click the Done button.
7. Drag the Table widget and perform the step as the chart widget.
8. Change to Table mode and select Values Table to show the data.
9. Select the following fields: Opportunity ID, Name, Account ID, Amount, and Close Date, then add filter Closed = false.
10. As you can see, we cannot show the Account Name because the Opportunity object only has the Account ID, so this is one of the limitations because we can't join the data as in the recipe.
11. Now you should see the dashboard as shown in Figure 9-12.

181

CHAPTER 9   ADVANCED TOPICS

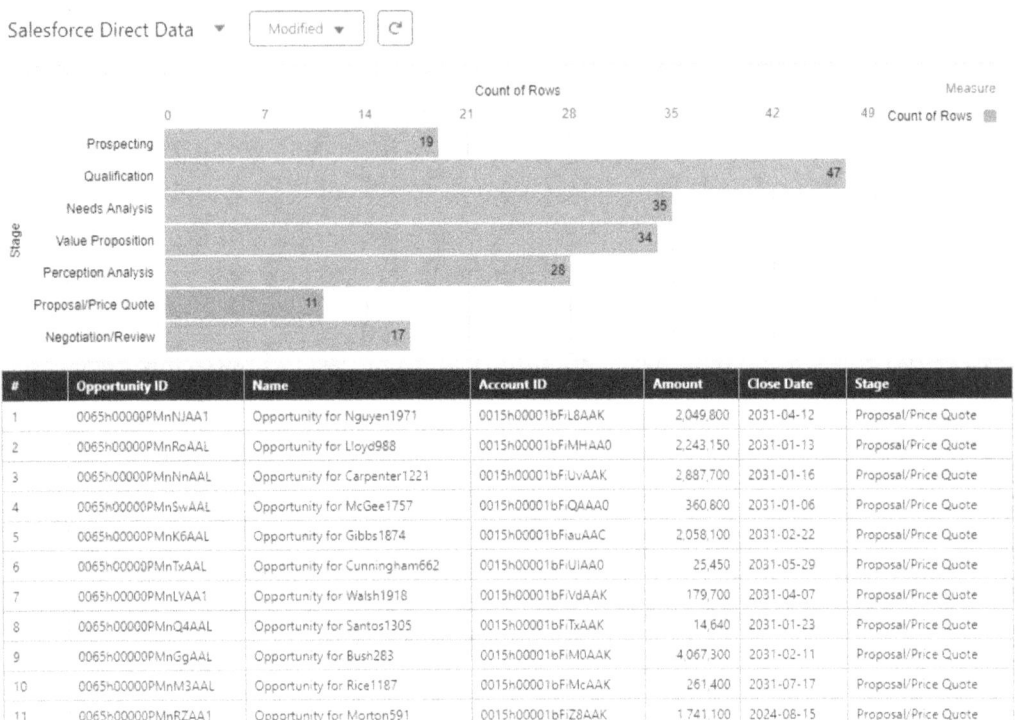

Figure 9-12. Dashboard with widget query data from Salesforce directly

Note

- Every time the dashboard opens or the browser refresh or the "Return to Initial View" button (next to the dashboard title) is clicked, it will pull data from Salesforce, so it is live data.

- As in Figure 9-12, when you click a stage from the chart, the selection will broadcast and facet by other widgets that query from the same object or child objects.

JSON

JSON stands for JavaScript Object Notation and is commonly used in data interchange language; however, we are not going to discuss JSON in depth in this book. But as you have read earlier in this book, we mentioned JSON many times. So, what is the

CHAPTER 9 ADVANCED TOPICS

relationship between JSON and CRM Analytics? Most CRM Analytics assets are stored in JSON format.

Although JSON is a subset of the JavaScript programming language, the good thing is that it is pretty friendly to human eyes; we do not need an extra tool to generate or decode it.

Dashboard and Lens

Open a dashboard or lens and hit Ctrl+E (for Windows OS) or Command+E (for Mac OS) to switch from the graphical interface to JSON mode, see Figure 9-13. You can make changes to the dashboard or lens in JSON mode, click the Done button to exit from JSON mode and save it, or use the Cancel button to exit without changes.

Figure 9-13. A dashboard in JSON mode

183

If you make changes in JSON manually, when you hit Done, the system will check if the JSON format is valid; otherwise, it will prompt for "Invalid JSON"; you may delete or add a comma or quote, etc., to fix it. If you cannot find the issue, you can copy and paste it into a text editor (such as Notepad++) as a backup, then hit the Cancel button to redo and edit the dashboard JSON.

You may also see the "Invalid JSON" error with some messages, which may be caused by some dependency issues or missing items, such as a step or query is deleted or renamed but is still used in a widget, see Figure 9-14; manually renaming a step in JSON mode will not rename the step in the widget automatically; therefore, the system will not exit from JSON mode as well.

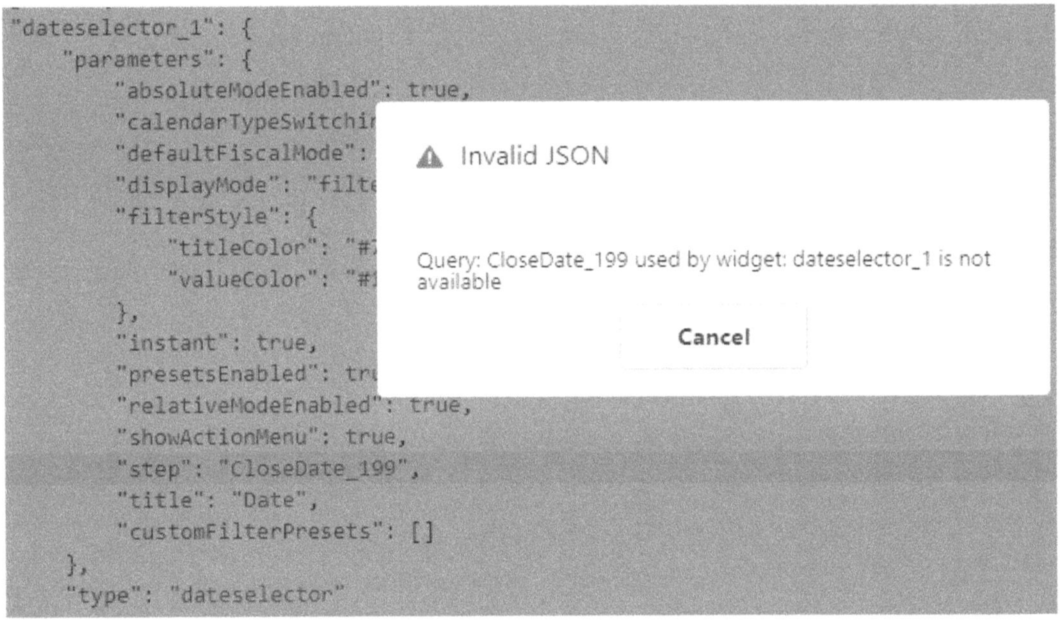

Figure 9-14. Invalid JSON error

Recipe

When we build a recipe using the graphical interface and produce the nodes, CRM Analytics will store it in JSON format. You can download the recipe into a JSON format file on the local computer (see Figure 9-15), open the file with a text editor to edit the JSON, and upload it back to overwrite the existing recipe.

It is always best practice to back up the original JSON file downloaded before making changes, then store the updated file as a new JSON file.

CHAPTER 9   ADVANCED TOPICS

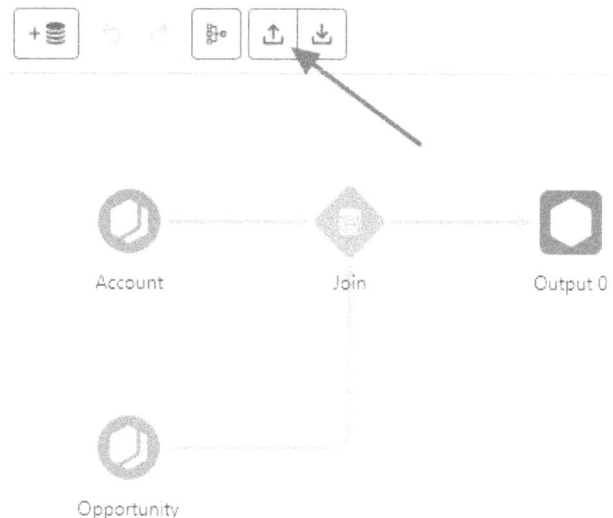

Figure 9-15. *Upload and download recipe as a JSON file*

Ideally, you do not need to update the recipe in JSON manually; however, it would be useful and faster to edit the recipe JSON for scenarios, such as mass adding fields to multiple nodes or removing fields that no longer exist. Another scenario for downloading a JSON file is to back up a working recipe locally.

Dataset

The Dataset's Extended Metadata File is also stored in JSON format. You make changes to the dataset metadata by exploring the dataset and editing the field, such as changing the number format; the changes will be stored in the Extended Metadata File.

To download the Extended Metadata File, edit the dataset (not explore), and look for the Extended Metadata File at the upper right (see Figure 9-16), download the file to your local computer, then use a text editor to open and change the JSON file. You can replace the Extended Metadata File by uploading the edited JSON file.

As mentioned earlier, it is always a good practice to back up the original JSON file before making any changes.

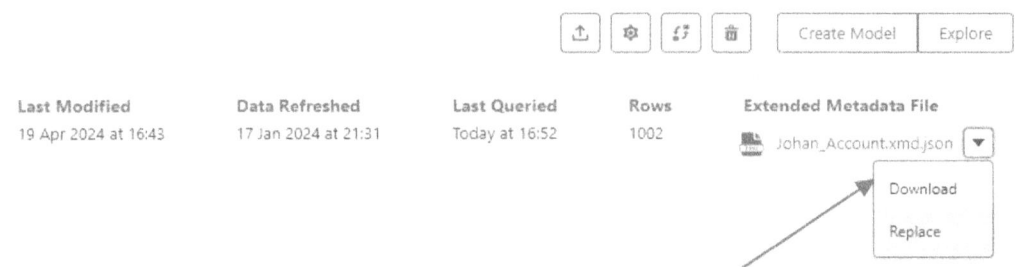

Figure 9-16. Download and upload the Extended Metadata File

SAQL

Same with JSON, we have discussed SAQL many times in this book. While JSON is used in CRM Analytics to store dashboards and other configuration items using industry standard format, SAQL is CRM Analytics' proprietary query language. If you come from a Salesforce developer or technical background, please do not relate SAQL with SOQL, SOSL, or SQL.

SAQL stands for Salesforce Analytics Query Language. CRM Analytics uses SAQL to query the dataset and produce the result in the widget for a dashboard or lens. When you build a widget with clicks in the dashboard designer, CRM Analytics builds the SAQL at the back end. You can see the query by clicking Show Details from the widget, then selecting the "View more details" icon and the "Final Query" tab, see Figure 9-17.

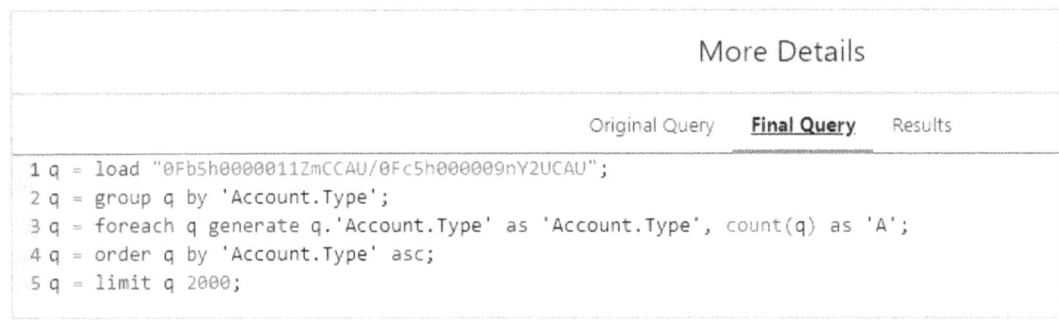

Figure 9-17. Sample of SAQL behind a dashboard widget

CHAPTER 9 ADVANCED TOPICS

Let us walk through each line from the preceding SAQL:

First Line: Load data from the Dataset

Second Line: Group data by Account.Type field

Third Line: Project Account.Type field and number of records for each Account.Type

Fourth Line: Order the data loaded by Account.Type field in ascending order

Fifth Line: Limit only for 2000 lines

We can also use SAQL when building a dashboard; let us open the Global Account dashboard that we built in earlier chapters:

1. Click the Edit button or hit the "e" key.

2. Click the number widget and click the pencil icon at the bottom to edit the widget.

3. Click the Query Mode icon at the upper right of the lens window. You should see something similar to JSON as follows:

   ```
   q = load "Open_Opportunities_more_than_0";
   q = group q by all;
   q = foreach q generate count(q) as 'A';
   q = limit q 2000;
   ```

4. Let us add a filter after load:

   ```
   q = load "Open_Opportunities_more_than_0";
   q = filter q by 'StageName' == "Closed Won";
   q = group q by all;
   q = foreach q generate count(q) as 'A';
   q = limit q 2000;
   ```

5. Click the Run Query button; you should now see the result change to show only the count of Closed Won opportunities.

6. Click the Update button, and the widget will be updated with SAQL.

Because the widget has been updated using SAQL, we are no longer able to configure the widget using a click, but we have to use SAQL.

If you go to the dashboard JSON by pressing Ctrl+E or Command+E, you will find the SAQL for the query that is used by the widget:

```
"query": "q = load \"Open_Opportunities_more_than_0\";\nq = filter q by 'StageName' == \"Closed Won\";\nq = group q by all;\nq = foreach q generate count(q) as 'A';\nq = limit q 2000;",
```

Binding and Custom Query

When building CRM Analytics dashboards, we often need to give our users more flexibility when exploring our dashboards, such as using the same widget and grouping by different fields, such as Region, Type, or Status. Typically, we need to have multiple widgets, and each has a different grouping. However, we have limited space for a dashboard, and it is not lovely to have too many widgets in a dashboard. With binding, we can use a widget and let users switch the grouping based on their selection.

When we drag a widget to the dashboard designer and select a field, without our awareness, CRM Analytics creates a "query" at the back end to power the widget; you can check this by flipping the dashboard to JSON mode; this is the standard step that auto-creates for the widget. But we can also manually create a query, select a dataset, group, and filter as necessary, and then drag the query created into the widget that has no query yet.

The other type of query is called Custom Query; with this query, we can apply our own defined values, including filters, groups, measures, order, and limits. We can use this query to facet other widgets using binding. To make it easier for you to understand both binding and static queries, let us have a hands-on that covers both in an exercise.

Hands-On Binding and Custom Query

1. Open CRM Analytics.
2. Create a new dashboard and select Blank Dashboard.
3. Click the "Create Query" button at the upper-right panel.
4. Click the "Create Custom Query" link at the bottom left of the window, see Figure 9-18.

CHAPTER 9   ADVANCED TOPICS

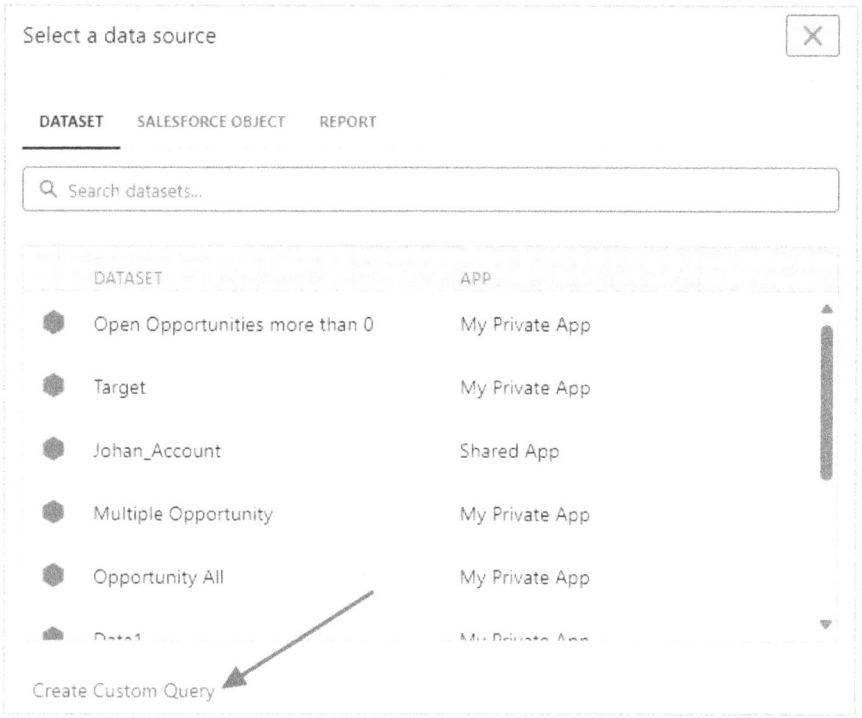

Figure 9-18. *Create Custom Query*

5. This exercise depends on your dataset fields, but for this sample, I will enter the following details:

    a. Change the label at the center from "New Custom Query" to "Static_Group."

    b. Add the following to the table, see Figure 9-19.

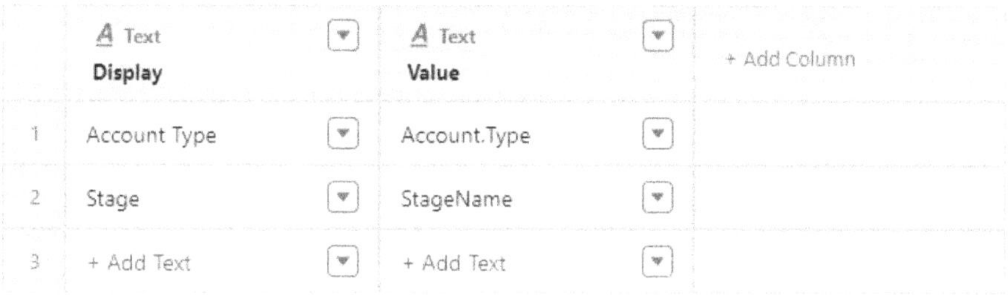

Display	Value	+ Add Column
1 Account Type	Account.Type	
2 Stage	StageName	
3 + Add Text	+ Add Text	

Figure 9-19. *New Custom Query*

189

CHAPTER 9 ADVANCED TOPICS

6. Click the "Done" button.

7. Notice that a new static query called "Static_Group" has been added.

8. Drag a toggle widget to the upper left in Dashboard Designer.

9. Drag the static query created to the toggle widget; now you should see two values in the toggle: Account Type and Stage.

10. Select the widget, click the Query tab at the right, and select "Single selection (required)."

11. Drag a chart widget to the dashboard designer.

12. Click the "Chart" icon inside the widget.

13. Select an Opportunity dataset and it must have the Account Type and Stage fields.

14. Select Account.Type as the grouping.

15. Click the Done button.

16. Save the dashboard as "binding," see Figure 9-20.

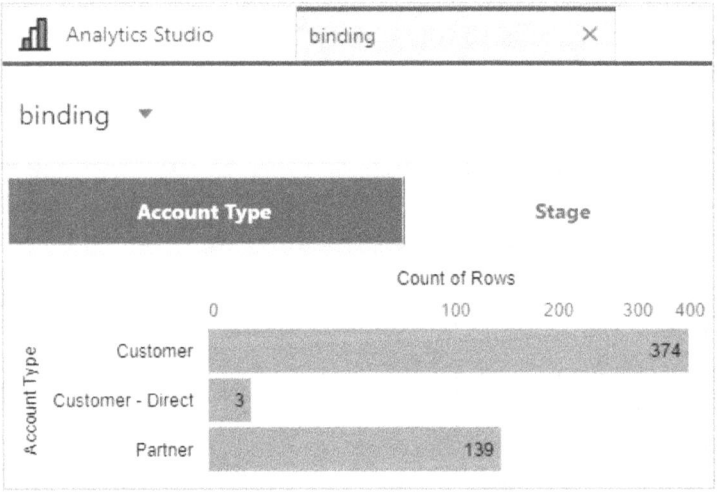

Figure 9-20. *A dashboard with toggle and chart widgets*

CHAPTER 9   ADVANCED TOPICS

17. Switch the dashboard to preview mode, but when you click the toggle, the chart grouping is not changed because we have not linked the toggle with the chart. Next, we need to create a binding for the chart to use the value from the selected toggle.

18. Switch back the chart to edit mode (hit the "e" key), click the chart, and click the "Advanced Editor" button below the Widget tab.

19. Under the Widget tab, look for "columnMap" under that widget, and delete the whole group of columnMap, as columnMap does not support binding.

20. Click the Query tab and do the same to delete the whole group of columnMap.

21. On the left panel, select Source Query = "Static_Group_1" and Source Data, as shown in Figure 9-21, and Interaction Type = "Selection."

Figure 9-21. *Advanced Interaction Editor*

191

CHAPTER 9   ADVANCED TOPICS

22. Click the Copy button and change "Account.Type" to {{cell(Static_Group_1.selection, 0, \"Value\"). asString()}} under groups and orders.

23. Click the Save button, and it will go back to the dashboard edit mode.

24. Hit "e" to switch to Preview mode. Now, let us try to change the toggle to Stage, and you should see the chart now grouped by Stage, see Figure 9-22.

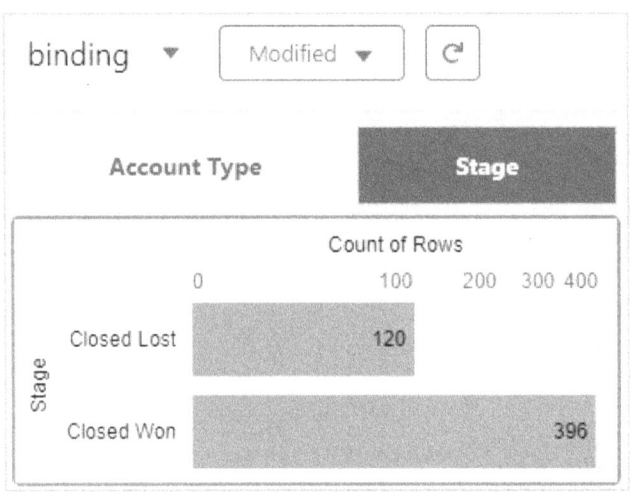

Figure 9-22. *Binding in action*

25. Notice that "Modified" and an arrow appear next to the dashboard title; this is the same when you filter or facet from the widget. You can click the arrow to restore to the initial selection.

With this hands-on experience, I hope you understand the concept of how binding works; you can make use of binding in many areas, such as changing grouping, filters, sorting, chart type, comparing data, etc. The preceding sample is binding using a selection, but we can also do binding from a result, so the binding is based on the result from another query.

CHAPTER 9   ADVANCED TOPICS

Widgets

We discussed most of the widgets available in CRM Analytics in Chapter 3, but there are three more that have not been discussed, which are newer and considered more advanced.

Input

There are a few settings that you can set for the input widget:

- Input Type: Slider or Freeform Input
- Display Format: None, Percent, Currency
- Minimum Value, Maximum Value, and Start Value
- Input Style

Different from other widgets, when you add an input widget, it will not ask to link to a dataset. How to use this widget? Let us do a quick hands-on.

Scenario: Calculate a formula based on the number of rows divided by two times the input value.

1. Create a new blank dashboard.
2. Add an input widget and set the following values:
   a. Minimum Value = 1
   b. Maximum Value = 100
   c. Start Value = 10
3. Add a number widget and link it to a dataset.
4. Edit query of the number widget created in step 3.
5. Click the + button under Count of Rows.
6. Click "Add Column" and select Input, see Figure 9-23.

CHAPTER 9   ADVANCED TOPICS

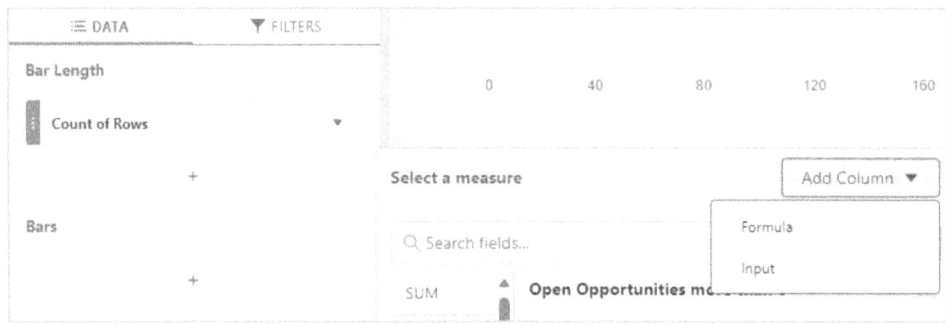

Figure 9-23. Add Column in a query

7. Select the input query that was created in step 2, then click the Add button.

8. Repeat steps 5 and 6, then select Formula under "Add Column."

9. You can add the Column Header, for example, Formula Result. Under the formula, enter A/(2*B); note that A = Count of Rows and B = value from the input widget. Click the Apply button, then the Update button.

10. Add another number widget; do not create a new query (click 123 Number in the widget), but drag the query created in step 3 to this new number widget.

11. You will see the same label and value as the existing Count of Rows widget; look at the right "Measure Field" and change the drop-down value from Count of Rows to Formula Result, then also change the Title to Formula Result.

12. Click the Preview button to test; as you drag the slider, the formula result will be updated, see Figure 9-24.

CHAPTER 9 ADVANCED TOPICS

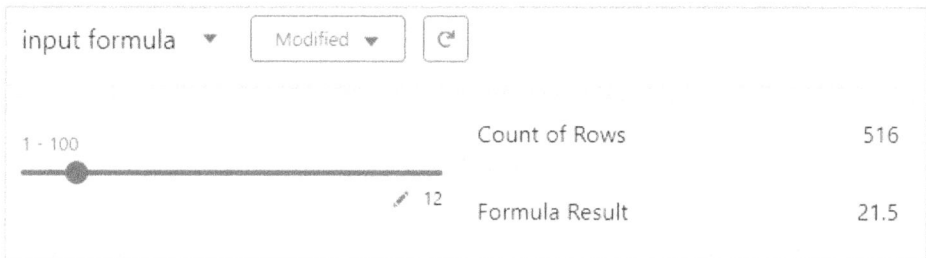

***Figure 9-24.** Input widget in action*

The input widget can also be used in SAQL and binding, so that the query result is filtered based on the selected input value.

Repeater

The concept of the Repeater widget is to show a query result as an individual value. There are two areas to configure for a repeater widget:

1. In the widget itself, configure the "Items per row."

2. In the repeater content, four types of widgets can be added: text, number, chart, and image. Styles such as Columns, Row Height, and Cell Spacing can also be configured.

Let's have a quick hands-on exercise to use the Repeater widget.

Scenario: Create a dashboard showing the Opportunity Total Amount for each Account in gauge charts; the target for each Account is 1,000,000.

1. Create a new blank dashboard.

2. Add a repeater widget and click the Repeater icon at the center of the widget.

3. The system will create a query; for this example, I will group by Account Name and change the Bar Length to the Sum of Amount.

4. Click the Done button, and we will be in the Editing Repeater Content window.

5. Change the Columns to 3.

195

CHAPTER 9   ADVANCED TOPICS

6. Add a Text widget, remove the default "Add text…," click the "Add Query Data" button, select Account Name from the "Dynamic Text Field," and click the Done button. To make it look better, change the text color to dark red; you need to select the [Account_Name], then select the color.

7. Add a Chart widget to the repeater content; change the chart widget to occupy the whole repeater, which is three boxes in width with four boxes in height; and change the chart type to Gauge. Notice that the available charts here are fewer than the standard chart widget.

8. Set the Title = Total Amount, Title Font Size = 12, Range Values Min = 0, and Max = 1,000,000.

9. Under the Gauge panel, uncheck "Show band range" and "Show band label."

10. Click Done at the upper-right corner to exit from the repeater content.

11. Resize the repeater content to occupy the whole dashboard width.

12. Update the "Items per row" under Content Layout to 6.

13. Here is your result, and you can switch to preview mode, see Figure 9-25.

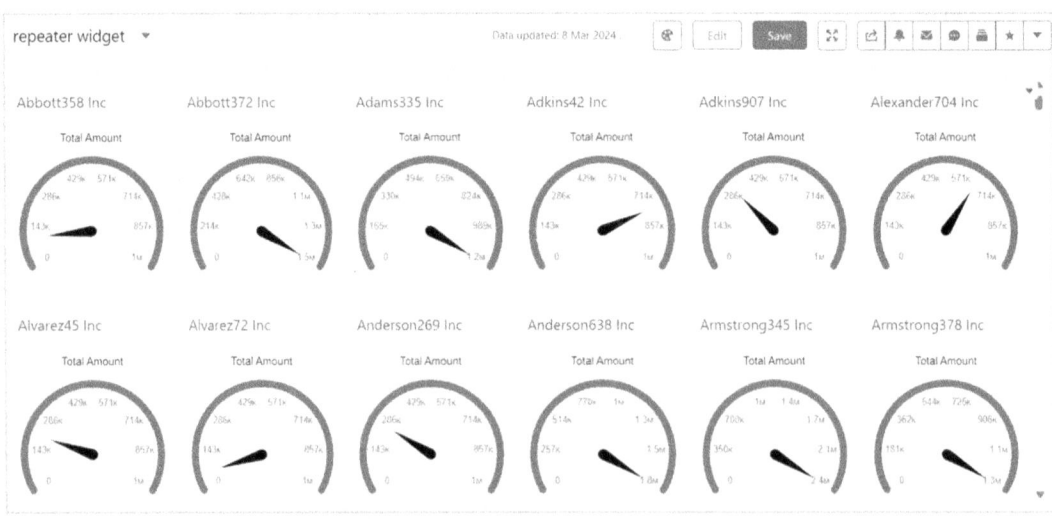

Figure 9-25. *Using the Repeater widget*

CHAPTER 9   ADVANCED TOPICS

Component

The Component widget is different from other widgets, where usually a widget is only built within, and for a dashboard, however, a Component can be used in multiple dashboards. So, you create a "mini dashboard" that contains a collection of widgets and reuse it.

When you update a component, it will update all dashboards that "use" the Component; by using the Component, the dashboard builder can maintain dashboards more easily.

Let's have a quick hands-on session using the Component widget.

Scenario: We need to create two similar dashboards, one for managers and one for team leads; the one for managers needs to have additional widgets.

1. From Analytics Studio, create a new Component, see Figure 9-26.

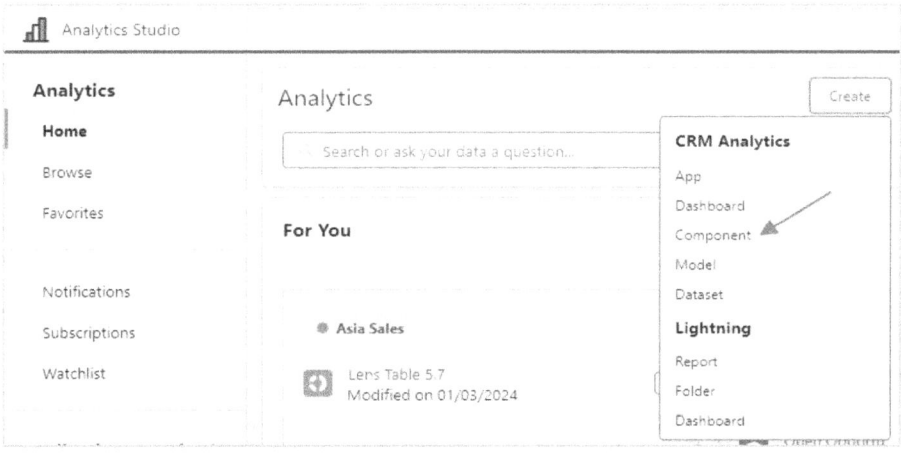

Figure 9-26. Creating a new Component

2. You will be landed in Component Designer; it looks very similar to Dashboard Designer.

3. Add two charts using the same dataset.

4. Add a global filter to filter only closed won opportunities.

5. Save the Component as "Won Opportunity" – notice from Figure 9-27, a component looks very similar to a dashboard, except the label at the top left is called "Component Designer," and you don't see the component icon at the left widget panel.

197

CHAPTER 9 ADVANCED TOPICS

Figure 9-27. A ready-to-use Component

6. Create a new dashboard and name it "Dashboard for Team Leads."

7. Drag the Component widget to Dashboard Designer and click the Component icon at the center of the widget.

8. Select the "Won Opportunity" Component and click the Done button.

9. You should see charts added to the component.

10. Drag a toggle widget to use the same dataset and group it by Account Type.

11. Drag a chart widget, change to Maps, select Location to Billing Country and Projection Type to Equirectangular, and enable Auto Zoom.

12. Click the Done button and switch to Preview mode.

Now, if you click the toggle widget, it will filter charts inside the component, and the same thing happens when you click the chart inside the component; it will filter other widgets, even if they are not part of the component, but using the same dataset, see Figure 9-28.

CHAPTER 9 ADVANCED TOPICS

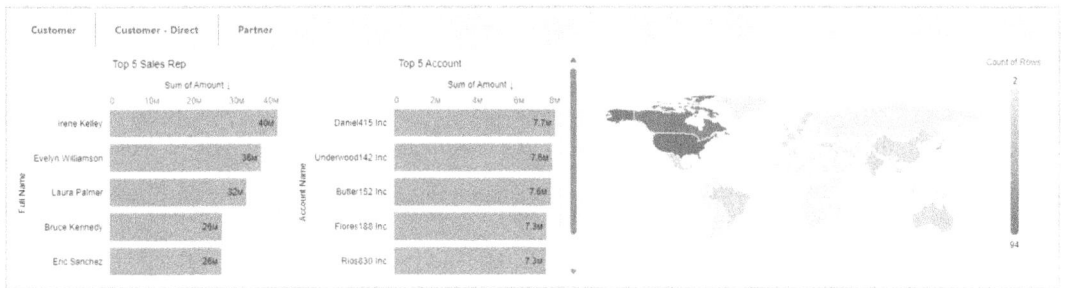

Figure 9-28. *A Dashboard with a Component*

For the other dashboard for managers, switch the existing dashboard to edit mode, clone the dashboard by clicking the arrow at the upper-right corner and selecting "Clone in New Tab," rename the dashboard to "Dashboard for Manager," and add more widgets as needed for the manager.

When you edit the Component, both dashboards will be updated, which makes it simpler and easier to maintain the dashboards.

Summary

Now, we have reached the end of this chapter, which is also the end of this book. I believe that by now, you have gathered basic skills in CRM Analytics and the ability to build powerful dashboards for your clients or your employer.

CRM Analytics is becoming popular as it is integrated well with Salesforce and also has the ability to get data from external sources. With Salesforce reporting and dashboard, you can only build a simple dashboard with many limitations; however, with the CRM Analytics platform, the power is limitless; you can build dashboards as per your creativity and also give your users the power to analyze, and slicing data easier with outstanding performance.

The more dashboards you build and the more challenges you face, the more skill you will acquire; practice makes perfect.

One more thing before ending this book: The CRM Analytics community is very powerful and massive; currently, it has more than 73,000 members. I would advise you to join the community: https://trailhead.salesforce.com/trailblazer-community/groups?tab=all. Click Log In with your Salesforce credentials, and search for **CRM**

CHAPTER 9　ADVANCED TOPICS

Analytics. There is a lot of information on Groups, from new features in every release, or you can ask questions about the technical issues or best practices, and you can also answer questions from other community members.

I wish you all the best in building awesome dashboards by applying the new skills acquired, and see you around!

Index

A, B

Analytics Studio app, 3, 7
Application programming language (API), 35

C

Comma-separated values (CSV)
    browse tab, 24
    dataset, 21, 23
    fields panel, 25
    field type, 25
    mapping/reference, 21
    pencil icon, 24
    Sales Rep Quota, 22
    upload file button, 23
CRM Analytics
    analytics tab, 6
    components
        apps, 8
        architecture, 10
        dashboards, 8
        dataset, 9
        lens, 9
    concepts/data integration, 21
    CSV files, 21–25
    dashboard (*see* Dashboard)
    dashboards, 6
    data manager, 10–16
    dataset, 20, 21, 65–79
    data sources (*see* Data sources)
    data visualization, 1
    definition, 2
    environment, 4, 5
    JSON format, 182–186
    lens, 81–99
    license information, 5
    lightning page, 6
    mobile app, 8
    permissions, 6, 7
    recipe, 37–63
    reports/dashboard features, 4
    Salesforce (*see* Salesforce platform)
    security, 157–170
    step-by-step instructions, 2
    Studio user interface, 7
Customer relationship management (CRM), *see* CRM Analytics

D

Dashboard
    data source connection, 130
    exploring (*see* Exploring dashboards)
    faceting options, 126, 127
    global filter/filter properties, 127–129
    layout, 102–105
    multiple datasets, 129–131
    pages, 124
        adoption/maintenance, 126
        dashboard tab, 125
        dataset pages, 125

INDEX

Dashboard (*cont.*)
    performance, 126
    sharing widget, 125
  templates, 105–108
  time series template, 107
  user permission, 102
  widgets
    chart, 108, 109
    container, 112
    date field, 113, 114
    filters, 111, 112
    image widget, 117, 118
    link, 115, 116
    list widget, 117, 118
    navigation, 124–126
    number, 118, 119
    queries, 109
    range, 120, 121
    record values/compare/pivot table, 110, 111
    text style/widget style, 120
    toggle, 121–124

Dashboards
  binding/custom query
    binding, 192
    Custom Query, 188, 189
    designer/field, 188
    details, 189
    interaction editor, 191
    preview mode, 192
    toggle and chart widgets, 190
  widgets, 193
    component, 197–199
    gauge charts, 195
    input, 193–195
    query, 194
    repeater, 195, 196

Dataflow
  conversion, 39, 40
  older version, 38
  save/run button, 39, 40
  source information, 39
  Wave/Einstein Analytics, 37

Data Manager
  accessing data, 10, 11
  connections tab, 15, 16
  data assets, 13
  data usage, 14
  external data, 27–29
  jobs monitor, 12
  recipe/dataflows, 13, 14
  user interface, 11

Datasets
  actions configuration, 77
    display fields, 79
    record action, 78
    types, 77
  extended metadata file
    configuration, 69
    edit field values, 72
    fields panel, 69
    format numbers, 73, 74
    grain label, 74, 75
    hide fields, 70
    rename, 70
    set default fields, 74, 75
  fields, 68
  information/actions, 67
  properties, 65–67
  replace/restore, 75, 76

Data sources
  API enables, 35
  existing datasets, 29
  external data source, 28–30

multiple connections, 28
salesforce trend report, 29–34

E, F, G, H, I

Exploring dashboards
  annotations
    feature, 140
    hands-on, 141, 142
    icon, 140, 141
  dashboard inspector
    details, 135
    features, 134
    icons, 136
    performance bottlenecks, 134, 135
    query details, 136
  explore action, 145
  hands-on, 146, 147
  learning process, 133
  Salesforce, 148–154
  SAQL, 147, 148
  set notifications
    features, 137
    lightning, 139, 140
    monitor, 139
    number widget, 138
  share widgets, 142–144
  show details action, 144, 145
Extended metadata (XMD), 9

J, K

JavaScript Object Notation (JSON)
  dashboard/lens, 183, 184
  error message, 184
  extended metadata file, 185, 186
  upload/download recipe, 184, 185

L, M, N, O, P, Q

Lens
  analyze data, 87
  chart mode, 85–87
  clip/designer button, 90, 91
  clone, 89
  collection, 94, 95
  completeness, 84
  conversational exploration, 97, 98
  CRM Analytics apps
    creation, 82, 83
    run app button, 83
    sharing, 84
    types, 82
  favorite feature, 95, 96
  present mode, 90
  quantity/quality, 84
  save button, 89
  sharing data, 91
    download data, 92
    posting/feed, 92
    URL tab, 91, 92
  subscription, 93, 94
  values table, 87–89
Lightning app page
  home page
    dashboard, 152
    hands-on, 150
    properties, 151
    recipe/dashboard, 150
    recipe pulls data, 150
  options, 149
  record page
    account page, 154
    dashboard, 152
    dashboard modification, 152
    hands-on, 152
    properties, 153

INDEX

R

Recipe
- aggregate node, 55, 56
- append node, 61
- backup/restore JSON file, 48, 49
- dataflow, 37–40
- data transformation, 49
- filter node, 54
- hands-on, 44–48
- input data, 49–51
- join
  - connecting node, 57
  - cross join, 60
  - datasets, 57
  - inner join, 59
  - left join, 58
  - LookUp, 58
  - nodes, 56
  - outer join, 60
  - right join, 59
  - types, 57
- objects/fields, 43, 44
- opportunities, 42, 43
- output node, 62, 63
- in progress, 46
- search dataset, 47
- Transform node, 51–54
- update node, 62
- user interface, 40–42
- version history, 48

Recipes
- nodes, 171
  - append node, 179
  - clean duplicate, 174
  - connecting nodes, 179
  - custom formula, 175–177
  - deleting links, 178
  - drop columns, 175, 176
  - duplicate names, 173
  - edit attributes, 172–174
  - filter node, 177–179
  - formula editor, 176
  - input nodes, 172
  - joining nodes, 180
  - options, 177
  - transform node, 174
  - value lookup, 180

S, T, U, V, W, X, Y, Z

Salesforce analytics query language (SAQL)
- CRM Analytics, 186–188

Salesforce platform
- direct data queries, 181
  - dashboard, 182
  - stage, 181
- integration, 2, 3
- Lightning page, 148–154
- local vs. external data, 26, 27
- retrieve data, 27
- sharing inheritance, 166–169
- trend report
  - benefits, 29
  - configuration, 30
  - dashboard, 34
  - fields, 33
  - hands-on, 30
  - monitor trend progress, 32
  - opportunity report, 30
  - schedule report, 31
  - snapshot date, 33
  - trend job progress detail, 33

204

INDEX

Security
    apps level sharing, 159
    learning process, 157
    permission set assignment, 157–159
    predicate
        definition, 160
        exception, 163
        flatten node properties, 165, 166
        flatten transform, 164
        hands-on, 161–163
        role hierarchy access, 163–166
        syntax, 160
    sharing inheritance, 166–169
Sharing inheritance
    configuration, 167, 168
    coverage assessment, 168–170
    definition, 166
    enable option, 167
    standard objects, 166
    user process, 169

GPSR Compliance

The European Union's (EU) General Product Safety Regulation (GPSR) is a set of rules that requires consumer products to be safe and our obligations to ensure this.

If you have any concerns about our products, you can contact us on

ProductSafety@springernature.com

In case Publisher is established outside the EU, the EU authorized representative is:

Springer Nature Customer Service Center GmbH
Europaplatz 3
69115 Heidelberg, Germany